S0-CCZ-102

CONTEXTS OF READING

Edited by

Carolyn N. Hedley

Anthony N. Baratta

Fordham University

Volume XVIII in the Series
Advances in Discourse Processes
Roy O. Freedle, Editor

Ablex Publishing Corporation

Norwood, New Jersey

Copyright © 1985 by Ablex Publishing Corporation

All rights reserved. No part of this publication may
be reproduced, stored in a retrieval system, or
transmitted, in any form or by any means, electronic,
mechanical, photocopying, microfilming, recording,
or otherwise, without permission of the publisher.

Printed in the United States of America.

Library of Congress Cataloging in Publication Data

Main entry under title:

Contexts of reading.

(Advances in discourse processes, v. 18)
Bibliography: p.
Includes index.
1. Reading—United States—Congresses. 2. Children—
Language—Congresses. 3. Reading—Social aspects—
United States—Congresses. I. Hedley, Carolyn N.
II. Baratta, Anthony N.
LB1049.95.C68   1985   372.4   85-13432
ISBN 0-89391-294-8
ISBN 0-89391-364-2 (pbk.)

Ablex Publishing Corporation
355 Chestnut Street
Norwood, New Jersey 07468

Contents

Preface to the Series

Roy O. Freedle
Series Editor

This series of volumes provides a forum for the cross-fertilization of ideas from a diverse number of disciplines, all of which share a common interest in discourse— be it prose comprehension and recall, dialogue analysis, text grammar construction, computer simulation of natural language, cross-cultural comparisons of communicative competence, or other related topics. The problems posed by multisentence contexts and the methods required to investigate them, while not always unique to discourse, are still sufficiently distinct as to benefit from the organized mode of scientific interaction made possible by this series.

Scholars working in the discourse area from the perspective of sociolinguistics, psycholinguistics, ethnomethodology and the sociology of language, educational psychology (e.g., teacher–student interaction), the philosophy of language, computational linguistics, and related subareas are invited to submit manuscripts of monograph or book length to the series editor. Edited collections of original papers resulting from conferences will also be considered.

Volumes in the Series

To Mae and to Gene

The Authors

ANTHONY N. BARATTA. Anthony Baratta is a professor at Fordham University School of Education. Currently, he is Chairman of the Division of Curriculum and Teaching; he is heavily involved in the doctoral program dealing with curriculum delivery systems and decision making as it effects educational planning. Additionally, he is head of the Human Resources and Adult Education Program. He served as Chairman of the Division of Administration and Supervision, later becoming Associate Dean of the School of Administration. He is past-president of the New York State COTE and the editor of the new *Journal of AACTE/NYS*.

DAVID BLOOME. David Bloome is an assistant professor at the University of Michigan at Ann Arbor, having recently received his doctorate at Kent State University. He is doing research in reading development, using ethnographic approaches to research in reading; he is also interested in classroom processes of interaction. He coauthored an article with Judith Green in Hutson's book *Advances in Reading/Language Research, Volume I,* and is currently doing an article in the *Handbook of Research on Reading* by Pearson, Barr, Mosenthal and Camille. He is an active participant in many professional organizations including the AERA SIG group on language and reading.

RITA S. BRAUSE. Rita Brause is an associate professor at Fordham University Graduate school of Education. She was the recipient of the National Council of Teachers of English "Promising Research" Award in 1975. Most recently she was invited to become a department editor with John S. Mayher for *Language Arts,* a journal published by the National Council of Teachers of English. The focus for much of her writing has been on the classroom teacher as researcher. Dr. Brause has published widely in language and reading journals, including *English Journal, Language Arts* and *Research in the Teaching of English* on such topics as language development and learning. She is working on research for the National Institute of Education on language in the classroom, which is expected to be a seminal work in the area.

BRYANT FILLION. Bryant Fillion has recently joined the Graduate School of Education at Fordham University, after having been at the Ontario Institute for Studies in Education (OISE); currently, he is head of the doctoral program in Language Literacy and Learning. As such, he teaches courses in language development, the cognitive bases of reading and psycholinguistics. He has degrees from the University of Michigan, Long Island University, the University of Illinois, and Florida State University. A major thrust of his work has been research relating language across the curriculum, inquiry as reading process, and the pedagogy of writing. Dr. Fillion has coauthored several books, including *Teaching English Today*, the *Inquiry into Literature* series, and *Writing for Results*.

ROY O. FREEDLE. Roy Freedle is a Senior Research Psychologist at Educational Testing Service. He received his degree from Columbia University in Psychology and has taught at both Columbia and the University of Pennsylvania. Currently he is doing research on transfer from narrative competence to expository competence. His chapter in the book *Developmental Issues in Discourse* is on the ability to transfer in a coherent mode from one level of writing competence to another. He is editor of the journal, *Discourse Processes*, and of the book series *Advances in Discourse Processes*.

DONALD R. GALLO. Don Gallo is a professor of English at Central Connecticut State University where he teaches courses in writing and in literature for young adults. He has been an English teacher in a Connecticut junior high school and a reading specialist in Colorado. Dr. Gallo has conducted seminars in teaching literature, writing, and reading in the content areas throughout the country. His publications include materials in the *Bookmark Reading Program, Novel Ideas*, and editorship of the *Connecticut English Journal*, as well as numerous articles and reviews in a variety of professional journals.

JUDITH GREEN. Judith Green is Director of Educational Leadership and Policy Studies at Ohio State University in Columbus, Ohio. She has been a professor at University of Delaware and at Kent State University. She is highly interested in language and ethnography in educational settings. She received her degree from University of California at Berkeley. Dr. Green is coeditor of the books *Ethnography and Language in Educational Settings*, and of the series of monographs Language and Learning for Human Service Professions.

ROSA HAGIN. Rosa Hagin is a professor in the Division of Psychological and Educational Services in the Graduate School of Education at Fordham University and Research Professor in Psychology in the Department of Psychiatry at New York University Medical Center. Her research interests have centered on prevention, diagnosis, and treatment of learning disorders in children and adults. Her publications include longitudinal studies of learning disabled children, investigations of neuropsychological development of children, and assessment of models of intervention programs. She is co-author of the *Search and Teach* program. She was principal investigator in a Handicapped Children's Model program funded by the U.S. Office of Education, titled *Links in Educating Emotionally Disturbed Children and Youth.*

CAROLYN N. HEDLEY. Carolyn Hedley is an Associate Professor and Director of Reading Programs at Fordham University Graduate School of Education. She has been involved in the development of the Master's Program in Reading and the doctoral program in Language, Literacy and Learning. Dr. Hedley has published widely in journals of reading *(Reading Horizons, Educational and Psychological Measurement, Elementary English,* as examples). She has contributed articles to several books, on such topics as *Career Education and the Language Arts* and *Reading Difficulties.* Dr. Hedley is a coauthor of the Scott Foresman *Life Long Series in Adult Education.* She has a book in press, titled *Assessment and Instruction of Reading: Problems of the Special Learner.*

BRIAN MONAHAN. Brian Monahan received his Ph.D. in 1982 from the Graduate School of Education at Fordham University. For a number of years he has been involved in the development of the *K–12 Communications Arts Curriculum Guides* for the Yonkers Public Schools and is working on writing computer software to support the objectives of those guides. Dr. Monahan's publications on the use of computers in English and language arts have appeared in *English Journal, Computers, Reading and Language Arts,* and *Educational Technology.*

P. DAVID PEARSON. David Pearson is a professor in the Department of Elementary and Early Childhood Education at the University of Illinois in Urbana-Champaign, where he also holds an appointment at the Center for the Study of Reading. He received a B.A. in History from the University of California at Berkeley and a Ph.D. in Education from Minnesota. He has held post-doctoral appointments at the University of Texas-Austin and Stanford University. He taught elementary school in California and worked several years at the University of Minnesota, Minneapolis before coming to Illinois. His current research has focused upon the role of questions in reading comprehension instruction and the strategies people use to accomodate student difficulties with content area reading material. He has published two books, *Teaching Reading Comprehension* and *Teaching Reading Vocabulary* with Dale D. Johnson of the University of Wisconsin. With S. Jay Samuels of the University of Minnesota, he edits the *Reading Research Quarterly.*

ROBERT J. TIERNEY. Robert Tierney is currently a researcher and teacher at the Center for Reading at the University of Illinois at Champaign-Urbana. He received his degree from the University of Georgia. As a teacher, researcher, and consultant in both the United States and

Australia, Dr. Tierney has authored numerous articles dealing with theory, research, and practice in the area of reading. He has carried out some of this research at Harvard and the University of Arizona, focusing on reading comprehension, schema, strategies, and experience that the reader brings to the reading process. He is a coauthor of the book, *Strategies for Teaching Reading.*

LOUISE CHERRY WILKINSON. Louise Cherry Wilkinson is a professor at the Graduate Center of the City University of New York. She is a graduate of Harvard University and has taught there, at Massachusetts Institute of Technology, at Boston University, and at Brooklyn College. She has long been interested in communicating in classrooms, and has organized conferences on such topics as *Instructional Groups in the Classroom.* She is consulting reviewer for *Child Development, Developmental Psychology*, and the *Journal of Education Psychology.* Her publications include *Communicating in Classrooms* as well as many publications in journals, such as *Child Development* and *Developmental Psychology.*

CARLOS A. YORIO. Carlos Yorio is a full professor at Lehman College and the Graduate Center of the City University of New York, where he teaches and does research in linguistics and directs the ESL program. He teaches second language acquisition courses, applied linguistics, and TESOL methodologies. He holds a B.A. in TESOL (Cordoba, Argentina), and an M.A. in Drama and Literature (Syracuse) and an M.A. and Ph.D. in Linguistics (Michigan). He has been president of TESOL, Ontario and Vice President of International TESOL. He has published numerous articles on reading, communicative competence, language errors, and the like. He is coauthor of *Who Did It?*

Preface

This book grew out of a series of lectures from the eighth annual Fordham University Reading Institutes, in 1983. The Reading Institute, titled *Contexts of Reading,* focused on the social, cognitive, and personal contexts in which reading occurs and which underlie the reading experience. The conference was designed to promote participants' consideration of the following:

1. Classroom contexts for learning.
2. The cognitive bases of literacy.
3. The language bases of the reading process.
4. The nature of text and of literature.
5. The role of the family in language and reading development.
6. The importance of community, including its bilingual and multicultural dimensions, in reading and language development.

In order to look at these aspects of the reading experience, the organizers and speakers at the conference felt that instructional and research methods that lent themselves to looking at reading context as a holistic phenomena rather than as an isolated function would be helpful. Thus speakers—and later the participants—viewed the classroom as the context for reading; these researchers felt that the teacher was crucial in creating this context, and that the teacher herself should be a participant-observer and researcher of reading and its contexts. Finally, the Reading Institute included speakers who were concerned about individual diversity and the personal constructs of the learner. These views were the basic outlook for the conference and for the book that followed.

In terms of the research outlook for the conference, reading was viewed as a complex process, which should be studied not only in the experimental mode, but through the use of descriptive analysis. Ethnographic techniques and probes, including such methods as discourse and conversational analysis, were the methods used in the social sciences that lend themselves to a fresh approach to language and reading research. Thus, the Institute included speakers who supported the notion of descriptive and naturalistic outlooks for reading research as they dealt with the concerns listed above.

The conference was enthusiastically received, and was evaluated favorably by participants in their role as speakers, directors, workshops leaders, and students. Those students who were familiar with more precise and perhaps limited descriptions of the reading process and to more traditional views of the research and inquiry process were skeptical but challenged. Most student-participants who were practitioners enjoyed their interactive role and the emphasis on social process. Thus, participants felt that the Reading Institute had an immediate, salutary, and practical effect on our group behavior, even before the Institute concluded. Most resolved to return to their respective classrooms with some sense of renewal about themselves, their roles as teachers, their methods of instruction, their students, and their evaluation of instruction and achievement.

Some persons were especially helpful to the Reading Institute and to the creation of this volume. We would particularly like to acknowledge their contributions. First we are grateful to the speakers who became the authors of this book. Their generosity of time and good will made both the Institute and this book possible. Additionally, the Institute workshop leaders made an important contribution and some of them, with their considerable background in the above areas, later became authors as well. The contribution and the inspiration of the students, who helped as we developed our ideas through discussion and evaluation, is gratefully acknowledged. Walter Naegle deserves credit and thanks for "word-processing" the original manuscript. Gene Hedley deserves our thanks for editing it. Thanks to John Hedley for some of the graphics. Finally, although the book is dedicated to our respective spouses, we wish to thank them formally for putting up with the pyrotechnics of dealing with two essentially Type A people who do not work on such projects without creating some stress.

Carolyn N. Hedley
Anthony Baratta
May 1985

Introduction

Reading is a part of language development and, as such, it occurs in contexts. It is a socially based, interactive language transaction that builds on personal and cultural constructs which motivate and limit comprehension of text. Even the decoding aspects of reading seem to be better learned when they are not isolated from social and personal meaning. If we are to look at the reading process and see what it is that happens in schools, we must necessarily find the means that accommodate the assessment of the complexity of the task. Fortunately, anthropology, sociology, and natural history among other disciplines, have provided us with ethnographic approaches for looking at just such complexity. That is what this book is about: the reading-thinking-learning process, the classrooms in which such reading and learning processes occur, and the means for studying these processes. Nearly all of the chapters in this book deal with the above concepts in terms of teaching, learning, and assessing the reading process. Each section and chapter has a focus, however. An overview of the book follows which provides the schema for its organization and the thrust of each chapter within the various sections.

Part I deals with learning contexts that are interactive and participatory. Louise Cherry Wilkinson, in Chapter 1, provides us with a study that she has done that shows us that children are effective speakers and learners in reading groups in the first and third grades. By doing a walkthrough of one of her recent studies in language competence, she gives valuable insight in methods of data collection and analysis along with an ethnographic analysis that provides "hard data" for the presentation of her results. Rita Brause, in Chapter 2, demonstrates that interpersonal relationships must be created along with academic goals. Based on her recent research, she indicates what teachers must do to create trusting relationships and supportive environments for students, while at the same time upholding the content-rich classroom. The last contributor to this section, Tony Baratta, provides a systematic way of breaking down and using the components of the decision-making process by teachers and principals in interactive classrooms.

Reading instruction itself—what's to be taught, how reading occurs, how the learner perceives the reading task, how reading and language support and transcend the subject matter curricula is discussed in Part II. Higher level thought and cognitive development as part of this instruction is discussed. Robert Tierney and David Pearson provide a composing model of reading process in Chapter 4. Bryant Fillion in Chapter 5 demonstrates how reading informs the writing and thinking process by listing ways in which teachers can implement such concepts. He supports the creation of school-wide language policies that foster language across the curriculum. Carolyn Hedley in Chapter 6 describes the philosophical underpinnings from pragmatism, existentialism, and ordinary language analysis to demonstrate how each of the disciplines demands a unique presentation of language. This presentation of language distinctions and common, yet differentiated, meaning derives from the social bases of language, and changing language functions in varying contexts. Dr. Hedley stresses teaching the regularities and conventions both within and across these disciplinary studies, while nothing the personal and social contexts in which such learning occurs. Roy Freedle's research in Chapter 7 demonstrates that restrictive settings may affect the generalizability of language across situations and tasks. He concludes by showing the reader how generalizability across language tasks may be fostered. Brian Monahan in Chapter 8 helps us to see how technology, especially the microcomputer, may be affecting just such "transfer" and suggests that we need even greater technological sophistication to be effective in classrooms.

Part III deals with personal and cultural variations in language and reading development. Rosa Hagin describes in Chapter 9 the special learner as language learner and points out where the sources of difficulty for language learning may be found. In Chapter 10, Carlos Yorio deals with cultural differences as a source of language and reading development difficulty with the second-language learner. The problem of using unrealistic materials, methods, and settings may be cause for some of the separation between student learning and in-school teaching. Techniques for greater integration of reading to reality are provided.

Part IV is closely aligned with the presentations in the preceding chapters. We considered putting David Bloome's and Judith Green's chapter in Part I, since it deals with classroom contexts as the social, personal, and interactive context in which reading occurs; we also considered that it was appropriate for Part II, since it deals with the instruction of reading as an academic task. Ultimately, it seemed to us that Drs. Bloome and Green, in Chapter 11, were dealing with the parameters and concerns of research, using ethnographic approaches in conducting assessment and looking at behaviors in reading which were highly contextualized—personally, academically, and culturally. From them, we get a sense of the dimensions of what must be looked at in language and reading research and evaluation. Finally, in Chapter 12, Don Gallo does a walk-through of the teacher as researcher; he points out that the participant-observer-researcher might best be the teacher. Since this book is for educators in many roles and at many levels, we find it appealing that the teacher may well "do it all." Thus, teachers and students as participant-observers are at the epicenter of all classroom language contexts; that they become their own best researchers and research-users is as it should be.

PART I
CONTEXTS FOR LEARNING

Chapter 1
Communicating in Classrooms: Research on Reading Groups

Louise Cherry Wilkinson

City University of New York

Within the last decade a new tradition of research has developed for the study of interaction in the classroom, that is, the sociolinguistic approach. This approach focuses on descriptions of teachers' and students' use of language in the classroom. These descriptions provide us with a rich understanding of life in real classrooms and reveal the diversity of students and the complexity of their communication with teachers and with each other. The descriptions can serve as reference points for the improvement and/or evaluation of specific educational intervention programs. They can also serve as a source for new ideas for the study of the processes of teaching and learning.

This chapter may serve as introduction to a sociolinguistic approach on research on the use of language in the classroom. Original research on the language used by students in their peer-directed reading groups will also be discussed. First, the work is placed in the larger context of the tradition from which it arises, that is, the sociolinguistic approach. The assumptions of this tradition, the approach, and the tools used by sociolinguistic researchers who study classroom interaction, and then the specific aims, are presented.

The Sociolinguistic Tradition

The first assumption underlying a sociolinguistic approach is that interaction in the classroom requires competence in both structural and functional aspects of language. Functional language has been referred to as communicative or interactional competence and, while it is an end in itself, it is also a means of achieving other educational objectives. It serves both cognitive as well as social goals and in order to participate effectively in classrooms, children must learn to be interactionally competent.

3

The second assumption underlying this approach is that the classroom is a unique context for communication. The kind of competence required is specific, although it may share some general characteristics with communicative competence and other contexts such as the home. For example, many communicative interchanges between teachers and students are structured in a way to facilitate the exchange, evaluation, and acquisition of information, in a different way than these language functions occur in the home.

The third assumption that underlies this approach is that there are individual differences in interactional and communicative competence that are required in the classroom. We cannot assume the special aspects of communicative competence are necessarily taught or learned and certainly some come to classrooms with a greater knowledge of what is required than others.

A variety of methods have been used by sociolinguistic researchers in their efforts to examine teachers' and students' use of language to communicate in the classroom. These tools have been borrowed and/or adapted from fields within the social sciences, psychology, anthropology, linguistics, education, and sociology, and they include such tools as naturalistic observation, coding, interaction, linguistic field descriptions, and ethnography.

One important dimension concerning the selection of tools or methods is the distinction between qualitative and quantitative research. Quantitative research can be distinguished by neutral scientific language that is free from the context-bound everyday use of language. Quantitative researchers seek the objective of reporting of facts as separate from values of researchers, and their goal is to describe, explain, and predict relationships among a succession of objects and events that occur within classrooms. In contrast, qualitative research is characterized by the everyday use of language, what is unique and true at that point in time and place. Values are reflected within the reporting and there can be no "facts" without particular values reflected within them. Qualitative researchers also seek an understanding of what goes on in classrooms. They believe that understanding is obtained by knowing and experiencing what happens to others within that unique and particular context (Smith, 1983).

The Effective Speaker

For the past several years the author has studied students' interactions in reading groups without the direct and continuous supervision by the teacher. This form of grouping for instruction is quite common in elementary schools for both math and reading. The focus of this work is the communicative processes within these groups; that is, how students use requests and responses with each other to exchange and evaluate information.

The idea of the effective speaker in these reading groups is a student who uses his or her knowledge of language forms, functions, and contexts to achieve communicative goals has been given. For example, in the case of requests, a student who asks a question is effective if s/he obtains an appropriate response to that question (Wilkinson & Calculator, 1982; Wilkinson & Spinelli, 1983).

The notion of speaker effectiveness is an abstract and a general one. One can consider being understood and obtaining communicative goals in any number of contexts: in the classroom, on the playground, in the kitchen, and in the supermarket. The aim of this model is a description of the effective speaker's use of requests to obtain appropriate responses in this particular and unique context of small instructional groups that are peer-directed within classrooms.

The model of the effective speaker holds that students, in instructional groups, who use requests that are direct, sincere, on-task, designated to particular speakers, and revised when they initially do not obtain an appropriate response are successful in obtaining appropriate responses from others. Effective speakers in this context must express speech acts clearly and directly in an attempt to minimize the ambiguity in multiple interpretations of the same utterance. For example, speakers must use direct forms and specifically designate them to one particular listener when making a request. Secondly, in the classroom, requests that are on-task—that is, those that refer to the shared activities in the teaching and learning situation—are most likely to be understood by listeners, and these types of requests are most likely to be successful in obtaining appropriate responses from listeners. Thirdly, requests that are understood by listeners as sincere are most likely to result in obtaining appropriate responses according to our model. And finally, effecive speakers are flexible in producing the requests so that, for example, they will revise their initial request when the appropriate response from the listener is not obtained.

The methodological approach taken in this research of the effective speaker's use of requests and responses in peer-directed instructional groups in the elementary school combines both qualitative and quantitative methods. It is an observational method that describes students' use of requests to obtain responses in this particular context. Terms define the bases of the model, and the particular and unique are illustrated by excerpts of real conversational interaction from classrooms. Three issues will be addressed: *the method of data collection*, audio and video recording and sampling of communicative processes; *analysis of data,* including the transcription and coding of these processes; and the *presentation of results,* that, is the description of aspects of communicative processes and reading groups' requests and responses. The results provide several levels of description: (1) characteristics of requests and responses, (2) the prediction of responses given requests, (3) individual differences, and (4) qualitative reporting of data that enhances the statistical descriptions of individual differences.

The Two Studies on First and Third Grade Students

In the two studies that are reported here, first and third grade students, in peer-directed reading groups, were observed. Audio and video recording of interaction were collected and transcribed, so that requests and responses could be identified and described. The following questions were addressed: (1) Are students effective in their use of requests for action and information in their instructional groups? (2) Are there individual differences in their use of requests and responses, and are the differences stable over the year? (3) Do particular aspects of requests predict whether appropriate responses will be obtained? (4) Is there a relationship between achievement in reading and students' use of requests and responses?

Study 1: First Grade Students

Previous research on first grade children provides support for the model of the effective speaker (Wilkinson & Calculator, 1982). Data were collected on 30 subjects interacting in their peer-directed reading groups during the academic year. The groups were audio- and videotaped eight times, and the segments of peer interaction were transcribed and coded to the characterization of requests that was identified in the model of the effective speaker. The data base, which consisted of more than 1,025 requests and their responses, showed that first grade students are, on the whole, effective speakers, since they obtained appropriate responses to their requests for action and information about two thirds of the time. The typical student usually produced requests that were direct, sincere, on-task, and designated to a particular listener. In cases when the listener did not comply with the speaker's request, students revised their requests two-fifths of the time. Figure 1-1 shows the characteristics of requests and appropriate responses (adapted from Wilkinson & Calculator, 1982). The data show individual differences in the characteristics of direct forms, revision, and appropriate responses.

Further analyses of the data set provided strong evidence for predictive nature of the model. A hierarchy of log-linear models was used to fit the data. The model that best fit the data assumed that there were associations among the five characteristics identified (direct, sincere, on-task, designated, revised) and whether the request obtained an appropriate response, and whether a request obtains that response depends upon all of the other six characteristics identified by the model.

Some of the most interesting results to emerge from the quantitative analysis of the first-grade data concern differences between the two types of requests and individual differences among the children in usage. The data show that requests for information in comparison with requests for action are used more frequently (57 versus 43 percent), twice as likely to take the direct form (88 versus 42 percent), and more likely to receive an appropriate response from listeners (82 versus 61 percent). The children showed the greatest individual differences in three of the characteristics: the directness of the form of the request; whether the request,

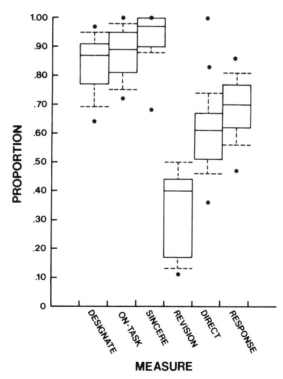

Figure 1-1. Characteristics of requests and appropriate responses: First grade students in reading groups.

if initially unsuccessful, was revised; and obtaining appropriate responses to requests.

The results of this study suggest that the model of the effective speakers' use of requests should be tested further.

Study 2: Third Grade Students in Reading Groups

Methods of Data Collection. Subjects. The subjects in the second study were 35 third-grade students who comprised seven reading groups in the third grade of one school (Wilkinson & Spinelli, 1983). The reading groups were determined by the teachers prior to the study, and there were between three and six subjects per group. According to the teachers, the students' reading skills at the beginning of the school year differed among the groups, even though no formal assessment of these skills had been given. All of the students were Caucasian, native speakers of English, and from middle-class families. They ranged in age from seven to eight years; they attended the school for the academic year. There were no students who were diagnosed to have learning disabilities or any language disorders. There were 16 males and 19 females.

Recording the reading event. Reading activities were the units of sample for data collection. Reading activity typically began at 9:00 and lasted until approximately 9:40 in each of the classrooms; teachers announced both the beginning and the end of the activity. Students chose their seats at the reading tables designated by the teacher. The teachers often provided instructions for the reading groups when the students were in the whole-group formation; however, some of the teachers provided instructions after the students had formed their small reading groups. In both situations, the completion of the instructions marked the beginning of the reading event.

All of the groups were similar in their organization and structure, such as the way that activities were initiated, maintained, and terminated. Initially, assignments and instructions were presented by the teachers: the teacher then left the reading group and the students functioned as a group in order to accomplish the individual tasks. In all cases, the task was the same for all of the members of the group for that particular reading activity (e.g., a worksheet or a workbook page). The final phase of the reading group included another teacher-directed period that occurred shortly before the groups disintegrated, where the teacher often provided evaluation.

All of the groups were seated at small tables within the classrooms that also contained other groups of students. Background noise and general environmental characteristics appeared to be comparable among the groups. And all of the groups performed one or more activities requiring a written response, such as completing worksheets, drawing a picture of events that the students had read about, or printing sentences from the stories that they had read.

The reading activities were audio- and videotaped in the classrooms for each of the reading groups. Data were collected in the fall, for the three-and-one-half weeks at the end of October and beginning of November, and then again in the spring for three-and-one-half weeks in April. There were three separate tapings for each reading group in each season for a total of six samples for each group; there were approximately 42 hours of recordings.

Two portable video cameras were used to record the reading activity of each group; cameras were visible to the students and were positioned across from one another so that nearly full-face views of all of the students would be recorded on one or the other camera. Two microphones were placed in the middle of each group's table.

Prior to, during, and following the recording, two observers prepared descriptions of the ongoing events in the group to supplement the recordings with relevant contextual information which may not have been included on the tapes. There were four adults in addition to the students, teachers, and school staff in the classrooms. The subjects were familiar with the presence of several adults in the classroom in addition to the teachers—including parents and aides, among others. According to the principal, videotaping of both teachers and students was common in these classrooms.

Individual assessment. Information concerning each student's language ability and reading achievement was collected by individual testing in the fall and in the spring; the assessments typically lasted for 45 minutes. A free speech sample consisting of approximately 50 spontaneous utterances from each student was obtained during an informal conversation in which an experimenter posed open-ended questions regarding topics presumed to be of interest to the children, such as television, friends, and so on. Grammatical complexity was assessed by segmenting each student's transcript into a series of communication units, then computing the average number of words per unit using a procedure based upon Loban (1976). Thirty communication units were used as an index of the Loban score.

Students' grammatical comprehension was assessed by their performance on the Miller-Yoder Test of Grammatical Comprehension (Miller & Yoder, 1975). This test, which consists of 84 items, requires the student to point to the picture, given a choice of four stimuli, that depicts the meaning of each utterance read by the experimenter. Various syntactic structures are tested, including prepositions, subject and object pronouns, possessives, and tenses.

Reading achievement was assessed in the fall and spring by the Metropolitan Reading Achievement Test.

Transcription of tapes. The videotapes collected for each group were transcribed by a member of the research team who had been present during data collection. The relatively long segment of all-student interaction for each group was chosen for detailed analysis in this study (10–30 minutes). During this segment, the teacher was not present in the group; typically, she was in the classroom assisting other students. Transcripts were rechecked against both of the tapes. Percentage agreement on these data had been established for word and utterance boundaries, and they exceeded 90 percent. Following transcription, the videotapes were viewed for relevant nonverbal and spatial information which then was included on the transcripts.

Two transcripts, one coded previously by the same observer, the second by an associate, were randomly selected and recoded by the second author. Interobserver agreement, represented as the proportion of coding agreements divided by the number of agreements plus disagreements, was then computed with respect to each of the variables included in this study. Agreement ranged from 90 percent to 100 percent for each coding category.

Coding: The samples of data selected for analysis were coded according to the following categories:

Utterance: A string of words communicating one idea.

Requests for action or directives: Attempts by speakers to get listeners to perform actions.

Requests for information or questions: Attempts by speakers to obtain information from listeners.

All requests were coded into the following categories:

On-task/off-task: An on-task request is related to the academic content, procedures, and/or materials of the assignment. Examples of on-task requests for information are: "Kara, what's that word/" "How do you do this page?" "Where can we get a dictionary?" Examples of on-task requests for action are: "Sit down and get back to work." "When can we get a dictionary?" An off-task request is unrelated to the task, such as "Did you watch that show about the magician last night?" "Where'd you get that T-shirt?"

Designated/nondesignated: A designated request is directed to a specific listener. The intended listener may be overtly signaled by behaviors such as naming, such as "Susie, give me the pen." or gaze or may not be overtly signaled by the speaker. Nondesignated requests are directed to two or more listeners.

Sincere/insincere: A sincere request for information is a request in which the speaker seeks information from a listener whom she expects to have the desired information when she herself does not have it, such as "What is the answer to number two?" A sincere request for action is a request in which the speaker wants an action carried out, cannot or does not want to perform the action herself, and is directed to a listener who is capable of complying with the request (Labov & Fanshel, 1977). Insincere requests for information and action violate the definitions for sincere requests: an example of an insincere request for information is one child saying to another about his drawing: "That is a pig?" "Go ask the chalk." is an example of an insincere request for action, which was given in response to the request "How do you spell chalk?"

Direct/indirect: For requests for action, direct forms include imperatives ("Give me that eraser"); direct requests for information include wh-questions ("How do you spell think?"), yes/no questions ("Is can spelled c-a-n?"), and tag questions "We're supposed to do this page, aren't we?"). All other forms were coded as indirect requests and included as commonly occurring forms of embedded requests ("Can I borrow your eraser?"), declarative statements ("I need help"), intonational questions ("Can is spelled c-a-n?"), and nonlexical requests ("Whaa?").

Revision/nonrevision: A revised request is the reinitiation of the same request made previously by the same speaker to the same listener within three turns (all speech by one speaker until another speaker speaks) of the initial request. Revisions may or may not be elicited by the listener. Examples include the following:

Jim: What's this supposed to be?
Tim: Huh?
Jim: What's this supposed to be?

Sue: You should put your books away.
        (no response)
        We should put our books away.

Nonrevisions are all requests that do not qualify as reinitiations defined.

Appropriate/inappropriate responses. Responses to requests were coded as appropriate if the requested action or information was provided or if a reason was given for the lack of compliance, as illustrated by the following examples:

Jay: Jeff, can I borrow your eraser?
Jeff: Don't have an eraser.
Jay: What goes here?
Jeff: Huh? oh, a bird.

Inappropriate responses included responses where the listener refused outright to comply ("No, I won't tell you."), nonresponses, postponements ("I'll tell you later"), irrelevant responses ("Doo-de-doo-de doo"), and indications that the listener did not know the appropriate answer ("Uh, I'm not sure . . .").

Measures. For each subject, the quantity of speech was computed as the number of utterances produced. In addition, the following proportional scores were computed: all requests divided by all utterances; appropriate responses divided by all requests; direct forms of requests divided by all requests; on-task requests divided by all requests; designated requests divided by all requests; sincere requests divided by all requests; revised requests divided by all requests which failed to elicit responses.

Results of Study. The data base included 11,915 utterances, of which 2,650 (22%) were requests, with 878 requests for action and 1,772 requests for information.

Differences in initial reading achievement and language ability. One standard score was computed for reading achievement from the two tests administered in the fall and spring. Kruskal-Wallis analyses revealed that there were significant differences in ability among the seven groups (χ^2 (6) = 12.90, p<.05). Further analyses revealed that the fall reading achievement was positively related to the spring achievement (tau = 0.53, p<.01). The groups differed to a greater degree in reading achievement in the spring (χ^2 (6) = 14.93, p<.01) in comparison to the fall (χ^2 (6) = 5.90, p<.42).

One standard score for language knowledge was calculated, based on scores from the two separate assessments in the fall and spring. Kruskal-Wallis analyses for overall language ability revealed that there were no significant differences among the groups.

Question 1: Are third graders effective in their use of requests?

The data for the characteristics of requests and appropriate responses are displayed in Figure 1-2. These displays are an adaptation of Tukey's (1977) "box and whisker" diagram, which has the advantage of displaying all the data and its variability. The following information is given for each variable: The lowest value in the sample (black circle), the 10th percentile (dash bar), the 25th percentile (solid bar), and the median (solid bar), the 75th percentile (solid bar), the 90th percentile (dash bar), and the highest value in the sample (black circle). The "box" represents the interquartile range, or middle half of the sample.

There seem to be two kinds of variables represented in Figure 1-2. One group of variables, represented on the extreme left-hand side of the figure, shows high medians and moderate interquartile ranges (0.04 to 0.16) indicating low spread and ceiling effects. This group of variables which includes designated-listener, on-task, and sincere requests, suggests a common competence among the children on these aspects of their communication. The second group of variables, which can be seen on the extreme right-hand side of the figure, shows medians in the middle range with moderate interquartile ranges (0.10 to 0.15) indicating medium spread. These variables, which include direct-forms, revisions, and appropriate responses to requests, show enough variation among children to suggest genuine individual differences.

Overall, the data showed this group of third graders were effective

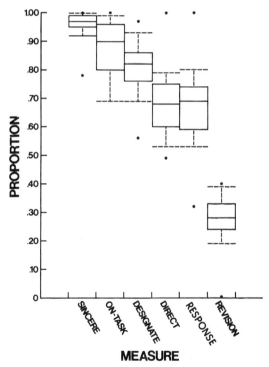

Figure 1-2. Characteristics of requests and appropriate responses: Third grade students in reading groups.

in obtaining appropriate responses to their requests for action and information more than two-thirds of the time. The typical child usually made requests that were direct, sincere, on-task, and to a designated listener. When the listener did not respond appropriately, the typical child tried again only one third of the time.

Question 2: Are there individual differences in use of requests and responses and are the differences stable?

Group data. With some exceptions, the patterns concerning both requests for information and requests for action were stable from fall to spring. Wilcoxon Matched pairs Signed Ranks Tests were used to examine the significance of differences between fall and spring, and between the two types of requests. There was only one significant difference between seasons. Designated requests ($z = 2.48, p<.01$) were used more often by the students in the spring than in the fall.

There were several differences between the two types of requests. Requests for action were more likely to be sincere ($z = 2.30, p<.02$) and to be designated to a particular listener ($z = 3.44, p<.01$). Requests for information were more likely to occur (rate of requests, $z = 4.87, p<.01$), to be revised when initially unsuccessful ($z = 3.43, p<.01$), to be direct in form ($z = 4.57, p<01$), and to receive an appropriate response ($z = 4.88, p< .01$).

This pattern of differential language usage for requests for information and action reflects increasing sophistication in language usage, including the differential uses of both types of requests. In contrast, adults' requests for information, typically, do not take a direct form, which is considered to be rude and impolite. For the students in this study, the probability of listener understanding may be increased by use of the characteristics of designated listener and by reference to the topic at hand. On the other hand, the probability of listener understanding and compliance seems to be increased by the use of sincere requests of a direct form.

Individual differences. Overall, individual differences among students are shown in Figure 1-2. In this section, we consider selected examples of students who are effective and ineffective speakers, including references to quantitative (see Figure 1-3) and qualitative data.

Student K is a good example of an effective and appropriate speaker. Karen designates her listeners, uses direct forms, and revises her unsuccessful requests at above average levels. Her performance on the sincere and on-task variables suggests that she speaks appropriately. Several factors may contribute to her high level of success in obtaining appropriate responses. She frequently obtains her listeners' attention in a direct manner by using names or tapping, rather than just looking at them. Her requests are specific; for example, she may ask her listeners to confirm her choice or to select one of two alternatives. She also tends to revise rather than repeat her requests. Although Karen frequently reinitiates when her requests are unsuccessful initially, she appears able to determine when a reinitiation will be unsuccessful and does not persist. Furthermore, this speaker makes relatively few requests; they are usually successful.

In the following exchange, Karen's requests to Diane demonstrate some of these behaviors.

Karen: Diane (touches) Does this say 'fazed, faced'?
Diane: Faced. I'm done with my first page.
Karen: None of them rhymes with blazed.
Diane: Fazed, faced, that's what I put down.
Karen: Diane (taps) I don't get this.
Diane: It's a siren.
Karen: I know but (reads) siren, lemon, siren, liken.
Diane: (circles correct answer on Karen's page)

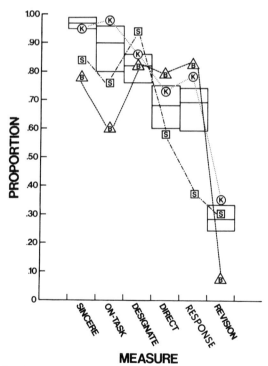

Figure 1-3. Individual differences in characteristics of requests and appropriate responses of students in reading groups.

Karen: (tapping) I don't get this.
Diane: (ignores)
Karen: Hey (looks at Diane) this could be 'hermit', couldn't it?
Diane: Yeah.
Karen: (smiles) Hermant.

Scott, shown as S in Figure 1-3, is an example of an ineffective speaker. His success in obtaining appropriate responses is below the tenth percentile. He tends to make fewer direct and sincere requests than his peers and is off-task more often than other children. Not only are Scott's direct requests less frequent than those of his peers, they are more aggravated, that is, stronger (Labov & Fanshel, 1977). Scott initiates or is drawn into arguments readily. These result in numerous unsuccessful requests. In the following example, Ben and Scott have been arguing over the possession of a pencil. Ben is taunting Scott in order to continue the argument.

Ben: Tell me more about it Scott, Big Scott boy.
Scott: Stop that or your're gonna get beat up outside at recess.
Ben: Gonna make me?
Scott: Yeah, outside for recess.
Ben: Big Scott Boy
Scott: You two be out there.

Although Scott's off-task behavior may contribute to his lack of success the content of this talk may be a more significant factor. He brings up socially "taboo" topics which appear to offend his classmates. The following example illustrates this point.

Ben: Scott, I can't stand that talk so please be quiet.
Scott: (unintelligible)
Ben: God, shut up.

Scott's insincerity may also contribute to his lack of success. In the following example, the group has been off-task for several minutes. Scott's attempt to get the group on-task is of questionable sincerity and Donald's response acknowledges this.

Donald: Scott, can't you ever stop laughing and making jokes?
Scott: Now let's all be serious.
Donald: How can you be serious, Scott?
Scott: I don't know. It's hard.

Bob, shown as B in Figure 1-3, is an inappropriate yet effective speaker. He exhibits low scores on sincerity and on-task, but his rate of obtaining appropriate responses is very high (0.82). He makes many direct requests and designates his listeners (0.82). In addition to specifying his listeners by name he makes frequent use of attention-getters such as "hey," "oh-oh," "see," and "y'know something?" as in the following example.

Bob: Oh-oh, Tim, lookit what's behind you.
Tim: (looks)

Bob's off-task comments may contribute to his high rate of obtaining appropriate responses. Although the children in the group do sometimes comment on the frequency of Bob's off-task behaviors, they often are interested in them. One reason is that Bob successfully uses these comments to entertain his peers as the following example illustrates.

Bob: Wanna see my funny hat?
Tim: Okay.
Bob: Da-da. (places book on his head)

Bob has learned that he can sometimes control the behavior of his peers by controlling their attention. When the children in his group threaten to report his actions to the teacher he distracts them by making attention-getting statements and requests for information. The children often respond to these requests, perhaps because they are already attending to him and because they know the answers. This tactic is occasionally successful. In the first example, Bob has taken Tim's notebook. He distracts Tim for a while but is unsuccessful in obtaining an appropriate response from his peer. In the second example, Cindy reprimands Bob for talking about and touching the experimenter's microphone. His distraction attempt is successful.

Tim: Gimme that.
Bob: Watch this. (plays with notebook)
Tim: Don't C'mon. I'm telling. I'm telling.
Bob: There. Two and two is four. Ain't I smart?
Tim: I'm telling.
Bob: Two times two is four.
Tim: I'm telling.
Bob: What's two times two?
Tim: It's four you dumb. (expletive deleted)

Bob: Two? Two twos?
Tim: I know, it's three, ya big dummy.
Bob: You think two times two is three, hey?
Tim: No, it's three ya dip. (expletive deleted)
Bob: Three times two are four. Four times four are eight. (singing)
Tim: Better erase that cause I'm telling the teacher.
Bob: 28 times 28 is 30, is 65, 65 times 65 is 232.
Tim: I'm going to tell. (leaves)
Cindy: Bobby, I'm telling on you.
Bob: What'd I do?
Cindy: You're talking and you're not supposed to talk about that stuff.
Bob: What stuff? OK, I'll get working. Ouch, my eyeball.
Cindy: Tell on you anyhow.
Bob: Tell on me, I'll tell on you.
Cindy: What am I doing?
Tim: You're crying.
Cindy: I am not crying.
Bob: Well you were, so there. (Children resume working)

Many of Bob's utterances suggest that he is an attentive listener. He frequently helps to maintain topics by requesting clarification and elaboration and by adding new information, as can be seen in the following examples.

Tim: Oh-oh, we're in trouble.
Bob: I know, I know, I know.
Tim: We better say our prayers. You know, my ma, when she saw my report card, she smacked me.
Bob: (giggle) How did she smack you?
Tim: She saw the report card and she went, she went (imitates nagging). And she went (imitates nagging, slap). Ooh!
Bob: You know what? Last year my mother saw my report card, said I went to Unit 3, and goes (slaps self) and then she goes, I go. What's your big problem—You're in Unit 3, why'nt you stay in Kindergarten?
Lisa: I don't get this.
Bob: What don't you get?

Question 3: Do particular characteristics of requests predict whether appropriate responses will be obtained?
This question was addressed by classifying the requests in a multi-dimensional way contingency table defined by the following dimensions: response, direct-form, designated-listener, on-task, sincere, revision, and request for action/information. Log linear models were fit to this table in an effort to find the simplest model that adequately predicted the

Rank-order correlations were computed between these variables and a standardized score for overall reading achievement. Rank-order correlations were used since they are as powerful as Pearson correlations, but are less likely to be biased by extreme cases, which occurred occasionally in these data. It was expected that the measures of the appropriate response, direct-form, and revision were likely to show a relationship with reading achievement, but the other measures were not likely to yield high correlations for purely statistical reasons of lack of variability in the measures showing ceiling effects.

The correlation between direct forms and reading achievement was tau = 0.23 ($p<.03$). One interpretation of this finding is that students who are direct in expressing their wants are securing appropriate responses to their on-task requests, which may contribute to their knowledge of reading. Another possible interpretation of the data is that the better readers are more sophisticated in their use of language and aware of multiple ways to obtain appropriate responses.

Conclusion

The results of these two studies have shown that first and third grade students are, on the whole, effective speakers in their all-peer reading groups, since they obtained appropriate responses to their requests for action and information most of the time. The data show progressive generalization of the model of the effective speaker's use of requests and responses. These data and previous data show consistency in the model across grade (first, third), and stability over time (longitudinal, one point in time).

The typical student in these situations produced requests that were direct, sincere, on-task, and designated to a particular listener. The use of language by these school-age children places a premium on explicitness, directness, and assertiveness. This pattern is consistent with findings reported by Ervin-Tripp (1976), Read and Cherry (1978), and Montes (1978). The pattern contrasts with that typically associated with adults, who express cooperation and politeness in requests through their use of indirect forms (Ervin-Tripp, 1976). Individual differences emerged in both characteristics of students' requests and in their effectiveness in obtaining appropriate responses.

The results also suggest the possible causes of the maintenance of differences in reading achievement throughout the year that are not actively directed by the teacher. Initial differences among students' achievement and effective use of language may be maintained by differences in communicative processes within these groups. Thus, the positive correlation between requests and reading achievement may reflect the true associations between them. These associations may be either directly or indirectly linked. In the direct case, students who obtain appropriate responses to their requests may learn skills as a consequence. In the indirect case, some other intellectual competence(s) promote both the production of requests and responses and skills. Further research should be directed to exploring these relationships, the sources of individual differences in language use, and their consequences for achievement.

Not much is known about peer-directed instructional groups, even though they constitute a significant educational task for students. Teacher-directed instructional groups have been a more common focus of previous research (Sorensen & Hallinan, 1984; Weinstein, 1976). The groups studied here are less structured than those directed by teachers, and more structured than peer play groups who interact cooperatively, but are not focused on a specific instructional task given by the teacher (e.g., Genishi & DiPaolo, 1982). We need to know more about these groups, since we already have evidence that shows that for some students, in some subcultures, achievement is facilitated in cooperative, peer-directed situations (Au, 1980).

References

Au, K. (1980). Participation structures in a reading lesson with Hawaiian children: Analysis of a culturally appropriate instructional event. *Anthopology and Educational Quarterly, 11* (2), 91–115.

Bishop, T., Fienberg, S., & Holland, P. (1975). *Discrete multivariate analyses: Theory and practice.* Cambridge, MA: MIT Press.

Ervin-Tripp, S. (1976). Is Sybil there: The structure of some American directives. *Language in Society, 5,* 25–66.

Genishi, C., & DiPaolo, M. (1982). Learning through argument in a preschool. In L. Cherry Wilkinson (Ed.), *Communicating in the Classroom.* New York: Academic Press.

Labov, W., & Fanshel, D. (1977). *Therapeutic discourse.* New York: Academic Press.

Loban, W. (1978). *Language development.* Champaign, IL: National Council of Teachers of English.

Miller, J. & Yoder, D. (1972). *The Miller-Yoder Test of Grammatical Comprehension.* Madison, WI: University of Wisconsin Press.

Montes, R. (1978). Extending a concept: Functioning directly. In R. Shuy & R. Griffin (Eds.), *Children's functional language in the early years.* Washington, DC: Center for Applied Linguistics.

Mosteller, F., & Tukey, J. (1977). *Data analysis and regression.* Reading, MA: Addison-Wesley.

Read, B., & Cherry, L. (1978). Preschool children's production of directive forms. *Discourse Processes, 1* (3), 233–245.

Smith, J. (1983). Quantitative verses qualitative research: An attempt to clarify the issue. *Educational Researcher,* March, 1983, 6–13.

Sorensen, A., & Hallinan, M. (1984). Rare effects on assignment to ability groups. In P. Peterson, L. Cherry Wilkinson, & M. Hallinan (Eds.), *The social context of instruction: Processes and organization of instructional groups.* Orlando, FL: Academic Press.

Tukey, J. (1977). *Exploratory data analysis.* Reading, MA: Addison-Wesley.

Weinstein, R. (1976). Reading group membership in the first grade: Teacher behavior and pupil experience over time. *Journal of Educational Psychology, 68,* 103–116.

Wilkinson, L. Cherry, & Calculator, S. (1982). Requests and responses in peer-directed reading groups. *American Educational Research Journal, 19* (1), 107–120.

Wilkinson, L. Cherry, & Spinelli, F. (1983). Using requests effectively in peer-directed instructional groups. *American Educational Research Journal, 20* (4), 479–501.

---

[1]Jackknifing is a method for assessing the degree to which an effect estimated from the data for all subjects persists when a subgroup of subjects is deleted from the analysis. In the present analysis, the subgroups are reading groups.

Chapter 2
Classroom Contexts for Learning

Rita S. Brause
Fordham University

The contexts of learning focused on in this chapter are those created by the people interacting in a classroom—the teacher and the students. The interaction between and among these individuals, rather than the organization of the furniture, seems to be the critical component in establishing effective learning environments. Using the lens provided by ethnography to study the tacit, implicit rules and practices evident in classrooms will help us bring to a level of consciousness what it is like to be a student in our classrooms. Once we are aware of what it is like to be a student once again, we can consider the effect of the classroom environment on student learning.

Media View of Classroom Interaction

Before looking at real classrooms, let's look at some classrooms depicted in recent movies, acknowledging the potential exaggeration inherent in such presentations. In the film *War Games*, the scene opens with the teacher criticizing the teen-age hero, David, for entering class late. The teacher continues to ostracize David by calling attention to his failing grade on a test that is being returned. When David is caught talking with his peers during class, he is suspended from school. The teacher humiliates David before his peers, without once finding anything positive or at least neutral to convey. The wonder is that David made the effort to get to class at all.

In the film *E.T.* we see the teacher lecturing students, while frogs, like the students, jump about in airtight containers. The students have no opportunity to participate in a dialogue or discussion. The teacher's monologue is the focus for the group. The students are not viewed as important in the conduct of the lesson. Rather, they are the audience for the teacher's comments. The interaction that occurs here is not an academic one. It is a display of power. The students' knowledge is not used as a base for development. There is little interaction—there is no involvement of students and teacher. An adversarial relationship seems to exist.

In both these films, the students are turned off. They have been humiliated, and they feel alienated. The teachers in both classrooms control the focus of the class. They interact negatively with the students, and fail to establish a mutually rewarding environment. The teachers do not seem to recognize the negative impact of their interactions with the students. The students are going through the motions of learning by attending class and completing writing assignments. But the dynamism apparent in productive, collaborative working environments contrasts with the setting the protagonist in each film provides outside of the classroom. Admittedly, these are not real classrooms, but they do present us with some truth. Many viewers sympathize with these students—and we all recognize these classrooms.

Children's Imaginary Classrooms

Another source of information for what classrooms are like is that of the children's game, where the youngsters, typically in the lower grades, "play school!" When I've observed these childhood simulations, I've heard children *reprimand* students for their behavior. They *test* student knowledge of rote facts. They *order* students to move about. But I've not heard them engage in cooperative activities or explore, inquire, investigate. Rather, they test and they ridicule . . . just as the teachers in the films did.

It is important to note the fact that children do play school. School is important in students' lives—so they want to get the rules right. They want to succeed. The rules for success which they have tacitly identified are behavioral ones. They obviously infer from their participation in classrooms that behavior is important because it seems to be a predominant concern in their role playing. Their games give added credibility to the model presented in the movies.

Learning Outside of School

We can look at another setting outside of schools as a basis for examining what we're doing in our classrooms. The *video game arcades* that have attracted many of our students provide important data for us to consider. The people (children and adults) who feed quarters into these machines voluntarily choose to participate and they pay considerably to do so.

(Students in classrooms pay with their time in contrast to the quarters paid in the arcade). Players are rewarded in the arcade in many ways including:

- success due to constant repetition of patterns without any negativism or condescension
- immediate feedback from multiple sources
- encouragement to try again
- difficulty set by the participant
- increasing scores (points never deducted, only added)
- privacy when desired—otherwise, interactive play as desired—with players seeking and receiving help and advice from others who are watching.

Although·very limited concepts are developed through these games, an important aspect of these games is that they provide an *exciting, challenging, risk-taking,* and *rewarding experience* which causes players to return for future games, and to attempt increasing *challenges.* These are critical attributes of learners which we see evidenced in game arcades. Can we establish classrooms where participants would voluntary exchange something they valued for their participation?

Ethnographic Approaches to Classroom Context

James Britton (1982, p. 197) tells us that "what happens in any classroom is the result of interacting teacher and pupil behaviors." According to Kounin (1970) and Good (1981), among others, students consider teachers responsible in large measure for establishing the classroom environment. The success of the group in achieving its goals is based on the *interactive* nature of the setting. We can look at classrooms from multiple perspectives. If we use the perspective of one individual in an interaction among 25 to 35 participants, we are not obtaining a comprehensive understanding of that setting. Some recent research in classrooms has focused on understanding the nature of interactions among the participants. Such investigations recognize the volatility of these settings. By seeking to understand the educational settings from the participants' perspectives, researchers have adopted methods used in anthropological research where the focus is to understand what it is like to walk in the shoes of the participants.

Shavelson (1983) tells us that each classroom is unique—as is each social situation. I have selected two factors of classroom interactions because I believe they are important in providing effective learning environments. The qualities I have identified are: *trusting environments,* and *supportive environments.* I will discuss the characteristics of each of these and note implications for providing students with classroom settings which encourage learning.

Trusting Environments

Trusting environments are essential for successful interactions. Some would suggest that we must trust ourselves before we can trust others. In an educational context this may be represented by trusting one's self to be successful as a learner. (An analysis of the complex task of language acquisition achieved by students prior to school entrance provides strong evidence of each individual's success at learning).

A more limited focus on trust would be concerned with worldly goods—such as trust that a pencil borrowed would not be intentionally retained. In viewing classrooms, what level of trust do teachers provide? Consider the following:

● Are your personal belongings locked up?
● Are your students' personal belongings locked up?
● How is access to teaching materials acquired? How is the hall pass acquired? How is access to the library gained?
● Do students cover their written work when you look over their shoulders?

Your answers reflect the trust in your classroom. Continuing our consideration of trust, let's analyze these hypothetical teacher utterances which may help convey some of the dimensions of a trusting environment:

(1) Let me know when you're ready.
(2) Are you doing your assignment?
(3) I'm watching everything you're doing.
(4) Do you need more time?
(5) Why don't you know this?
(6) How can I help you?

Utterance (1), (4), and (6) convey trust while (2), (3), and (5) suggest a suspicious stance.

Civikly (1982) identified six conditions for the teacher to address to convey trust in the classroom. These include:

1. The teacher must be perceived by the students as a significant other.

2. The teacher must be perceived by the student as a credible appraiser and evaluator.
3. The teacher must be consistent in evaluations of the student.
4. The teacher must be accurate in evaluations and not exaggerate opinions of the student. Compliments must be genuine and traceable to behaviors actually accomplished by the student.
5. The teacher must be perceived by the student as personally concerned with the student's development and interests.
6. The student must believe that he or she is responsible for personal achievements.

McDermott (1977) discusses trusting relations as "a crucial subset of working agreements people use to make sense of one another's classroom behavior. In the classroom these issues translate into how the teacher and children understand each other's behavior as directed to the best interest of what they are trying to do together and how they hold each other accountable for any breach of the formulated consensus" (p. 199).

Teachers and learners work together in many ways. *They respect each other.* This respect may take many different forms. We see respect for privacy in a classroom when we don't probe into others' lives; we see respect for individuals when care is taken to eliminate ridicule of others' dress, language, or behavior. A basic, tacit agreement is reached among the participants in a classroom that includes: I won't ridicule you if you don't ridicule me; I'll respect your privacy if you respect mine. This level of trust which is found in many classes, although necessary for establishing a trusting environment, is not sufficient.

Not only must the participants be *ridicule-free* and physically safe in a nonthreatening environment, but the academic setting must be *content-rich* as well. A trusting educational environment must provide the opportunity for all participants, including the teacher, to learn. The agreement must be understood as:

> "I'm here to learn—you're responsible for helping me accomplish that objective." or
> "I'll help you teach me if you help me learn." or
> "I believe I can learn—you have to believe I can as well." or
> "Help me learn what is important for me to know."

These beliefs must be jointly held and realized by the teacher as well as the students in an ideal trusting relationship.

The ways in which each person's language and dress are accepted in the classroom are concrete examples of the respect each receives and the trust present in the class. Piestrup (1973) studied the interactions between children using Black English Vernacular (BEV) and teachers using a more standard dialect. She found: "To the extent that the teachers of children speaking BEV tried to stop them from using BEV dialect in the classroom, the children were unable to get to the task of learning to read. These children's use of dialect either remained the same or increased depending on how often the teachers corrected their speech. For children whose use of dialect was often corrected, reading scores tended to be low. In classrooms where the children were allowed to talk and read in dialect, vernacular use did not increase and reading scores were higher. When the dialect was not treated as a barrier to communication, the children and the teacher were able to spend time on reading tasks. However, when dialect was treated as a problem in the relations between the teacher and children, the criticism interfered with their formulating trusting agreements" (p. 209).

In a trusting relationship, the student and the teacher understand each others' behaviors as directed to the best interest of what they are trying to do *together*. What they are trying to do together in the classroom is increase one anothers' conceptual background while learning how to participate productively in the classroom society. A trusting environment must simultaneously provide a safe setting while increasing conceptual knowledge.

In this regard, Britton, Burgess, Martin, McLeod, and Rosen (1975) remind us of the need for establishing classroom environments wherein the students and teachers are willing to take risks, explore new experiences, accept new information, and move to a new viewpoint. A trusting environment is one which frees the learner to explore with the knowledge that these efforts will not be taken lightly or ridiculed. Risk-taking by all (including the teacher) will make it possible for participants to understand in new ways. In place of restraining behavior, a trusting environment liberates the student to learn with the assurance of support as needed.

The trusting environment may provide differing amounts of trust. Even within the same classroom one student may be placed in a more trusting relationship than another. So we need to consider the ways in which we are communicating our trust to each of our students. If we don't trust them—or they don't trust us—we will not have a successful relationship.

Supportive Environments

Educational settings that support learning are optimistic ones, recognizing on the one hand that learners need to succeed while acknowledging on the other hand that success is not possible without some failure or frustration. But those failures and frustrations are used as a basis to achieve success. Persons in supportive environments *expect participants to succeed eventually;* the setting facilitates the achievement of success. The participants are engaged cooperatively in an activity; students, teachers, and administrators collaborate to achieve this objective. McDermott (1977) suggests that "successful learning environments provide children with the possibility of discovering clearly defined tasks and the time to work on them until mastery is achieved . . . unsuccessful environments are marked by children spending years struggling to get organized and to pay attention rather than learning" (p. 198).

Brause & Mayher, 1982, 1983 and Brause, Mayher, & Bruno, 1982 reported important examples of this cooperative principle from a study of elementary classes. Some characteristics which distinguish cooperative settings are identified in the ranges presented in Table 2-1 and scaled to resemble a semantic differential.

The interaction evidenced in classroom activities may be evaluated for evidences of cooperation using these contrasts. The closer the score is to 50, the more cooperative the environment. If a cooperative setting facilitates learning as suggested by many, including McDermott (1977) and Cahir and Kovac (1981), the objectives for all participants in an interaction will be to achieve a high rating. This continuum may be divided into four quadrants reflecting a range of cooperation listed from most to least cooperative. These are labelled: ADVOCATING, FACILITATING, ACCEPTING and OBSTRUCTING. Table 2-2 presents distinguishing attributes of each type of cooperative behavior. To systematize the evaluation of settings using Table 2-1, representative criteria are presented in Table 2-2.

TABLE 2-1. CONTINUUM OF COOPERATION

Most Cooperative										Least Cooperative
United										Fractious
	10	9	8	7	6	5	4	3	2	1
Responsive										Antagonistic
	10	9	8	7	6	5	4	3	2	1
Pliant										Contrary
	10	9	8	7	6	5	4	3	2	1
Alacritous										Laggardly
	10	9	8	7	6	5	4	3	2	1
Collaborative										Restrained
	10	9	8	7	6	5	4	3	2	1

TABLE 2-2. TYPES OF COOPERATION IN STUDENT-TEACHER INTERCHANGES

I ADVOCATING	II FACILITATING
Seeks turn at talk Responds appropriately Presents adequate information Active pacing	At least one characteristic identified as advocat- ing

III ACCEPTING	IV OBSTRUCTING
Accepts imposed turn Presents restricted or limited information Moderate pacing	Rejects imposed turn Presents irrelevant information Pacing delayed Unacceptably bidding for turn at talk

The following examples of actual classroom interactions indicate how verbal exchanges can be classified as advocating, facilitating, accepting, and obstructing behaviors. These were collected by Brause, Mayher, and Bruno (1982).

ADVOCATING

(1) T: Who remembers what a synonym is?
            (Several students raise hands)
      T: (Addressing student who is raising his hand): Pharoh.
(2) T: Who can tell me what antonyms are?
            (Students raise hands, while attempting to make eye contact with the teacher. The teacher looks around the class without making any eye contact . . . several seconds elapse).
      S: (calling out without being acknowledged by the teacher) Happy, sad.
      T: (Ignoring student who called out and addressing student whose hand is raised and who has not called out): Tele.
      S   (Tele): Opposites

FACILITATING

(3) T: Who would like to give me two [words that are opposites]?
      Ss: (Calling out without being recognized): Coward. Brave
      T: Coward: brave . . . Raise your hand if you can think of two words that are opposites.
(4) T: Ruth, give me a sentence with this one . . . (teacher points to the blackboard and other students raise hands)
      Other Ss: (call out) Oh! Oooooh!

T: Let her think. Put your hands down. (to Ruth) You know what it
    means, don't you?
S: (Ruth) Yes.
T: Alright, give me a sentence with that word. .
S: (Ruth) Number one is the first number.

ACCEPTING

(5) T: (Soliciting student responses for a sentence including the word *witch*)
         Somebody who hasn't said anything. (Teacher surveys class ignoring
         students with raised hands). Christian (whose hand was not raised)
         give me a sentence with this *witch* . . .
     S   (Christian): I didn't saw no witch on Halloween.

OBSTRUCTING

(6) T: (after rejecting several sentences proposed by students using *would*,
         the teacher inquires): Who else would like to give me a sentence?
     (No students raise their hands).
(7) T: We are going to review what we studied yesterday in social studies and
         afterwards, mixing one thing with others, I have a story to read to
         you.
     S   (raising hand which is acknowledged by the teacher): I didn't see the
         little book.
     T: You'll see the little book during English tomorrow. There's no time
         for that anymore.
(8) T   (reviewing definitions for *Slavery* brought in by students as a home-
         work assignment): So you have to say "the condition of being owned
         therefore, not being free." Let's write it down if you didn't look in
         the dictionary [and therefore did not do your homework].
     S   (raising hand to be acknowledged, not having written definition for
         homework but having done another assignment): I've got a calendar
         [therefore don't chastise me for no homework].
     T: Good. We'll save it for some other time, though, O.K.? *Now, going back
         to what I was saying*, um, let's give the best definition that we can,
         alright? (Italics added).
(9) T: Numero cuatro, Demetrio. (Number 4, Demetrio)
     D: (No response).
     T: Demetrio, numero cuatro. (Demetrio, number 4)
     S2 (speaking softly to Demetrio): Esos, Esos (Those, Those)
     T: Esos perros. . . . (Those dogs)
     D: Esos perros (Those dogs)
     T: Son (are) . . . Demetrio, tu tienes que practicar más (Demetrio, you
         must practice more).

We have grouped these instances as representative of four different categories as displayed in Table 2-2. In these instances we note that there are times when the teacher is cooperative but students are not, or students are cooperative and the teacher is not. When all the participants are cooperating to achieve a particular objective, there is a cohesiveness that facilitates accomplishment of the task. If we look at our own actions, as well as those of our students, we will be able to see whether we are being cooperative. When cooperation breaks down, the success of the interaction diminishes, so we need to notice cues that will help us recognize when cooperation is waning and find ways to recreate the cooperative setting. Cooperation behaviorally defined is one characteristic of a supportive environment. Another important aspect of a supportive environment is one that is *content-rich*—thereby helping students acquire knowledge.

If we believe educational settings should be content-rich, and exploratory risk-taking settings as we discussed before, then we should provide these essential components in our classrooms. Studying typical classroom transcripts helps us focus on this issue. Let's examine the content of Example 1, which is a transcript of the beginning of a second grade lesson in which the topic of synonyms is reviewed. This transcript represents a large data base of classroom interactions collected by Brause, Mayher and Bruno (1982).

EXAMPLE 1: CLASSROOM INTERACTION

T: (addressing class) Who remembers what a synonym is? (students raise hands)

T: (acknowledging student who is raising hand) Pharoh.

P: Same words

T: Uh, close. Who can say it better?

Ss: (raising hands and calling out) Me, Oooooh, Me.

T: Me, me. I don't know. (acknowledging student) Karen.

K: The same meanings

T: OK, but the same meaning what? You didn't say the whole sentence. (acknowledging another student with hand raised) Yes

S: The same meaning, that means the same

T: The same meaning, that means the same of what?

S: Of the word.

T: Right. Two words that have the same or similar meaning. Now we're learning similarity also in math, so we know very clearly what both terms mean. Um, if I say *glad,* what's a synonym?

S: (calling out) Happy

T: Happy. If I say *sad,* what's a synonym?

Ss: (calling out) Mad.
T: No.
Ss: (calling out)   I mean happy
                    Happy
                    Synonym? Grouch.
T: (repeating question) If I say *sad,* what's a synonym?
Ss: (calling out)   Selfish
                    Unhappy, unhappy
T: Who said that? . . Right . . Unhappy. *Unhappy* is a synonym of sad, not
     mad. You could be sad and you don't have to be mad. *Mad* is a synonym
     of what?
S: (calling out)   Happy
                     Angry
T: That's right. *Mad* is synonym of *angry.* (walking towards blackboard) Al-
     right, so we know synonyms. Let's review another example. Alright let's
     write this (writing on blackboard) Words . . . that have . . . that have what,
     children? (students are copying into their notebooks)
Ss: (calling out) the same meaning
T: Same or similar meaning . . . such as . . .
S: Such as what?
T: Give me an example.
S: Ill, sick.
T: *Ill* and *sick,* very good. This is an example, allright . . ill and the ones we
     just gave . . unhappy and sad . . glad and happy . . . and whatever else.

In analyzing this transcript we note a testing environment in contrast
to a content-rich one. To clearly see the contrast, John Mayher and I
(Mayher & Brause, 1983) modified the real transcript. (See Example 2.)
We placed the concept of synonyms within the considerations of an
activity where the students were conveying their feelings (the composition was written by another student). They were becoming sensitive to
the power of words by weighing the impact of their options. In Example
1 students were discussing synonyms in isolation. In Example 2 the issue
is contextualized, thereby creating a more meaningful setting.

EXAMPLE 2: CLASSROOM INTERACTION—REVISED

T: Yesterday we wrote reactions to our storytime. I enjoyed reading them
     because I found out about your feelings about that activity and I got some
     good ideas for our next storytime. Now I would like all of us to look at one
     of these, without saying whose work it is. I have picked this one because
     it is very similar to many others. Let's read it. (Places text on overhead

frequencies that were observed in the table (Bishop, Fineberg, & Holland, 1975).

In the simplest model, it was assumed that the six characteristics of requests were completely independent of each other. This model was rejected (χ^2 (120) = 378.32, $p<.01$). In a more complex model, it was assumed that appropriate responses depended on the other characteristics but that these other characteristics did not depend on each other. This model was rejected, (χ^2 (114) = 265.89, $p<.01$), but it was a significant improvement over the first model, (χ^2 (6) = 112.73, $p<.01$). In a still more complex model, it was assumed that there were associations between every pair of characteristics but no higher order associations. This model did fit the data (χ^2 (99) = 94.44). Moreover, it fit better than the preceding model in which it was assumed that only appropriate response was associated with other characteristics, (χ^2 (15) = 171.15, $p<.01$). Finally this model fit better than the one in which it was assumed that all pairs of characteristics were associated except the pairs involving appropriate responses, (χ^2 (6) = 97.93, $p<.01$). The major conclusions, therefore, are (1) that characteristics of requests are correlated and (2) that whether a request received an appropriate response depended upon the other characteristics of the request. This latter effect received support from two sources; the goodness of fit improved when the effect was added to the model and worsened when it was removed.

Because the observations are dependent, the significance levels which were obtained are not completely trustworthy. One solution to this problem is to select a statistic which measures an effect of interest and to jackknife that statistic by groups (Mosteller & Tukey, 1977). The log linear effect of each characteristic upon appropriate responses was computed and jackknifed by groups. The results suggested that all characteristics predicted appropriate responses if they were for information for action, ($t(6)$ = 15.17, $p<.01$); if they were of a direct form ($t(6)$ = 4.23, $p<.01$), and if they were revised (after initial attempt), ($t(6)$ = 4.08, $p<.01$). These results confirm the validity of the model.

Question 4: Is there a relationship between reading achievement and use of requests?

Analyses were conducted to examine whether students' requests and appropriate responses differed in ability groups which may affect reading achievement. The relationship between characteristics of requests and reading achievement was examined. Appropriate responses to requests are predicted by characteristics of requests (action/information, direct-form, designated-listener, revision, on-task, sincere). Since the content of these requests usually refers directly to some aspect of the reading assignment, selected aspects of requests were expected to show relationships to reading achievement.

projector and reads aloud to class: I think that the story "The Funny Man's First Case" was a nice funny story and a nice one to read. Writing stories was fun. And Mrs. Rogers said, "We should do this more often." And that you told the story nicely.) How do you think this person felt about yesterday's story?

S: Good.

S: OK.

T: How can you tell?

S: It says it was nice.

S: It says it was funny.

S: A nice story.

T: OK. What do you think the person meant by "It was a nice funny story"?

S: The story was funny.

S: The story was nice.

T: What makes a story nice for you?

S: Exciting.

S: Adventure.

S: Happy.

S: Short.

T: You're suggesting many different kinds of stories can be nice. Do we know why this person thought the story was "nice"?

S: It was funny.

T: Is funny the same as nice in this sentence?

S: No. Then it would say a funny funny story. I don't think it means the same thing. Maybe the person meant to say an exciting funny story.

T: Perhaps. The word appears two other places. Do you think we might try to find other words that might express the ideas more precisely (seek additional options) . . . The word funny was used a lot too. I know the word was used in the title. Are there other words that mean the same as funny, that we might use?

S: Humorous.

S: A laugh.

S: Happy.

S: Good.

S: Exciting.

T: Let's see how these words fit with the writer's meaning. Let's try the first one. It was a nice, *humorous* story. How do you like that as a choice?

S: It's OK.

T: OK. There does not seem to be any dispute about that one. Let's go on to the next. Writing short stories was *a laugh*. How do you like that as a choice?

S: It sounds strange.

T: What sounds strange about it. . . . . (After discussion) OK, let's all look at our own compositions and see if we can improve the effectiveness of them by using more precise words. After you've read your own, exchange papers with your partner and make suggestions for each others' work.

When students draw on their own experiences students understand the concepts being discussed. Students are encouraged to explore connections and they are exposed to additional information in contrast to being tested on their knowledge.

The importance of providing content is emphasized by Richard Allington (1983) who noted the differential focus in classroom reading groups. He decries the fact that some students have such a limited opportunity to learn to read because they are required to complete exercises which are meaningless to them prior to having an opportunity to learn to understand text. Collins (1977) suggests that the dialogues provided in classrooms, although using a question-answer format, are not Socratic dialogues. Socratic dialogues are characterized by the interchange of ideas on an issue; they are not focused on a "skill." Participants in Socratic dialogues discuss content and ideas. It is not a game of turn-allocations. It is an intellectual exchange. Real Socratic dialogues provide the essence of education—the cognitive component of the curriculum.

Instead of students being asked questions which require them to present knowledge of facts, the focus is on inquiry—which more accurately represents our state of limited knowledge—doubt—rather than absolutism. If we want students to learn to inquire, to take risks, to doubt, to explore, to question the possibility of multiple meanings, then we must provide models and settings which encourage these cognitively-based activities. Students in Example I are neither given an enriched conceptual environment nor an enriched experience. The paucity of their educational experience is in contrast to that students provide for themselves in other activities such as computer access to multiple knowledge bases.

If we as teachers really want to get students to be at the center of their own learning, then we must encourage them to pose questions. We can't get students to take charge of their own learning by wishing it were true—saying something like, "Today is question day!" Rather, we must set up an environment that is conducive to questioning. For example, let me tell you of some questions my nieces posed to me when we went to see *Merlin*, the Broadway play:

Is it difficult to get a job as a musician?
What does abstinence mean? . . . So why were they making such
    a big thing of it?
How did the water support the woman?
Where did the man go? What happened to the man?
Is water from a fountain different from water from a tap?

These are real questions—and the context in which they occurred is an important issue for us, as teachers, to consider. They were drinking from a fountain, viewing magic acts, and observing the orchestra rehearse. These examples suggest the need for getting our students involved in projects and activities where they are trying to figure out how things happen. Such a setting is representative of life—more so than the teacher-student dialogues which typify classroom interactions as in Example 1. The modifications in the transcript suggested earlier might be a good basis for reconsidering our classroom dialogues.

Civikly (1982) provides us with a list of some characteristics of a supportive environment. Classroom factors identified by her are: (a) challenge, (b) freedom, (c) respect, (d) warmth, (e) control, and (f) success. If we provide the opportunity for students to become involved in activities which challenge their intellect while nurturing their interests, we will be operationalizing these concerns. The examples cited above provide specific criteria for us to use in evaluating and redesigning classroom interactions.

Conclusion

In analyzing classroom contexts which facilitate learning we have identified two major issues: *trust* and *support*. These concepts include an environment that is at once ridicule-free and content-rich. A dichotomous scale (Table 2-3) characterizing these settings is useful as a basis for considering the new environments we establish daily in our classroom. The higher the score, the more congruent the classroom is with the characteristics we have identified.

References

Allington, R. (1983, May). The reading instruction provided readers of differing reading abilities. *Elementary School Journal, 83*(5).

Brause, R.S., & Mayher, J. S. (1982, May). Students, teachers and classroom organization. *Research in the Teaching of English,* 16 (2), 131–148.

Brause, R.S., & Mayher, J.S. (1983). Learning through teaching: The classroom teacher as researcher. *Language Arts,* 60 (6), 758–765.

Brause, R. S., Mayher, J. S. & Bruno, Jo. (1982). *An investigation into bilingual students' classroom communicative competence: Final report to the National Institute of Education.*

Britton, J. (1970). *Language and learning.* Montclair, NJ: Boynton/Cook.

Britton, J. (1982). *Prospect and retrospect: Selected essays of James Britton.* (G. Pradl, Ed.) Montclair, NJ: Boynton/Cook.

Britton, J. (1982). Language in the British primary school. In Gordon Pradl (Ed.), *Prospect and retrospect.* Montclair, NJ: Boynton/Cook.

TABLE 2-3. CRITERIA FOR DESCRIBING CLASSROOM ENVIRONMENTS

MOST INTERACTIVE										LEAST INTERACTIVE
Liberating										Restraining
	10	9	8	7	6	5	4	3	2	1
Respectful										Denigrating
	10	9	8	7	6	5	4	3	2	1
Assisting										Adversarial
	10	9	8	7	6	5	4	3	2	1
Friendly										Alienating
	10	9	8	7	6	5	4	3	2	1
Challenging										Mindless
	10	9	8	7	6	5	4	3	2	1
Risktaking										Error-free
	10	9	8	7	6	5	4	3	2	1
Content-rich										Content-poor
	10	9	8	7	6	5	4	3	2	1
Cooperative										Fractious
	10	9	8	7	6	5	4	3	2	1
Rewarding										Inhibiting
	10	9	8	7	6	5	4	3	2	1
Safe										Unknown
	10	9	8	7	6	5	4	3	2	1
Peaceful										Unsettling
	10	9	8	7	6	5	4	3	2	1
Accountable										Random
	10	9	8	7	6	5	4	3	2	1
Consistent										Boring
	10	9	8	7	6	5	4	3	2	1
Systematic										Distracting
	10	9	8	7	6	5	4	3	2	1

Britton, J., Burgess, T., Martin, N., McLeod, A., & Rosen, H. (1975). *Development of Writing Abilities*. Urbana, IL. National Council of Teachers of English.

Cahir, S., & Kovacs, C. *Transition: Activity between activity*. Washington, DC: Center for Applied Linguistics.

Civikly, J. (1982). Self-concept, significant others and classroom communication. In L. Barker (Ed.), *Communication in the classroom*. Englewood Cliffs, NJ: Prentice-Hall.

Collins, A. (1977). Processes in acquiring knowledge. In R. Anderson, R. Spiro, & W. Montague (Eds.) *Schooling and the acquisition of knowledge*. Hillsdale, NJ: Erlbaum.

Good, T. (1981). Teacher praise: A functional analysis. *Review of Educational Research, 51*.

Kounin, J. (1970). *Discipline and group management in classrooms*. New York: Holt, Rinehart & Winston.

Mayher, J. S. & Brause, R. S. (1983, April). *Teachers can make a difference*. Symposium at Conference on English Education National Council of Teachers of English, Seattle, WA.

McDermott, R. P. (1977, May). Social relations as contexts for learning in school. *Harvard Educational Review, 47*(2), 198-213.

Piestrup, A. (1973). *Black dialect interference and accommodation of reading instruction in first grade.* Berkeley: University of California, *Monograph of the Language Behavior Research Laboratory,* Vol. 4.

Shavelson, R. J. (1983, April). Review of research on teachers' pedagogical judgments, plans and decisions. *Elementary School Journal,* 83 (4).

Vygotsky, L. S. (1962). *Thought and language.* Cambridge: MIT Press.

Vygotsky, L. S. (1978). *Mind in society.* Cambridge: Harvard University Press.

Chapter 3
Decision Making in School and Classroom Contexts

Anthony N. Baratta

Fordham University

Day-to-day activities in classrooms and other school contexts may be placed on a continuum of simple to complex activities. Among the many activities are the innumerable thoughts, actions, events, feelings, and sensations that occur and recur each day. Descriptions of such contexts in classrooms and schools are a function of elementary task analysis, the act of breaking wholes into parts. This process of task analysis enables us to understand the interrelation of functions as these interrelations apply to the work of classroom teachers and school administrators.

A comprehensive analytical approach for decision-making can be constituted in terms of task categories, hereafter referred to as the *Seven Analytical A's*: (1) Axiologicals, (2) Axiomatics, (3) Alternatives, (4) Architectures, (5) Allocations, (6) Actions, and (7) Appraisals. These categories provide a system or process for assisting educators to conceptualize and analyze the numerous activities that are typical of a principal's or teacher's managerial decision making. The *axiologicals* deal with the values that persist in the environment which surrounds decision making; the *axiomatics* are the givens which must be taken into account; the *alternatives* deal with various possibilities one might construct for dealing with a problem; *architecture* deals with the planning of such alternatives; *allocations* deal with the provisions of human and material resources for these alternatives; *actions* deal with the implementation and execution of the decision making associated with alternatives; and *appraisals* deal with the evaluation of this decision making and its products. Thus, the Seven Analytical A's comprise the decision functions of people who assess values, consider givens, deal with alternatives, design plans, allocate resources, see that the plans are implemented, and then judge the process and the results. In Figure 3-1, the comprehensiveness and the interrelatedness of the Seven Analystical A's in decision making are indicated by the lines and arrows connecting the categories.

Figure 1. THE SEVEN ANALYTICAL A's

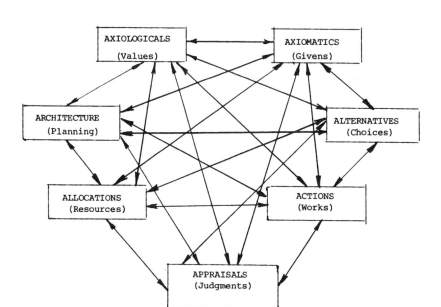

Figure 3-1. THE SEVEN ANALYTICAL A's

ANALYSIS OF AXIOLOGICALS

The analysis of the *axiologicals,* or value dimensions, includes several aspects: (1) values definition, (2) values development, (3) values constancy, (4) complexity of values positing, (5) effects of values on behaviors, (6) values changes, and (7) values imperatives.

Values definition. The definition of values for this analysis is that provided by Blackmon:

> A value is a motivating force, a selecting factor, an appraising concept which enables us to make choices among alternative paths of action. Values are decisive agents in formulating hypotheses and judging consequences. A value might be said to be the comparative weight, esteem or price attached by the individual to a given idea, person, or object. (Blackmon, 1968, p. 97)

Blackmon's definition of values provides an interesting point of departure for strategic behaviors utilized in the Seven Analytical A's. Note that this definition indicates that a value is a motivating force, a selecting factor, and an appraising concept which are key components in the system.

Values development. How are human values developed? Research done by Blackmon (1968) indicates that the role of the home, the importance of the early childhood experience, and the socioeconomic context were most influential in values development. Several of the main findings of Blackmon are.

1. *At what period in life are an individual's basic or governing values developed?* Sixty percent of the subjects responded that their basic or governing values were developed in early childhood, 20 percent responded that adolescence was the period in life most dominant in developing values, 12 percent responded that puberty and early adulthood was the period that was most formative of values and 10 percent responded that their values developed during infancy.

2. *What do you consider the single most effective institution in the order of importance in developing or inculcating values?* Eighty-nine percent of these educators indicated that the home was the most effective single institution for developing or inculcating values. Eight percent stated it was the school and two percent indicated it was the church. Nevertheless, considering the middle rank order of importance of institutions in developing or inculcating values, the school was given recognition by 56 percent of the professors and the church received a ranking of 28 percent of them.

3. *What influence does community exercise over values?* The educators indicated that the socioeconomic environment plays a dominant role in the development of a person's value system. They stated that one develops his or her value system primarily as a result of one's socioeconomic environment (72%), through education (20%) and through the intellectual ability (5%).

Blackmon's research indicated that the home during early childhood within the context of the socioeconomic environment was important in the values development of educators who responded in the study. Nevertheless, the role of the school in the development of values may assume more challenging dimensions as the home and family structure undergo substantial transformations in contemporary society. The implications of this phenomena are of vital importance to the school, to teachers in particular, and to the broader society in general.

Values constancy. The basic proposition of this component of the analysis of the axiological dimension is that certain universal values exist in even the most dynamic and fast-moving society. The following researchers and practitioners find:

Some values are universally held. No society has ever approved of suffering as a good thing in itself. No society approves of killing in itself, lying or stealing. Rape is universally disapproved. (Kluckhohn, 1956)

We have come to appreciate that values which schools should promote—such as orderliness, inhibition of aggressive impulses, rational approach to a problem situation, desire for a work career based on skill and knowledge, desire for a stable family life, and desire for freedom for self and others—are not class values. The teaching of fundamental values basic to adequate living in a democratic technological society will occupy a significant place in schools in the future. (Conovan, 1967, p. 19)

The identification of universal values is difficult and often controversial, but there seem to be certain commonalities underlying value systems. School administrators and teachers are guided in a minimal way in the identification of universal values through the weight of formal legal statues at the national and state levels, within the context of the political process—with its pragmatic shortcomings and blemishes.

Complexities of values positing. In the analysis of axiological dimensions of decision making, there is wide recognition that the positing of values is a complex undertaking in a society such as the United States. Worthen's (1968) statement in this regard is to the point:

It is interesting to observe these universally held values, but the justification for different actions, when committed, varies a great deal according to the culture. Although it is worthy to consider values as absolute, attempts of philosophers, theologians and other thoughtful men to seek absolute values have proved confusing. Values are essentially relative—not only to the culture but also to the diverse varieties of human nature in history and relative to opportunities and limitations of human situations. (Worthen, 1968, p.71)

For the school administrator and teacher, the current emphasis on what is commonly called "values clarification" is the pragmatic approach to identify and posit values which have a broad base of support and acceptance for transmission in the formal school experience. Furthermore, the analysis of values is constantly tested through the requirements and challenges of the typical day-to-day decision-making tasks that face school administrators and teachers. What texts do we order next year? Who is to be the new reading teacher? These two questions are examples of decisions which require values positing in their implementations.

Values as determinants of human behaviors. Recognizing that values serve as determinants of human behaviors, this phase focuses on values as behavioral guidelines. Blackmon (1968) writes: "Values exist and have an important bearing upon the behavior of the individual" (Blackmon, 1968, p. 3). This statement is supported by Sachs (1968), who writes:

> Each person "plays many parts"—one may assume one role at one time and another in some other situation. But the first step to awareness and self-evaluation is to bring to the conscious level how we might be behaving and under what value structure we are operating. (p. 39)

> Among psychologists, there is a consensus that values refer to implicit and explicit standards for choices and evaluations . . . To be concerned with the best choice rather than just which choice, a social or behavioral scientist must have courage to take a position concerning values conducive to optimal psychological health. (Worthen, 1968, pp. 71–73)

To summarize, values serve as determinants of human behavior; values have a pervasive impact upon human behaviors; and therefore, values analysis is important to teachers and administrators.

Analysis of values changes. Although there is a high degree of constancy in a human being's value system, values do change, however slowly. Values are not static. As individuals mature and as the society changes due to innovation and technology, values alter to meet the changing condition. Thus, we see that values changes are related to our contemporary society in a more accelerated way than in any previous time. Worthen writes:

> Successful personality functioning requires one to take care of value changes fostered at a rapid rate in our culture. When an individual is required to give up or exchange values, his personality mechanisms are involved. Successful value adjustment is essentially the person's ability to make compromises. (Worthen, 1968, p. 77)

The implications of the impact of value systems in the day-to-day work of school administrators and teachers is not readily apparent. It is a common propensity to retain one's cultural values, roots, or foundations. The task of analyzing values changes within the context of complex educational systems and environments presents a challenge for school administrators and teachers. There is the constant tug to strike a balance between antecedent values and the changing values for tomorrow. This struggle for equilibrium is a fertile domain of the school as a social institution—as it endeavors to serve several major purposes that is, the transmission of universal values and the improvement of existing value systems.

Analysis of values imperatives. Rational directions for American education are the subject matter for the analysis of axiological or values imperatives. These imperatives connote the minimum foundations for American education. They are intertwined with values universals and values changes. Axiological imperatives are often the decision points regarding the values that will be definitive in the curriculum of the school.

How do school administrators and teachers analyze axiological imperatives? The process of identifying and distilling the axiological literature from philosophers, religious leaders, psychologists, social scientists, political scientists, technocrats, legislators, government officials, educators, leaders in the community, leaders in the arts, leaders in the media, parents, and children is only a small part of their task. In the past, special commissions have been formed by professional organizations and governmental units to state the goals, objectives, and imperatives of education. Often the statements of such groups were only minimally helpful in the day-to-day decision-making of the school.

ANALYSIS OF AXIOMATIC FACTORS

To analyze axiomatic factors in the decision making process implies dealing with the *givens* in the situation. The dictionary defines an axiom as a self-evident or necessary truth; a consideration of any proposition or principle that people universally accept. How do axiomatic factors relate to school and classroom decision-making processes? Are the axiomatic factors, components, or dimensions important in the process of school decision making? In this phase of the Seven Analytical A's model we will conceptualize, identify, and illustrate several axiomatic factors. Extrapolating from the formal definition of axiomatic, we call attention to obvious factors that persons universally accept as extant in a situation and then say that these *givens* must be considered in the decision-making process.

Propositions in decisions making must be screened through the axiomatic filter. For example, during the school year, school principals are formally involved in the decision-making process of selecting teachers for their schools. This responsibility of the principal goes through the axiomatic filter process. There are several primary axiomatic factors which are generally part of this filter listed below.

Territorial givens. Territorial givens are a key component of the axiomatic factors filter. Territorial givens imply a particular place, domain, location, and jurisdiction. Whatever is unique and indigenous to a particular territory, be it mountain, valley, seacoast, farm area, urban, rural, upstate, suburban, downstate, metropolitan, inner city, "Park Avenue," industrial, resort, harbor, plains, ghetto, residential, and so on, becomes part of that axiomatic factors filter system. These territorial givens are connected to the process of the selection of the teachers of a school, as an example of the numerous decision-making responsibilities in the complex system of the school. The school principal of a particular territory will consider the candidates in the light of the congruency needs of that system as analyzed through territorial givens of the axiomatic filter.

Socioeconomic givens. Socioeconomic givens assume a pivotal place in the axiomatic filter. An analysis of the socioeconomic givens requires an understanding by principals and teachers of the social systems and the economic systems in the school district. Does the social system consist of single dominant, multiple, or diverse peoples? Is the community stable or mobile? What is the cultural level of the community? What are the various areas of worker's roles? Is the economic level of the community low-, middle- or high-income? What economic givens have been precedent during the last decade for municipal services, cultural services, and particularly educational services? Again, we submit that an analysis of the socioeconomic givens becomes an integral part of the axiomatic filter as the principal seeks to appoint new teachers.

Significant people givens. Significant people givens are of primary concern in the screening process using the axiomatic filter. Who are significant people? The significant people for the selection of teachers would be the few people who are formally members of the board of education and who have a legal function in that selection. It may include a few people who serve in the role of consultants to a school board, involved in the search and screening of candidates for a school superintendency. Then again, the significant people could include the many who voted to elect the school board members. The significant people may include the many citizens who vote to either approve or reject the school budget at the public referendum. The significant people registered by an axiomatic factors filter are those who have or are perceived to have power or influence in the decision-making process.

In dealing with the significant people givens within this axiomatic filter, there are some human tendencies which need to be identified.

1. *Approbativeness.* What is the approbativeness factor or approvement record of the significant people related to the decision-making process in question? What is the level or potency of latent or private approbation on the part of the significant people? Is this latent or private approbative tendency of significant people effective? Who are the significant people

who manifest public or outspoken approbation on the decision-making issue at hand? The axiomatic factors will be affected by the number of significant people as they speak and relate to majority or minority clusterings in the decision-making process. Finally, within the category of analysis of axiomatic factors, many complex situations occur in dealing with significant people. For example, in the selection of a superintendent, this writer observed a situation in which a majority of the school board had decided on a particular person. However, the president of the board had been away during the development of selection criteria and he was not involved. Upon his return, this single significant person had enough persuasive power to cause the majority members to reconsider the criteria and to make a different selection.

2. *Opposition.* What are the oppositional tendencies of the significant people as they relate to the decision-making process? What is the past record of opposition on the part of the significant people? What is the level or potency of latent or private opposition on the part of the significant people? Is this latent or private opposition effective? Who are the influential people who manifest public or outspoken opposition? What is their past record on potency or effectiveness to block various proposals? What is the nature of the opposition from these persons? The axiomatic factor includes the number of significant people who relate to majority and/or minority clusterings within the community.

Significant coalitions as givens. Significant coalitions become a powerful factor within the axiomatic function because of their formalized power when these groups choose to be influential. March (1976) emphasized in analyzing coalitions that their interests vary in their mutual compatibility partly as a consequence of the form they take, but also partly as a consequence of the alternative combinations of policies and options that are considered. What was said about the significant people givens in terms of approbativeness or opposition is applicable to the significant coalitional givens, with the differentiation that the latter often becomes more potent because of the publically recognized influence or weight of the coalition. Therefore, using the Seven Analytical A's model, the significant coalitional givens are interconnected with the other dimensions of the model. Skilled school administrators and teachers must understand these axiomatic factors or givens in order to move the decision-making process.

Organizational givens. Organizational givens, as part of the axiomatic factor, are a complex composite of numerous phenomena. Sergiovanni and Starratt (1983) succinctly synthesize several well-recognized theoretical conceptualizations that are included in this section to assist in the analysis of axiomatic organizational givens. Skilled school administrators and teachers might wish to understand the following organizational givens:

1. Administrative roles and functions
2. The importance of administrative orientation
3. Implementational levels of supervisory and administration and behavior
4. Power bases and authority systems
5. Compliance systems within the organization
6. Organizational styles, managerial systems, managerial emphases, and bureaucratic style within the organization
7. Organizational climates

Greater knowledge regarding these functions may be found in their volume, which deals with these components.

For many skilled school administrators and teachers their understanding of the axiomatic factors has come about through "on the job training"—which may be painful at times. One of the purposes of the conceptualization of the Seven Analytical A's is to serve as educational training for prospective and practicing school administrators and teachers who may need this type of professional understanding. Figure 3-2 indicates the primary components of this axiomatic factors filter system.

ANALYSIS OF ALTERNATIVES

The purpose of the analysis of alternatives in decision making is to improve the rationality among the selection of two or more choices. Within the literature on the analysis of alternatives in decision making, there is a rapidly developing and sophisticated body of knowledge of decision science or operations research which is relevant to this phase of the Seven Analytical A's. The concepts in this section are derived from that body of knowledge. Yet, the sophistication of the specialists in the field of decision science is not available to many that function in school systems. In the future more of these specialized concepts of the decision scientists may become part of the typical school administration and supervisory decision-making process. Some of the salient components of decision science concepts that may be utilized by general administration and supervisory practitioners in ways that are adapted to the highly humanistic enterprise of the schools are presented below. In the analysis of alternatives, our model will deal with three distinct aspects:

1. Congruency with axiological components

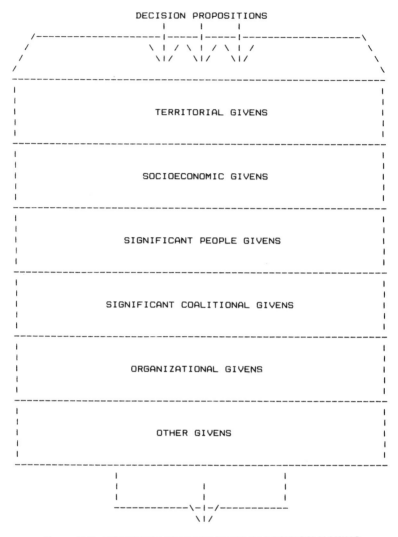

Figure 3-2. AXIOMATIC FACTORS FILTER IN DECISION MAKING

2. Examination according to axiomatic factors
3. Elements of decision science.

Congruency with axiologicals. One of the key steps in analyzing alternatives in decision making is to consider the congruency of alternatives to the axiological or values imperatives of the organization—in this case, the school system. Blackmon's (1968) definition bears repetition: "A value is a motivating force, a selecting factor, an appraising concept which enables one to make choices among alternatives." In order to operationalize the congruency to values concept, an organization should have a codified statement or document which serves as a practical guide in this assessment. The best example of this type of document is the United States Constitution in the governance process of our nation. Analogous to this type of document, school systems are guided by formal policy statements as well as by legal statutes at the local, state, and national levels.

Examination of axiomatic factors. Another key step in analyzing alternatives for decision making is the examination of axiomatic factors—that is, the givens. We submit that decision makers are guided or influenced intuitively by axiomatic filters in the selection of alternatives. Perhaps the primary message of the Seven Analytical A's approach is to formalize the analysis of the axiomatic factors in the decision-making process as a means of improving the rationality of the selection of alternatives. An operational step for implementing the analysis of axiomatic factors, a number of checklists may be developed. We suggest several checklists because there are diverse axiomatic factors which bear upon decisions dealing with programs, personnel, curriculum materials, sites, buildings, transportation, sports, pupil personnel, and so forth. Further, it is suggested that the checklists be broad in their perspectives of these functions.

Decision science elements. The value of the theoretical constructs of decision science is that they assist and improve rational selection among alternatives. Scientific and empirical methods have been brought to the decision-making process. This is particularly true since the advent of the computer, which pointed up the importance of minute decisions, the kind educators make on a day-to-day basis. In the normal process of decision making some aspects of the decision have predominant value and other aspects have contributing value. Although science has tried to bring rational process to decision making, the complexities of operationalization of that process force decision makers to try to identify the obvious and more understandable elements. Therefore, decision making dealing with products and tangible alternatives may be easier than decision making dealing with human resources or processes with the complexity and unpredictabilities of human behavior. The following decision science elements may provide a checklist for assisting with the complexities of choosing among alternatives:

1. *Utility.* The *utlity* of alternatives must be analyzed in terms of the purposes, values, and goals of the organization. Decision makers may

study the degrees of utility given below: the *maximum utility* principle which stresses the selection of alternatives which maximize the minimum usefulness of the decision outcome; the *minimax principle* means that the decision maker should study all the consequences of each alternative and then select the alternative whose worst outcome has the highest utility; *minimax risk or regret* means that the decision maker should or could choose the alternative which is considered to offer the minimum of maximum risk or regret; *satisficing utility* means that the decision maker chooses the alternative that is good enough.

2. *Cost.* The cost of the alternative deals with the economic affordability that is often a basic consideration in the decision making process. Many factors come into play in the economic aspect such as guarantees, expected life of the alternatives, durability, adequacy, appropriateness, style, quality of materials, reputation of manufactures or institutions, and short- or long-range needs.

3. *Decision making under certainty.* There are decisions that are made by school administrators and teachers which fall into the category of decision making under certainty. Taylor (1965) defined decision under certainty as "that in which not only the alternatives in the choice to be made are known, but also each alternative is known invariably to lead to a specific outcome."

4. *Decision making under risk.* There are various decisions that are made by school administrators and teachers which fall under the category of decision making under risk. These are defined by Taylor (1965) as "those in which the alternatives are known and in which each alternative leads to one of a set of possible specific outcomes, each outcome occurring with a known probability." Taylor indicated that there are several related principles to be considered in decision making under risk. Choices involving risk should maximize expected value and the decision maker under risk should know all of the consequences which may result from each alternative.

5. *Decision making under uncertainty.* There are many decisions that are made by school administrators and teachers which fall under the category of decision making under uncertainty. Taylor (1965) states that in these decisions, as in decision under certainty or under risk, the decision maker knows with some certainty all of the alternatives. As in the decision under risk, he also knows most of the consequences. Taylor indicated that uncertainty arises in that the probabilities of specific outcomes are unknown or, in some cases, not even meaningful. The decision maker under uncertainty is less completely informed than the decision maker under risk because he lacks knowledge of the probablities of specific outcomes. There are also several related principles to be considered by decision makers under uncertainty. The first is the maximum utility

principle, which stresses the selection of alternatives which maximize minimum usefulness of the decision. The second is the minimum risk or regret principle, which stresses the selection of the alternative which minimize maximum loss or regret in the decision-making process.

6. *Decision under ambiguity.* The principle of decision under ambiguity is related to the concept of decision under uncertainty. Decision under ambiguity was developed by Mintzberg (1973) who termed the concept "unstructural decision-making." Unstructural decision-making deals with problems and solutions when alternatives, information, and objectives are ambiguous. March (1976) connected the work of school administrators and supervisors to decision under ambiguity by indicating that, at times, not only are they uncertain about the consequences of alternatives, but are also unclear about their goals, uncertain of their technology, and unaware of their alternatives.

7. *Satisficing.* Satisficing is a concept defined by Simon (1957) and Taylor (1965) as the decision of choice which replaces the goal of maximizing with the goal of satisficing, that is to say, of finding a course of action that is "good enough." The decision maker who seeks to satisfice searches until he finds an alternative which is "good enough." This concept is also related to the concept of minimax regret.

In summary, the purpose of the *analysis of alternatives* in the decision-making process is to improve the rationality of the selection of two or more choices. So many factors come into play in the selection of choices, that some degree of priority within decision science factors develops pragmatically, while other factors are given minimal attention. Nevertheless, this component of the Seven Analytical A's dealt with the intricacies of what sometimes are thought of as simple decision-making issues.

ANALYSIS OF ARCHITECTURE

The analysis of architecture deals with planning the implementation of alternatives. The architecture of decision making deals with the functional designing or specific planning for a particular project. There is an abundance of sophisticated literature about planning. Knezevich (1975) graphically depicts the primary role of planning which is incorporated in the administrative process. Knezevich uses Dror's definition of planning as "a process of preparing a set of decisions for action in the future, directed at achieving goals by optimal means." (Knezevich, 1975, p.29) In this section of the analysis of architectures the main purpose will be to focus on the designing of the blueprints or plans. The focus of the Seven Analytical A's is utilitarian; often planning is frequently conceived and utilized in decision making as a global or umbrella concept, but a more functional aspect is considered here. The analysis of architecture includes: (1) the selection and definition of the plan and (2) the design of the plan.

Selecting and defining the plan. After analyzing the axiological, axiomatic, and alternative dimensions in decision making, the selection of the specific plan occurs. Of course, a great deal of preliminary work has preceded this step. For example, in planning for the operations in one school, Banghart and Trull (1973) indicate a comprehensive process is integral to the selection of a plan. They include the following aspects in their comprehensive process: (1) establish goals; (2) develop objectives; (3) study in an exploratory manner the population, education, economics, technology, legalities, and finance of the system; (4) develop scheme 1, scheme 2, and scheme 3; (5) conduct policy review; (6) select a scheme; (7) investigate in a preliminary manner the population, education, economics, technology, legalities and finance of the problems under consideration; (8) develop sketch 1, sketch 2, and sketch 3; (9) conduct policy review; (10) select sketch; (11) study in detail population, education, economics, technology, legalities, and finance; (12) develop educational models, transportation models, land development models, transportation models, land development models, and economic models; (13) develop alternative 1, alternative 2, and alterntive 3; (14) test and evaluate alternatives and (15) adopt a comprehensive school plan. Planning may consist of a simple plan one carries in one's head or an elaborate plan consisting of reports and PERT charts.

Curriculum planning and program development is a critical professional function in the educational organization. McCarthy (1980) presented six major principles as possible guides for administrators in approaching curriculum planning. They were: (1) the principle of purpose, which relates activities to overall school purposes; (2) the principle of priority, relating activities to one another, or other program options, and to the overall evaluation of the school; (3) the principle of continuity, which relates curriculum activities sequentially within the school, coordinating school activities with each other and with nonschool education activities, formal and informal; (4) the principle of practicality, which involves the study of costs and of effectiveness of curriculum activities, and relates curriculum practices to the resources of the school in terms of time, material, and personnel; (5) the principle of collegiality, which requires that curriculum decisions be reached cooperatively and on multilateral levels that include both the professional and the client, and (6) the principle of subsidiarity, which requires that decisions be made at the lowest operational level at which the problem can be handled efficiently. Specific guidelines for selecting a particular curriculum plan are given.

Designing the plan. The phase of planning focuses on the actions of the persons responsible for carrying out the plans of the decision. For example, in the construction of school buildings, Mohair speaking of the preparation of architectural specifications, states:

> Next, working drawings and specifications are developed to indicate the precise design of the building, to specify the materials and methods of construction and the exact dimensions of each space specified. The working drawings must be accompanied by . . . descriptions of all details which cannot be conveyed by the drawings alone and minimum standards of materials and worksmanship are set in these descriptions. From engineers working with him, the architect obtains plans for the heating, plumbing, ventilating and electrical components and these became a part of the total drawings and specifications. (Mohair, 1980)

Thus in the process of designing a plan for a program, activity, process, or physical facility, this phase includes the specific written, graphic, and other specifications of human, economic, and material resources. These elements are considered in the allocation of human and material resources. In addition, legal factors must be incorporated in the design of the plans.

ANALYSIS OF ALLOCATION OF HUMAN AND MATERIAL RESOURCES

The analysis of allocations of human and material resources in the Seven Analytical A's model was considered indirectly in our discussion of the axiological, axiomatic, alternatives, and architecture phases. Values, givens, alternatives, sufficiency, adequacy, cost, utility, availability, durability, and specializations are among the basic criteria and principles that pertain to the analysis of allocation of human and material resources. This section will be divided into two primary segments:

Allocations of human resources. What human resources are needed for the plan? The analysis of human allocations runs the gamut of personnel requirements. Among the primary concerns for the allocation of human components are: kinds of roles, training and specialization requirements, existing and/or new personnel requirements, costs and benefits, legal factors, the nature and length of services required, and systems of authority, power, hierarchy, and status.

The analysis of allocations of human resources in the decision-making process within the context of educational organizations is a complex undertaking that is often misunderstood by leaders or by persons who view themselves as "change agents." The field of organizational development has emerged as an attempt to improve the allocation and effectiveness of human resources. Because educational organizations allocate from 60 to 80 percent of their budgets to human resources, because these persons are protected by legal statutes through negotiated contractual agreements as well as state tenure laws, because these persons have specialized and professional training, and because of the normal human propensity for self-preservation and survival—many "new plans" have too frequently suffered or perished when they have been whimsically or capriciously imposed. The values of democratic systems, professional autonomy, and collegial, participatory arrangements are not idle or meaningless concepts in their influence on the normal day-to-day operations of the school. The analysis of the allocations of human resources must take into consideration whether the environment, in which the new plan is proposed, is amenable to growth and development or whether it is subject to the consolidations or retrenchment of a declining interest or priority in education. Whatever the circumstances are in an organization, a high priority must be given to the analysis of allocation of human resources.

Allocation of Material and Economic Resources. What material and economic resources are necessary for the plan? Decisions regarding utility, cost, minimax and maximin principles must be taken into account. Generally speaking, this phase of the analytic process in decision making is benefited because of the more concrete and tangible characteristics of these resources.

ANALYSIS OF ACTION

Analysis of action, in the Seven Analytical A's system, is the part of the design concerned with the most optimal implementation of the planning in the decision-making process. Values have been expressed, givens considered, alternatives chosen, and resources allocated. Now the plan is made operational.

The best made plans are wanting if the actual work or operations are fraught with mistakes or unsatisfactory or mediocre implementation occurs. A detailed and comprehensive literature has been developed for the implementation of the planning. This section includes the components of work flow, timing, performance of workers, initial phase operations, medial phase operations, and ongoing operations.

Work flow. The work flow should be developed so that it is simple, practical, clear, and logical. There are two basic principles that operate to control work flow. The first basic principle that should be observed in the development of new projects is the tolerance for ambiguous work flow. The concept of "new", in this instance, means uncharted terrain. The tolerance for ambiguous work flow is necessary to deal with such matters as undefined role expectations, false starts, trial and error learning, uncoordinated efforts, weak communications systems, lack of resources, and contingency planning.

The expectancy for work flow is that its nature will be a mature and highly specified work flow. This concept of a highly definitive work flow is the general expectation for a new project. The most efficient and effective work flow is an optimal ideal. However, so many internal and external variables press upon this optimal ideal of work flow that it is imperative to understand that the nature of the work flow ranges from relatively simple dynamics to highly complex ones. In the context of this analytical treatment, it is imperative that the "executive" facet of the principal and teacher comes into play.

Timing. The phenomenon of timing is important in the analysis of action. Timing of action is defined as the period of time in which work is accomplished. There is a developmental element involved in the timing function. In the analytical treatment of action, the notion of initial, medial, and ongoing operations is treated. Moreover, timing is a function of multiple factors, such as readiness, seasons, cyclical, and durational variables. For example, new shows for the TV are made ready during the spring, for the new season, usually in the fall. The garment industry in New York City has their Christmas in July. They are working on the clothing to be sold at Christmastime in the summer. In school work, a principal and teachers must work on the opening of the new school year six months ahead. The timing of work must take into account many economic, social, political, and psychological factors.

Performance of the workers. Successful worker performance must take into account the principles of (1) competency, (2) readiness, (3) collaboration, (4) involvement, (5) understanding, (6) legal factors, (7) norm factors, (8) attitudes, and (9) actual accomplishment.

Initial phase operations. The necessary confluence of people and materials to implement plans is basic. A single responsible person must be assigned the task of executing an initial phase. Critical monitoring and appraisal operations are necessary at this time. Provisions for contingency plans or modifications are often very critical when discrepancies are identified between the ideal statement or design of the plans and the working out of the plan. Time and scheduling factors are key in this phase.

Medial phase operations. The medial phase of activity should profit from the initial phase, with progress occuring as a result of the appraisal of action and the contingencies made during the initial phase. The medial phase should benefit from growth, advancement, and maturity of the human resources especially when new or uncharted plans are operationalized. Leadership and monitoring are key components of this phase.

Final or ongoing operations. The final or ongoing operations of the action should profit from the growth and experience of the initial and particularly the medial phase. The final operations phase implies that the plans are completed. We should like to consider that the decisional operation terminates in a product. For example, if the plan was to build a new reading lab, the final operations are completed, when the reading laboratory begins functioning.

When this final phase of the action is completed, then the ongoing operations phase, the use of the reading lab for specific activities begins. This ongoing phase requires its own particular set of decisions and actions. This clear example is illustrative of much of our work in school operations, that is, the completion of one final operation is the prelude to the initiation of a whole new set of decisions.

ANALYSIS OF APPRAISAL

The final component of the Seven Analytical A's is the analysis of appraisal. It is well known through the study of the elementary foundations of evaluation, that ongoing evaluation is an integral component of each of the functions in the system. Appraisal and evaluation are the process of ascribing worth or value to a product, system or process. Appraisal of contexts and phenomena, as a result of planful decision behavior, within the parameters of validity, reliability, and goodness, gives rise to the following questions:

1. In the decision-making process, have you considered the salient axiological, or values component and are you assisted in considering the appropriateness of the decision?

2. In the decision-making process, which axiomatic factors or givens are dominant, crucial, or imperative in conceptualizing the new plan?

3. In the decision-making process, does the analysis of alternatives in terms of utility, cost and decision science principles assist you in making the optimal choice?

4. In the decision-making process, have you designed the best plan

to achieve the goals and objectives of the organization consistent with the other analytical factors in the system?

5. In the decision-making process, have the allocations of human and material resources been valid, and appropriate for the designed plan?

6. In the decision-making process, has the full system of action been valid, beneficial, and appropriate in realizing the plan?

7. In the decision-making process, has appraisal been integrally, adequately, and validly, utilized throughout the entire process?

CONCLUSION

At the outset of this chapter, we made the point that there are numerous and complex activities in classrooms and schools. The Seven Analytical A's system was conceptualized as an instructional modality or strategy to analyze the complexities of even simple decision-making processes. Admittedly, there are omissions and gaps in the conceptualization. Further, the taxonomical arrangement of the Seven Analystical A's is but one conceptualization for dealing with many complexities involved in problem solving in the schools. The best case that can be made for such an ordering is that too frequently the axiological and axiomatic components have been given minor or relatively little attention in decision making. This new ordering of decision-making components gives the process a different focus.

At a functional level, teachers in classrooms are provided a practical mnemonic (Table 3-1) for strategic behavior in making decisions. Few teachers consider themselves decision makers and managers. Yet, much of the literature regarding life in classrooms tells us that the teacher is the critical person in creating a classroom climate. These strategies may aid teachers to become facilitators of greater participation and interaction in classrooms.

Table 3-1. The Seven Analytic A's

A Mnemonic for Decision Making
Axiologicals
Axiomatics
Alternatives
Architecture
Allocations
Actions
Appraisal

References

Anderson, B.F. (1980). *The complete thinker: A handbook of techniques for creative and critical problem solving.* Englewood Cliffs, NJ: Prentice Hall.

Argyris, C. (1957). *Personality and organization.* New York: Harper and Row.

Banghart & Trull. (1973). *Educational planning.* New York: Macmillan.

Blackmon, C.R. (1968, August). A preliminary report of data from a survey of professors of educational administration concerning values. In C.R. Blackmon (Ed.), *Selected papers on values.* Lafayette, LA: University of Southwestern Louisiana.

Blake, R., & Mouton, J. (1966). *The managerial grid.* Houston: Gulf Publishing.

Conovan, C. (1967). Tradition and innovation in teacher education. *The Eighth Charles W. Hunt Lecture,* Washington, DC: American Association of Colleges for Teacher Education.

Delbecq, A.L., Van de Ven, A.H., & Gustafson, D.H. (1975). *Group techniques for program planning.* Glenview, IL: Scott Foresman.

Dror, Y. (1963). Planning process: A facet design. *International Review of Administrative Sciences, 29* (1).

Etzioni, A. (1961). *A comparative analysis of complex organizations.* New York: The Free Press.

Florida State Department of Education. (1962). *A guide: Teaching moral and spiritual values in Florida schools.* Bulletin 14–1962. Tallahassee, FL.

French, J.R.P., & Raven, B. (1960). The basis of social power. In D. Cartwright & A.F. Zander (Eds.), *Group dynamics: Research and theory.* Evanston, IL: Row Peterson.

Garan, J. (1985). *High school juniors' perceptions of the importance and use of analytic strategies in academic decision making.* Unpublished doctoral dissertation. Fordham University, New York.

Getzels, J.W. & Guba, E.G. (1957, Winter). Social behavior and administrative process. *The School Review.*

Gibb, J.R. (1964). Communication and productivity. *Personnel Administration, 27* (1), 8–13, 45.

Hage, G. (1967). An axiomatic theory of organization. *Administrative Science Quarterly, 10* 289-320.

Halpin, A. (1967). *Theory and research in administration.* New York: Macmillan.

Hammond, K.R., McClelland, G.H., & Mumpower, J. (1980). *Human judgment and decision making: Theories, methods, and procedures.* New York: Praeger.

Janis, T.L., & Mann, L. (1977). *Decision making: A psychological analysis of conflict, choice, and commitment.* New York: The Free Press.

Kluckhohn, C., & Murray, H.A. (Eds.) (1956). *Personality in nature, society, and culture.* New York: Alfred A. Knopf.

Knezevich, S. (1975). *Administration of public education* (3rd ed). New York: Harper and Row.

Likert, R. (1968). *The human organization: Its management and value.* New York: McGraw-Hill.

Lerner, M. (1976). *Values in education: Notes toward a values philosophy.* Bloomington IN: Phi Delta Kappa.

March, J.G. (1978). Bounded rationality, ambiguity, and the engineering of choice. *The Bell Journal of Economics, 9,* 587–608.

March, J.G. (1976). Analytical skills and the university training of educational administrators. In J.D. Herring and R.E. Klimes, (Eds), *Walter D. Cocking lectures: The NCPEA series of prominent papers in educational administration.* Berrian Springs, MI: Center for Studies and ... in Education, Andrews University.

March, J.G., & Olsen, J.P. (Eds.). (1976). *Ambiguity and choice in organizations.* Bergen: Universitetsforlaget.

McCarthy, J.F.X. (1980) *Curriculum Planning.* Unpublished manuscript. Fordham University.

McGregor, D. (1960). *The human side of enterprise.* New York: McGraw-Hill.

Mintzberg, H. (1973). *The nature of management work.* New York: Harper and Row.

Mohair, M. (1980). *School Planning.* Unpublished manuscript. Fordham University.

President's Commission on National Goals. (1960). *Goals for Americans,* New York: The American Assembly Columbia University.

Sachs, B.M. (1968). Values, perception and leadership behavior. In C.R. Blackmon (Ed.), *Selected papers in values.* Lafayette, LA: University of Southwestern Louisiana.

Sergiovanni, T., & R. J. Starratt (1983). *Supervision: Human perspectives* (3rd ed.). New York: McGraw-Hill.

Simon, H.A. (1976). *Administrative behavior.* (3rd ed.). New York: The Free Press.

Simon, H.A. (1957). *Models of man.* New York: Wiley and Sons.

Taylor, D.W. (1965). Decision making and problem solving. In J.A. March (Ed.), *Handbook of organizations.* Chicago: Rand McNally Co.

Thompson, V.A. (1961). *Modern organizations.* New York: McGraw-Hill.

Waters, R.H. (1958). Behavior: Datum or abstraction. *American Psychology,* 13: 278–282; 1958.

Weick, K.E. (1969). *The social psychology of organizing.* Reading, MA: Addison-Wesley.

Worthen, RE.. (1968, August). The relevance of values to psychological health. In C.R. Blackmon (Ed.), *Selected papers on values.* Lafayette, LA: University of Southwestern Louisiana.

PART II
THE CONTEXT OF READING INSTRUCTION

Chapter 4
Toward a Composing Model of Reading*

Robert J. Tierney
P. David Pearson
University of Illinois, Center for Reading

We believe that at the heart of understanding reading and writing connections one must begin to view reading and writing as essentially similar processes of meaning construction. Both are acts of composing. From a reader's perspective, meaning is created as a reader uses his background of experience together with the author's cues to come to grips both with what the writer is getting him to do or think and what the reader decides and creates for himself. As a writer writes, she uses her own background of experience to generate ideas and, in order to produce a text which is considerate to her idealized reader, filters these drafts through her judgments about what her reader's background of experience will be, what she wants to say, and what she wants to get the reader to think or do. In a sense, both reader and writer must *adapt* to their perceptions about their partner in negotiating what a text means.

Witness if you will the phenomenon which was apparent as both writers and readers were asked to think aloud during the generation of, and later response to, directions for putting together a water pump (Tierney, LaZansky, Raphael, & Cohen, in press; Tierney, 1983). As Tierney reported:

> At points in the text, the mismatch between reader' think-alouds and writer's think-alouds was apparent: Writers suggested concerns which readers did not focus upon (e.g., I'm going to have to watch my pronouns

*Reprinted by permission of the publisher and the authors from *Language Arts*, May 1983 (copyright © 1983 by the National Council of Teachers of English).

This work was supported in part by the National Institute of Education under Contract No. NIE 400-81-0030. Selected aspects of relevance to the model are also discussed in a paper *On Becoming a Thoughtful Reader: Learning to Read Like a Writer* by P. David Pearson & Robert J. Tierney and *Writer-reader transactions: Defining the dimensions of negotiation* by Robert J. Tierney. Special thanks go to T. Rogers and others, including A. Crismore, L. Fielding, J. Hansen, and J. Harste for their reactions to and help with the paper.

here . . . It's rather stubborn—so I better tell how to push it hard . . . he should see it looks very much like a syringe), and readers expressed concerns which writers did not appear to consider (I'm wondering why I should do this . . . what function does it serve?). As writers thought aloud, generated text, and moved to the next set of subassembly directions, they would often comment about the *writer's craft* as readers might (e.g., no confusion there . . . that's a fairly clear descriptor . . . and we've already defined what that is). There was also a sense in which writers marked their compositions with an "okay" as if the "okay" marked a movement from a turn as reader to a turn as a writer. Analyses of the readers' *think alouds* suggested that the readers often felt frustrated by the writer's failure to explain why they were doing what they were doing. Also the readers were often critical of *the writer's craft,* including the writer's choice of words, clarity, and accuracy. There was a sense in which the reader's *think-alouds* assumed a reflexive character as if the reader were rewriting the texts. If one perceived the readers as craftpersons, unwilling to blame their tools for an ineffective product, then one might view the readers as unwilling to let the text provided stand in the way of their successful achievement of their goals or pursuit of understanding. (p. 150)

These data and other descriptions of the reading act (Bruce, 1981; Collins, Brown, & Larkin, 1980; Rosenblatt, 1976, 1978; Tompkins, 1980) are consistent with the view that texts are written and read in a tug of war between authors and readers. These think-alouds highlight the kinds of internal struggles that we all face (whether consciously or unconsciously) as we compose the meaning of a text in front of us.

Few would disagree that writers compose meaning. In this paper we argue that readers also compose meaning (that there is no meaning on the page until a reader decides there is). We will develop this position by describing some aspects of the composing process held in parallel by reading and writing. In particular, we will address the essential characteristics of effective composing: planning, drafting, aligning, revising, and monitoring.

As a writer initially plans her writing, so a reader plans his reading. Planning involves two complementary processes: goal-setting and knowledge mobilization. Taken together, they reflect some commonly accepted behaviors, such as setting purposes, evaluating one's current state of knowledge about a topic, focusing or narrowing topics and goals, and self-questioning.

Flower and Hayes (1981) have suggested that a writer's goals may be procedural (e.g., how do I approach this topic?), substantive (e.g., I want to say something about how rockets work), or intentional (e.g., I want to convince people of the problem). So may a reader's goals be procedural (e.g., I want to get a sense of this topic overall.) substantive (e.g., I need to find out about the relationship between England and France.) or intentional (e.g., I wonder what this author is trying to say.) or some combination of all three. These goals can be embedded in one another or addressed concurrently; they may be conflicting or complementary. As a reader reads (just as when a writer writes) goals may emerge, be discovered, or change. For example, a reader or writer may broaden, fine-tune, redefine, delete, or replace goals. A recent fourth-grade writer, whom we interviewed about a project he had completed on American Indians, illustrates these notions well: As he stated his changing goals, "I began with the topic of Indians but that was too broad, I decided to narrow my focus on Hopis, but that was not what I was really interested in. Finally, I decided that what I really wanted to learn about was medicine men . . . I really found some interesting things to write about." In coming to grips with his goals our writer suggested both procedural and substantive goals. Note also that he refined his goals prior to drafting. In preparation for reading or writing a draft, goals usually change; mostly they become focused at a level of specificity sufficient to allow the reading or writing to continue. Consider how a novel might be read. We begin reading a novel to discover the plot yet find ourselves asking specific questions about events and attending to the author's craft . . . how she uses the language to create certain effects.

The goals that readers or writers set have a symbiotic relationship with the knowledge they mobilize, and together they influence what is produced or understood in a text (Anderson, Reynolds, Schalleert, and Goetz, 1977; Anderson, Pichert, & Shirey, 1979; Hayes and Tierney, 1982; Tierney & Mosenthal, 1981). A writer plans what she wants to say with the knowledge resources at her disposal. Our fourth grade writer changed his goals as a function of the specificity of the knowledge domain to which he successively switched. Likewise readers, depending on their level of topic knowledge and what they want to learn from their reading, vary the goals they initiate and pursue. As an example of this symbiosis in a reader, consider the following statement from a reader of *Psychology Today*.

I picked up an issue of *Psychology Today*. One particular article dealing with women in movies caught my attention. I guess it was the photos of Streep, Fonda, Lange, that interested me. As I had seen most of their recent movies I felt as if I knew something about the topic. As I started reading, the author had me recalling my reaction to these movies (Streep in *Sophie's Choice*, Lange in *Tootsie*, Fonda in *Julia*). At first I intended to glance at the article. But as I read on, recalling various scenes, I became more and more interested in the author's perspective. Now that my reactions were nicely mobilized, this author (definitely a feminist) was able to convince me of her case for stereotyping. I had not realized the extent to which women are either portrayed as the victim, cast with men, or not developed at all as a character in their own right. This author carried me back through these movies and revealed things I had not realized. It was as if I had my own purposes in mind, but I saw things through her eyes.

What is interesting in this example is how the reader's knowledge about films and feminism was mobilized at the same time as his purposes became gradually welded to those of the author's. The reader went *from* almost free association, *to* reflection, *to* directed study of what he knew. It is this directed study of what one knows that is so important in knowledge mobilization. A writer does not just throw out ideas randomly; she carefully plans the placement of ideas in text so that each idea acquires just the right degree of emphasis in text. A successful reader uses his knowledge just as carefully; at just the right moment he accesses just the right knowledge structures necessary to interpret the text at hand in a way consistent with his goals. Note also how the goals a reader sets can determine the knowledge he calls up; at the same time, that knowledge, especially as it is modified in conjunction with the reader's engagement of the text, causes him to alter his goals. Initially, a reader might "brainstorm" his store of knowledge and maybe organize some of it (e.g., clustering ideas using general questions such as who, what, when, where, or why—*or* developing outlines). Some readers might make notes; others might merely think about what they know, how this information clusters, and what they want to pursue. Or just as a writer sometimes uses a first draft to explore what she knows and what she wants to say, so a reader might scan the text as a way of fine tuning the range of knowledge and goals to engage, creating a kind of a "draft" reading of the text. It is to this topic of drafting that we now turn your attention.

Drafting

We define drafting as the refinement of meaning which occurs as readers and writers deal directly with the print of the page. All of us who have had to write something (be it an article, a novel, a memo, a letter, or a theme), know just how difficult getting started can be. Many of us feel that if we could only get a draft on paper, we could rework and revise our way to completion. We want to argue that getting started is just as important a step in reading. What every reader needs, like every writer, is a first draft. And the first step in producing that draft is finding the right "lead." Murray (1982) describes the importance of finding the lead:

> The lead is the beginning of the beginning, those few lines the reader may glance at in deciding to read or pass on. These few words—fifty, forty,

thirty, twenty, ten—establish the tone, the point of view, the order, the dimensions of the article. In a sense, the entire article is coiled in the first few words waiting to be released.

An article, perhaps even a book, can only say one thing and when the lead is found, the writer knows what is included in the article and what is left out, what must be left out. As one word is chosen for the lead another rejected, as a comma is put in and another taken away, the lead begins to feel right and the pressure builds up until it is almost impossible not to write. (p.99)

From a reader's perspective, the key points to note from Murray's description are these: (1) "the entire article is coiled in these first few words waiting to be released," and (2) "the lead begins to feel right . ." The reader, as he reads, has that same feeling as he begins to draft his understanding of a text. The whole point of hypothesis testing models of reading like those of Goodman (1967) and Smith (1971) is that the current hypothesis one holds about what a text means creates strong expectations about what the succeeding text ought to address. So strong are these hypotheses, these "coilings," these drafts of meaning a reader creates that incoming text failing to cohere with them may be ignored or rejected.

Follow us as we describe a hypothetical reader and writer beginning their initial drafts.

A reader opens his or her textbook, magazine, or novel; a writer reaches for his pen. The reader scans the pages for a place to begin; the writer holds the pen poised. The reader looks over the first few lines of the article or story in search of a sense of what the general scenario is. (This occurs whether the reader is reading a murder mystery, a newspaper account of unemployment, or magazine article on underwater life.) Our writer searches for the lead statement or introduction to her text. For the reader, knowing the scenario may involve knowing that the story is about women engaged in career advancement from a feminist perspective, or knowing that the murder mystery involves the death of a wealthy husband vacationing abroad. For the writer, establishing the scenario involves prescribing those few ideas which introduce or define the topic. Once established the reader proceeds through the text refining and building upon his sense of what is going on: the writer does likewise. Once the writer has found the "right" lead, she proceeds to develop the plot, expositions, or descriptions. As the need to change scenarios occurs so the process is repeated. From a schema-theoretical perspective, coming to grips with a lead statement or, if you are a reader, gleaning an initial scenario, can be viewed as schema selection (which is somewhat equivalent to choosing a script for a play); filling in the slots or refining the scenario is equivalent to schema instantiation.

As our descriptions of a hypothetical reader suggests, what drives reading and writing is the desire to make sense of what is happening—to make things cohere. A writer achieves that fit by deciding what information to include and what to withhold. The reader accomplishes that fit by filling in gaps (it must be early in the morning) or making uncued connections (he must have been angry because they lost the game). All readers, like all writers, ought to strive for this fit between the whole and the parts and among the parts. Unfortunately, some readers and writers are satisfied with a piecemeal experience (dealing with each part separately), or, alternatively, a sense of the whole without a sense of how the parts relate to it. Other readers and writers become "bogged down" in their desire to achieve a perfect text or "fit" on the first draft. For language educators our task is to help readers and writers to achieve the best fit among the whole and the parts. It is with this concern in mind that we now consider the role of alignment and then revision.

Aligning

In conjunction with the planning and drafting initiated, we believe that the alignment a reader or writer adopts can have an overriding influence on a composer's ability to achieve coherence. We see alignment as having two facets: stances a reader or writers assume in collaboration with their author or audience; and roles within which the reader or writer immerse themselves as they proceed with the topic. In other words, as readers and writers approach a text they vary the nature of their stance or collaboration with their author (if they are a reader) or audience (if they are a writer) and, in conjunction with this collaboration, immerse themselves in a variety of roles. A writer's stance toward her readers might be intimately challenging or quite neutral. And, within the contexts of these collaborations she might share what she wants to say through characters or as an observer of events. Likewise, a reader can adopt a stance toward the writer which is sympathetic, critical, or passive. And, within the context of these collaborations, he can immerse himself in the text as an observer or eyewitness, participant or character.

As we have suggested alignment results in certain benefits. Indeed, direct and indirect support for the facilitative benefits of adopting alignments comes from research on a variety of fronts. For example, schema theoretic studies involving an analysis of the influence of a reader's perspective have shown that if readers are given different alignments prior to or after reading a selection, they will vary in what and how much they will recall (Pichert, 1979; Spiro, 1977). For example, readers told to read a description of a house from the perspective of a homebuyer or burglar tend to recall more information and are more apt to include in their recalls information consistent with their perspective. Furthermore, when asked to consider an alternative perspective these same readers were able to generate information which they previously had not retrieved and which was important to the new perspective. Researchers interested in the effects of imaging have examined the effects of visualizing—a form of alignment which we would argue is equivalent to eyewitnessing. Across a number of studies it have been shown that readers who are encouraged to visualize usually perform better on comprehension tasks (Sadoski, in press). The work on children's development of the ability to recognize point of view (Hay and Brewer, 1982; Applebee, 1978) suggests that facility with alignment develops with comprehension maturity. From our own interviews with young readers and writers we have found that the identification with characters and immersion in a story reported by our interviewees accounts for much of the vibrancy, sense of control, and fulfillment experienced during reading and writing. Likewise, some of the research analyzing proficient writing suggests that proficient writers are those writers who, when they read over what they have written, comment on the extent to which their story and characters are engaging (Birnbaum, 1982). A number of studies in both psychotherapy and creativity provide support for the importance of alignment. For purposes of generating solutions to problems, psychotherapists have found it useful to encourage individuals to exchange roles (e.g., mother with daughter). In an attempt to generate discoveries, researchers have had experts identify with the experiences of inanimate objects (e.g., paint on metal) as a means of considering previously inaccessible solutions (e.g., a paint which does not peel).

Based upon these findings and our own observations, we hypothesize that adopting an alignment is akin to achieving a foothold from which meaning can be more readily negotiated. Just as a filmmaker can adopt and vary the angle from which a scene is depicted in order to maximize the richness of a filmgoers's experience, so too can a reader and writer adopt and vary the angle from which language meanings are negotiated. This suggests, for language educators, support for these questions or activities which help readers or writers take a stance on a topic and immerse themselves in the ideas or story. This might entail having students project themselves into a scene as a character, eyewitness, or object (imagine you are Churchill, a reporter, the sea). This might occur at the hands of questioning, dramatization, or simply role playing. In line with our hypothesis, we believe that in these contexts students almost spontaneously acquire a sense of the whole as well as the parts.

To illustrate how the notion of alignment might manifest itself for different readers, consider the following statement offered by a professor describing the stances he takes while reading an academic paper:

> When I read something for the first time, I read it argumentatively. I also
> find later that I made marginal notations that were quite nasty like, "you're
> crazy!" or "Why do you want to say that?" Sometimes they are not really
> fair and that's why I really think to read philosophy you have to read it
> twice . . . The second time you read it over you should read it as sympa-
> thetic as possible. This time you read it trying to defend the person against
> the very criticisms that you made the first time through. You read every
> sentence and if there is an issue that bothers you, you say to yourself,
> "This guy who wrote this is really very smart. It sounds like what he is
> saying is wrong; I must be misunderstanding him. What could he really
> want to be saying?" (Freeman, 1982, p.11)

Also consider Eleanor Gibson's description of how she approaches
the work of Jane Austen:

> Her novels are not for airport reading. They are for reading over and
> over, and savoring every phrase, memorizing the best of them, and getting
> an even deeper understanding of Jane's "sense of the human comedy" . . . As
> I read the book for perhaps the twenty-fifth time, I consider what point
> she is trying to make in the similarities and differences between the char-
> acters . . . I want to discover for myself what this sensitive and perceptive
> individual is trying to tell me. Sometimes I only want to sink back and
> enjoy it and laugh myself. (Gibson & Levin, 1975, pp.458–460)

Our professor adjusted his stance from critic to sympathetic coauthor
across different readings. Our reader of Austen was, at times, highly
active and sympathetic collaborator and, at other times, more neutral
and passive.

Obviously the text itself prompts certain alignment. For example,
consider how an author's choice of words, arguments, or selection of
genre may invite a reader to assume different stances and, in the context
of these collaborations, different roles. The opening paragraph of
Wolfe's *Electric Kool-Aid Acid Test* (1977) illustrates how the use of first
person along with the descriptive power of words (e.g., cramped, metal
bottom, rising, rolling bouncing, etc.) compels the reader to engage in
a sympathetic collaboration with an author and be immersed as an active
participant in a truck ride across the hills of San Francisco.

> That's good thinking there, Cool Breeze. Cool Breeze is a kid with 3 or
> 4 days' beard sitting next to me on the cramped metal bottom of the open
> back part of the pick up truck. Bouncing along. Dipping and rising and
> rolling on the rotten springs like a boat. Out the back of the truck the city

of San Francisco is bouncing down the hill, all those endless staggers of
bay windows, slums with a view, bouncing artd streaming down the hill.
One after another, electric signs with neon martini glasses lit up on them,
the San Francisco symbol of "bar"—thousands of neon, magenta martini
glasses bouncing and streaming down the hill, and beneath them thousands
of people wheeling around to look at this freaking crazed truck we're in,
their white faces erupting from their lapels like marshamallows—streaming
and bouncing down the hill—and God knows they've got plenty to look
at. (p.1)

Also, consider the differences in collaboration and role taking the
following text segments invite. While both texts deal with the same information, on one text the information is presented through a conversation between two children, and in the other text, the information is
presented in a more "straightforward" expository style.

FLY

Lisa and Mike were bored. It was Saturday and they did not know what
to do until Lisa had an idea.
"I know a game we can play that they play in some countries.

All over the world children like to play different games. In some countries,
children enjoy playing a game called "Fly."

We have found that readers of the first text usually assume a sympathetic
collaboration with the writer and identify with the characters. They view
the game through the eyes of the children and remain rather neutral
with respect to the author. Our readers of the second text tend to have
difficulty understanding the game at the same time as they are critical
of the author. They adopt a role more akin to an observer who, lacking
a specific angle, catches glimpses of the game without acquiring an overall understanding. Some of us have experienced a similar phenomenon
as viewers of an overseas telecast of an unfamiliar sport (e.g., the game
of cricket on British television). The camera angles provided by the
British sportscasters are disorienting for the naive viewer.

Obviously a number of factors may influence the nature of a reader's
alignment[1] and the extent to which his resulting interpretation is viable.
A reader, as our last example illustrated, might adopt an alignment

---

[1]It is not within the scope of the present paper to characterize the various mechanisms
by which writers engage readers we would encourage our readers to examine different
texts for themselves and some of the analystic schemes generated by Bruce (1981) and
Gibson (1975) among others.

which interferes with how well he will be able to negotiate an understanding. Sometimes a reader might adopt an alignment which overin-
dulges certain biases, predispositions, and personal experiences. Doris
Lessing (1973) described this phenomenon in a discussion of readers'
responses to her *The Golden Notebook:*

> Ten years after I wore [it], it can get, in one week, three letters about
> it . . . One letter is entirely about the sex war, about man's inhumanity to
> woman, and woman's inhumanity to man, and the writer has produced
> pages and pages all about nothing else, for she—but not always a she—can't
> see anything else in the book.
> The second is about politics, probably for old Red like myself, and he or
> she writes many pages about politics, and never mentions any other theme.
> These two letter used, when the book was as it were young, to be the most
> common.
> The third letter, once rare but now catching up on the others, is written
> by a man or a woman who can see nothing in it but the theme of mental
> illness.
> But it is the same book.
> And naturally these incidents bring up again questions of what people see
> when they read a book, and why one person sees one pattern and nothing
> at all of another pattern, and how odd it is to have, as author, such a clear
> picture of a book, that is seen so very differently by its readers. (p.xi)

Such occurrences should not be regarded as novel. It is this phenomena of reader-author engagement and indiosyncratic response which has
been at the center of a debate among literary theorists, some of whom
(e.g., Jakobson and Levi-Strauss, 1962) would suggest that a "true" reading experience has been instantiated only when readers assume an alignment which involves close collaboration with authors. Others would
argue that readers can assume a variety of alignments, whether these
alignments are constrained by the author (Iser, 1974) or initiated freely
by the reader (Fish, 1970). They would rarely go so far as to suggest the
destruction of the text, but instead as Tompkins (1980) suggested they
might begin to view reading and writing as joining hands, changing
places, "and finally becoming distinguishable only as two names for the
same activity" (p.ii). We do not wish to debate the distinctions represented
by these and other theorists, but to suggest that there appears to be at
least some consensus that effective reading involves a form of alignment
which emerges in conjunction with a working relationship between readers and writers. In our opinion, this does not necessitate bridling readers
and writers to one another. Indeed, we would hypothesize that new
insights are more likely discovered and appreciations derived when readers and writers try out different alignments as they read and write their

texts. This suggests spending time rethinking, reexamining, reviewing, and rereading. For this type of experience does not occur on a single reading; rather it emerges only after several rereadings, reexaminations, and drafts. It is to this notion of reexamination and revision to which we now turn.

Revising

While it is common to think of a writer as a reviser it is *not* common to think of a reader as someone who revises unless perhaps he has a job involving some editorial functions. We believe that this is unfortunate. We would like to suggest that revising should be considered as integral to reading as it is to writing. If readers are to develop some control over and a sense of discovery with the models of meaning they build, they must approach text with the same deliberation, time, and reflection that a writer employs as she revises a text. They must examine their developing interpretations and view the models they build as draft-like in quality—subject to revision. We would like to see students engage in behaviors such as rereading (especially with different alignments), annotating the text on the page with reactions, and questioning whether the model they have built is what they really want. With this in mind let us turn our attention to revising in writing.

We have emphasized that writing is not merely taking ideas from one's head and placing them onto the page. A writer must choose words which best represent these ideas; that is, she must choose words which have the desired impact. Sometimes this demands knowing what she wants to say and how to say it. At other times, it warrants examining what is written or read to discover and clarify one's ideas, Thus a writer will repeatedly reread, reexamine, delete, shape, and correct what she is writing. She will consider whether and how her ideas fit together, how well her words represent the ideas to be shared, and how her text can be fine-tuned. For some writers this development and redevelopment will appear to be happening effortlessly. For others, revision demands hard labor and sometimes several painful drafts. Some rework the drafts in their heads before they rewrite; others slowly rework pages as they go. From analyses of the revision strategies of experienced writers, it appears that the driving force behind revision is a sense of emphasis and proportion. As Sommers (1980) suggested, one of the questions most experienced writers ask themselves is "what does my essay as a *whole* need for form, balance, rhythm, and communication?" (p.386). In trying to answer this question, writers proceed through revision cycles with sometimes overlapping and sometimes novel concerns. Initial revision cycles might be directed predominately at topical development; later cycles might be directed at stylistic concerns.

For most readers, revision is an unheard-of experience. Observations of secondary students reveal that most readers view reading competency as the ability to read rapidly a single text once with maximum recall (Schallert & Tierney, 1982). It seems that students rarely pause to reflect on their ideas or to judge the quality of their developing interpretations. Nor do they often reread a text either from the same or a different perspective. In fact, to suggest that a reader should approach text as a writer who crafts an understanding across several drafts—who pauses, rethinks, and revises—is almost contrary to some well-established goals readers proclaim for themselves (i.e., that efficient reading is equivalent to maximum recall based upon a single fast reading).

Suppose we could convince students that they ought to revise their readings of a text; would they be able to do it? We should not assume that merely allowing time for pausing, reflecting, and reexamining will guarantee that students will revise their readings. Students need to be given support and feedback at so doing. Students need to be aware of strategies they can pursue to accomplish revisions, to get things restarted when they stall, and to compare one draft or reading with another. The pursuit of a second draft of a reading should have a purpose. Sometimes this purpose can emerge from conferencing or discussing a text with the teacher and peers; sometimes it may come from within; sometimes it will not occur unless the student has a reason or function context for revision as well as help from a thoughtful teacher.

Monitoring

Hand in hand with planning, aligning, drafting, and revising, readers and writers must be able to distance themselves from the texts they have created to evaluate what they have developed. We call this executive function monitoring. Monitoring usually occurs tacitly, but it can be under conscious control. The monitor in us keeps track of and control over our other functions. Our monitor decides whether we have planned, aligned, drafted, and/or revised properly. It decides when one activity should dominate over the others. Our monitor tells when we have done a good job and when we have not. It tells us when to go back to the drawing board and when we can relax.

The complexity of the type of juggling which the monitor is capable of has been captured aptly in an analogy of a switchboard operator, used by Flower and Hayes (1981) to describe how writers juggle constraints:

She has two importants calls on hold. (Don't forget that idea.)
Four lights just started flashing. (They demand immediate attention or the'll be lost.)
A party of five wants to be hooked up together. (They need to be connected somehow.)
A party of two thinks they've been incorrectly connected. (Where do they go?)
And throughout this complicated process of remembering, retrieving, and connecting, the operator's voice must project calmness, confidence, and complete control. (p.33)

The monitor has one final task—to engage in a dialogue with the inner reader.

When writers and readers compose text they negotiate its meaning with what Murray (1982) calls the other self—that inner reader (the author's first reader) who continually reacts to what the writer has written, is writing, and will write—or what the reader has read, is reading, and will read. It is this other self which is the reader's or writer's counselor, and judge and prompter. This other self oversees what the reader and writer is trying to do, defines the natural collaboration between reader and author, and decides how well the reader as writer or writer as reader is achieving his or her goals.

A Summary and Discussion

To reiterate, we view both reading and writing as acts of composing. We see these acts of composing as involving continuous, recurring, and recursive transactions among readers and writers, their respective inner selves and their perceptions of each other's goals and desires. Consider the reader's role as we envision it. At the same time as the reader considers what he perceives to be the author's intentions (or what the reader perceives to be what the author is trying to get the reader to do or think), he negotiates goals with his inner self (or what he would like to achieve). With these goals being continuously negotiated (sometimes embedded within each other) the reader proceeds to take different alignments (critic, coauthor, editor, character, reporter, eye witness, etc.) as he uses features from his own experiential arrays and what he perceives to be arrayed by the author in order to create a model of meaning for the text. These models of meaning must assume a coherent, holistic quality in which everything fits together. The development of these models of meaning occurs from the vantage point of different alignments which the reader adopts with respect to these arrays. It is from these vantage

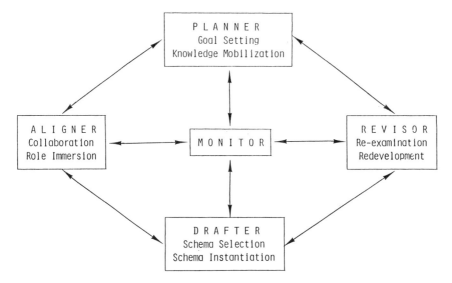

Figure 4-1. Some Components of the Composing Model of Reading

points that the various arrays are perceived, and their position adjusted such that the reader's goals and desire for a sense of completeness are achieved. Our diagrammatic representation of the major components of these processes is given in Figure 4-1.

Such an account of reading distinguishes itself from previous descriptions of reading and reading-writing relationships in several notable ways:

1. Most accounts of reading versus writing (as well as accounts of how readers develop a model of meaning) tend to emphasize reading as a receptive rather than productive activity. Some, in fact, regard reading as the mirror image of writing.
2. Most language accounts suggest that reading and writing are interrelated. They do not address the suggestion that reading and writing are multidimensional, multimodal processes—both acts of composing.
3. The phenomenon of alignment as integral to composing has rarely been explored.
4. Most descriptions of how readers build models of meaning fail to consider how the processes of planning, drafting, aligning, and revising are manifested.
5. Previous interactional and transactional accounts of rereading (Rosenblatt, 1978; Rumelhart, 1980) give little consideration to the

transaction which occurs among the inner selves of the reader and writer.

What our account fails to do is thoroughly differentiate how these composing behaviors manifest themselves in the various contexts of reading and writing. Nor does it address the pattern of interactions among these behaviors across moments during any reading and writing experience. For example, we give the impression of sequential stages even though we believe in simultaneous processes. We hope to clarify and extend these notions in subsequent writings.

References

Anderson, R. C., Pichert, J. W., & Shirey, L. L. (1979, April). *Effects of the reader's schema at different points in time* (Tech. Rep. No. 119). Urbana: University of Illinois, Center for the Study of Reading. (ERIC Document Reproduction Service No. ED 169 523)

Anderson, R. C., Reynolds, R. E., Schallert, D. L., & Goetz, E. T. (1977). Frameworks for comprehending discourse. *American Educational Research Journal, 14,* 367–382.

Applebee, A. N. (1978). *The child's concept of story.* Chicago: University of Chicago Press.

Birnbaum, J. C. (1982). The reading and composing behavior of selected fourth and seventh grade students. *Research in the Teaching of English,* 1982, *16*(3), 241–260.

Bruce, B. (1981). A social interaction model of reading. (1981). *Discourse processes, 4,* 273–311.

Collins, A., Brown, J. S., Larkin, K. M. (1980). Inference in text understanding. In R. J. Spiro, B. C. Bruce, & W. F. Brewer (Eds.), *Theoretical issues in reading comprehension.* Hillsdale, NJ: Erlbaum.

Fish, S. (1970). Literature in the reader: Affective stylistics. *New Literary History, 2*(1), 123–162.

Flower, L., & Hayes, J. R. (1981). A cognitive process theory of writing. *College Composition and Communication, 32*(4), 365–387.

Freeman, M. (1982). *How to read a philosophical text.* Unpublished paper. Harvard University.

Gibson, E. J., & Levin, H. (1975). *The psychology of reading.* Cambridge: MIT Press.

Goodman, K. S. (1967). Reading: A psycholinguistic guessing game. *Journal of the Reading Specialist, 6,* 126–135.

Hay, A., & Brewer, W. F. (1982). *Children's understanding of the narrator's point of view in prose* (Tech. Rep. No. 294). Urbana: University of Illinois, Center for the Study of Reading.

Hayes, D., & Tierney, R. (1982). Developing readers' knowledge through analogy. *Reading Research Quarterly, 17,* 256–280.

Iser, W. (1974). *The implied reader: Patterns in communication in prose fiction from Bunyan to Beckett.* Baltimore: John Hopkins University Press.

Jakobson, R., & Levi-Strauss, C. (1962). Les chats de Charles Baudelave. *L'Homme, 2,* 5–21.

Lessing, D. (1973). *Introduction to The Golden Notebook.* New York: Bantam Books.

Murray, D. (1982). *Learning by teaching.* Montclair, NJ: Boynton/Cook Publishers.

Murray, D. (1982). Teaching the other self: The writer's first reader. *College Composition and Communication, 33,* 140–147.

Pichert, J. W. (1979, November). *Sensitivity to what is important in prose* (Tech. Rep. No. 149).

Urbana: University of Illinois, Center for the Study of Reading. (ERIC Document Reproduction Service No. ED 179 946)

Rosenblatt, L. M. (1976). *Literature as exploration* (3rd ed.). New York: Noble and Noble. (Originally published 1939).

Rosenblatt, L. (1978). *The reader, the text, the poem: The transactional theory of the literary work.* Carbondale: Southern Illinois University Press.

Rumelhart, D. (1980). Schemata: The building blocks of cognition. In R.J. Spiro, B. C. Bruce, & W. Brewer (Eds.), *Theoretical issues in reading comprehension.* Hillsdale, NJ: Erlbaum.

Sadoski, M. (in press). An exploratory study of the relationships between reported imagery and the comprehension and recall of a story. *Reading Research Quarterly.*

Schallert, D., & Tierney, R. J. (1982). *Learning from expository text: The interaction of text structure with reader characteristics.* Final report. National Institute of Education.

Smith, F. (1971). *Understanding reading.* New York: Holt, Rinehart & Winston.

Sommers, N. I. (1980). Revision strategies of student writers and experienced adult writers. *College Composition and Communication, 31,* 378–388.

Spiro, R. J. (1977). Remembering information from text: The "state of schema" approach. In R. C. Anderson, R. J. Spiro, & W. E. Montague (Eds.), *Schooling and the acquisition of knowledge.* Hillsdale, NJ: Erlbaum.

Tierney, R. J. (1983). Writer-reader transactions: Defining the dimensions of negotiation. In P. Stock (Ed.), *Forum: Essays on theory and practice in the teaching of writing.* Montclair, NJ: Boynton/Cook.

Tierney, R. J., LaZansky, J., Raphael, T., & Cohen, P. (in press). Author's intentions and reader's interpretation. In R. J. Tierney, P. Anders, J. Mitchell (Eds.), *Understanding readers' understanding.* Hillsdale, NJ: Erlbaum.

Tierney, R. J., & Mosenthal, J. (1981, October). *The cohesion concept's relationship to the coherence of text* (Tech. Rep. No. 221). Urbana: University of Illinois, Center for the Study of Reading. (ERIC Document Reproduction Service No. ED 212 991)

Tompkins, J. P. (Ed.). (1980). *Reader-response criticism.* Baltimore: John Hopkins University Press.

Wolfe, T. (1977). *Electric Kool-Aid Acid Test.* New York: Bantam.

Chapter 5
Writing, Reading, and Learning

Bryant Fillion
Fordham University

A major problem in both teaching and research in language education has been our tendency to study particular skills and acts in isolation, apart from each other, and often apart from their significant use. Only recently, with increased interest in writing as a central concern of schooling and a focus of serious research, have we begun to explore the relationship of reading to other aspects of language development and use.

Although study of the reading–writing relationship is still in its infancy, my intention here is to examine our present understanding of the relationship and its implications for classroom practice. This examination will consider (1) the context of present writing research, (2) similarities between reading and writing processes and influences on their development, (3) the ways that reading and writing influence each other, and (4) the relationship of reading and writing to learning and school language policies.

Writing: "The New Kid on the Block"

Educational interest in writing, and support for writing research, has increased markedly since 1970. Public concern for writing increased with the increasing demand for writing skills on the job and in post-secondary training programs, and the criticism from employers and universities that many school graduates were inadequately prepared in writing. Pioneering research into the nature of writing processes (Emig, 1971; Flower and Hayes, 1981), and writing development and use (Britton, 1970; Britton et al. 1975) has stimulated widespread interest in the educational research community, especially among cognitive psychologists, who recognized writing and composing behaviors as important sources of information about mental processes. Perhaps most important to the nature of writing research over the past decade has been the growing awareness that school writing is intimately connected with learning (Britton, 1970; Emig, 1977), and with the development of critical thinking and reasoning (Scribner and Cole, 1981), high-priority cognitive skills thought to be lacking among many of today's students (Maeroff, 1984; National Assessment of Educational Progress, 1981; Petrosky, 1982).

Recent research in writing and the teaching of writing has tended to bring together specialists and practitioners who had previously worked in isolation: linguists, psycholinguists, educational psychologists, and language arts and reading specialists. One salutary result of this interdisciplinary enterprise has been the development of a promising body of theory and research concerning the relationship between writing and reading, and the more general relationship of literacy to learning, thought, and cognitive development. A second beneficial result has been that writing research has informed and been informed by work in language development, language pedagogy, cognition, and reading. It is much more difficult today than it was twenty years ago for specialists in reading, writing, linguistics, or psychology to remain ignorant of developments in related fields.

Despite its established place as a concern of formal education (Heath, 1981), writing has been relatively unencumbered by a well-established, traditional pedagogy and strong public opinions about how it should be taught. Unlike reading teachers, most teachers of writing have been quick to admit that they are operating largely by instinct in a trial-and-error fashion, with little or no academic training for the job they are asked to do. As a result, such pedagogy of writing as exists has probably been shaped as much by theory and research as by tradition, and that pedagogy has placed primary stress on writing as an active, intentional, largely mental process that is learned in purposeful use rather than by being told about it, or by acquiring separate, discrete skills taught in isolation.

The emphasis in writing research on processes rather than skills may prove especially insightful for the teaching of reading. Reading pedagogy and research have made extensive use of the terms "skills" and "skill development." "Skills" are essentially descriptions of ends rather than of means, of desired achievements, abilities, talents, or acts that someone can or should be able to perform. The relationship of a particular skill to a larger action (which may also be termed a skill) may or may not be self-evident in the labeling of the skill itself. "Comprehension" and "thinking" skills name the larger acts; "phonics" does not. Furthermore, many of the so-called "reading" and "writing" skills are themselves complex combinations of behaviors and abilities that suggest virtually nothing about how they might be achieved.

At least since 1970, writing research and theory have favored the term "process" over "skills." Processes are dynamic, intentional sequences of behaviors—distinct from abilities or talents which imply a degree of stasis. Unlike skills, processes are virtually always descriptions of means, rather than ends, and they are clearly associated with their purposes, usually being named for the intended end of the sequence. The composing process ends with something being composed; the revision process concludes with a changed text.

In writing and in reading, the shift from "skills" to "processes" has had promising results. It is much more difficult to identify the critical behaviors involved in complex acts, especially when many of these behaviors are mental and unobservable directly, than to list the skills involved. But the end result of process specification is the identification of means: a pedagogically useful description of behavioral sequences, rather than a list of discrete goals. I believe one of Frank Smith's major contributions to reading, in *Understanding Reading* (1978), was to explain in detail the processes involved in the act of reading, demonstrating that many of the behaviors named as "reading skills" (such as translating from sight to sound to meaning) could not, in fact, be part of the process of fluent reading, given the proven limitations of the brain's information-processing capacities.

Knowing the processes, of course, does not insure that we will know how to teach them, and we are still far from understanding many of the processes themselves. Much recent research on the pedagogy of writing and of reading, however, has demonstrated promising results by focusing on the behaviors and sequences already identified in theory and research. We seem much better able to improve students' language proficiency through their mastery of purposeful behavioral sequences and strategies than through their learning of discrete skills.

Significant developments in any aspect of language education are likely to affect language education generally. Thus, these emphases in recent writing research on processes rather than skills, on writing development and use, rather than on teaching per se, and on writing related to language, learning, and cognitive development, rather than as an isolated behavior, all seem likely to influence our thinking about reading as well.

Similarities of Reading and Writing and How They Develop

As Tierney and Pearson (Chapter 4) indicate, we are beginning to recognize essential similarities in the processes of reading and writing. Both involve the use of written language in meaning construction, both are largely mental processes that cannot be observed directly, and both are purposeful, intentional actions rather than passive behaviors. Given these very basic similarities, it appears likely that the conditions of their development are also similar. That is, proficiency in reading, as in writing and language development generally, will be positively influenced by its meaningful use (practice) in interaction with other language behaviors (talking, writing, and listening), supported by good advice (precepts), the observation of effective techniques (modeling), and information about outcomes (feedback).

The concepts of development and proficiency emerging from writing research suggest a considerable shift in emphasis from traditional North American views. Development is seen not as the accumulation of separate skills and knowledge, or as the elimination of error, but as the mastery of largely cognitive processes, and the willingness and ability to use writing for an increasing range of purposes. The relative importance of meaningful use and of direct skills instruction remains a critical issue in all language education, with British theorists generally stressing the former and North American theorists the latter. Concisely stated in the influential Bullock Report (1975), the argument for meaningful use has had a definite influence on writing research and theory:

> The kind of approach which we believe will produce the language development we regard as essential . . . involves creating situations in which, to satisfy his own purposes, a child encounters the need to use more elaborate forms and is thus motivated to extend the complexity of language available to him. (p.67)

> A writer's intention is prior to his need for techniques. The teacher who aims to extend the pupil's power as a writer must therefore work first upon his intentions, and *then* upon the techniques appropriate to them. (p.164)

The notion of reading as an active, intentional, goal-driven process, rather than a passive exercise of mechanical skills is certainly consistent with Tierney's and Pearson's view. The processes of planning, drafting, aligning, revising, and monitoring that Tierney and Pearson describe all presuppose a reader's active involvement with the text that can only be powered by engagement and intention. In a discussion of the nature and processes of learning, Torbe and Medway (1981) stress the importance of students answering for themselves the question "What has this got to do with me?," suggesting that "arriving at a clear sense of 'why I'm choosing to get involved with this' is inseparable from the more obvious processes by which learners make knowledge their own" (pp.32–33).

The importance of purpose and intention is, of course, not a new discovery in language education. Motivation is a constant concern of teachers, at least at the precollege level, and James Moffett (1968) re-minded teachers in 1968 that "for the learner, basics are not the small-focus technical things but broad things like meaning and motivation, purpose and point, which are precisely what are missing from exercises" (p.205). What research into writing and reading has done, however, is to emphasize intentional activity in pedagogically useful ways, suggest-ing, for instance, a crucial role for talk, for the integration of reading and writing activities, and for the inclusion of student goal setting in our lessons.

Traditional methods of motivation generally involve some form of telling students why the coming activity will be useful or important to them. Most school readers and anthologies introduce selections or ac-tivities with a form of advertising blurb, intended to develop students' interest and active involvement. Motivational techniques that are emerg-ing from work on writing, however, make much greater use of the students' own language—including their questions—and of game-like problems to promote students' involvement in lessons and activities. Torbe and Medway (1981), for instance, suggest letting students talk their way into topics and readings, beginning with what they already know. Scardamalia et al. (1981) describe sixty "consequential writing tasks" patterned after games, in which the goal of the assignment (e.g., obtaining classmates' agreement about the true author of a paper) is made clear and students are encouraged to find their own ways to achieve the goal. A related approach in literature (Fillion & Henderson, 1980) encourages students to conduct their own inquiry into selections, rather than relying upon the teacher or the textbook to provide the questions.

To what extent are classroom reading activities purposeful and sig-nificant for our students? Courtney Cazden identifies this as a key issue in language education:

> The most serious problem facing the language arts curriculum today is an imbalance between means and ends—an imbalance between too much attention to drill on the component skills of language and literacy and too little attention to their signficant use. (1977, p.40)

Research into actual classroom uses of writing (Applebee, 1981) and into the writing produced in schools (Fillion, 1979; Graves, 1978) sug-gests that Cazden's concerns are well-founded. Although students spend much of each school day with pen or pencil in hand, the amount of actual composing done is minimal, and the level of mental activity re-quired for most school writing is low. Similarly, extensive observations of secondary school reading in England (Lunzer and Gardner, 1979) found very few instances of reflective, thoughtful reading, or thoughtful discussions about materials that students had been assigned to read. Instead, teachers often by-passed reading as a means of presenting material to students, substituting lectures and recitations in place of reading. The main reading activity observed in most classrooms was characterized as "short burst" reading primarily to locate specific information called for by the teacher.

If such research findings regarding student performance in reading and writing are indicative of present practices, the probable reasons are not hard to find. Lacking experience and instruction in the use of reading to learn and of writing to compose and clarify thoughts, many students are understandably poor at and reluctant to do either. Aware of their students' reluctance and inability, teachers have found ways to reduce the reading and writing demands made by their courses, often substituting oral or visual presentation of subject matter for reading, and discussions or "objective" tests for substantive writing. This allows the teacher to cover the subject matter and evaluate student knowledge without taxing students' reading and writing abilities and without taking on the added burden of teaching language skills.

The Interaction of Reading and Writing

Reading and writing are not merely similar language activities with likely similarities in the way they are learned. They also influence each other. We have long realized that proficiencies in reading and in writing tend to correlate, and that all language uses are related at least to the extent that they contribute to knowledge and to general linguistic proficiency. Reading adds to the information one has to write about; writing and speaking clarify our understanding of topics so that subsequent reading about topics is easier. And although skill in reading or writing requires practice of the activity itself, either one may increase our familiarity with the linguistic resources needed for the other. However, we have only recently begun to explore the nature of these influences, with research focused mainly on how reading influences writing.

Frank Smith (1982) maintains that reading and writing are in an "asymmetrical if not parasitical relationship," since writers must read but readers do not necessarily have to write. Smith identifies reading as a writer's "essential fundamental source of knowledge about writing" (p.177), claiming that "to become writers children must read like writers" (1983, p. 565).

Current writing research at the Ontario Institute for Studies in Education is exploring the question of what it means to "read like a writer," to determine whether there are particular reading strategies that lead to improved writing and that might be taught to students as a way to increase their writing proficiency. A working assumption of the project is that reading and writing play reciprocal roles in developing sensitivity to how things are written. The more immersed one is in the craft of writing, the more likely one is to notice how other writers do things.

One early study in this research suggests that readers may differ considerably from one another in what they attend to, at least in repeated readings of the same text. "Aesthetic readers," while showing a primary interest in the meaning and content of a selection, differed markedly from "information-getting readers" in being more aware of the language of the text and of links with other texts and their own experiences. In addition to their interest in the text's meaning and the information it provided, aesthetic readers "voiced opinions about it and related it to other texts and to their own experiences. They also attended to language and responded affectively more than the others," responding "in a holistic way both to content and to the way it was expressed." In contrast, information-getting readers appeared to have the attitude that "once the meaning has been extracted there is nothing more to be gained from reading a text" (Church & Bereiter, 1983, pp. 471–472). Since the aesthetic readers also demonstrated greater writing proficiency in being able to translate given passages from one style to a constrasting style, the study may offer some indirect support for the contention that writing may affect reading as well as vice versa.

Several conclusions drawn from the Church and Bereiter study have implications for reading instruction intended to improve student's writing as well as their reading. If we want students to engage in the close reading and analysis of texts, we must still begin with comprehension: "Until students have understood a text to their satisfaction, they have little tendency to respond to style, either affectively or analytically" (p. 474). Also, students "should be encouraged to respond freely to the text," since aesthetic readers tend to do this, and "it would seem risky to impose criteria of relevance or appropriateness, especially with young readers" (p. 475). A teacher is seldom in a position to determine the ultimate relevance to the readers of the links they forge between the text and their own prior knowledge. Although, "being instructed to notice how the passage was written had no significant effect on student's attention to style" (p.472), such attention can be increased by the design of reading tasks. For example, the structure of a text can be highlighted by requiring students to reconstruct texts from sentences presented in scrambled order, and style may be emphasized by having students compare different versions of the same text or transform a text from one style into a contrasting style (p. 475).

Despite the obvious importance of comprehension, the narrow focus of our reading instruction on "reading for meaning" may deprive students of two major potential benefits of reading: the improvement of their writing, and the development of an aesthetic stance (Rosenblatt, 1978) that will enhance their sensitivity to and appreciation of literature and critical thinking in their responses. Classroom work by poet Kenneth Koch (1970, 1973) suggests that children who write poetry are better able to read, respond to, and appreciate poetry. Critical thinking by information-getting readers is likely to be limited to postreading assessments of the meanings in a text: whether they agree or disagree with the perceived ideas. Aesthetic readers, by attending as well to the style, structure, and craft of the text, are in a better position to consider the internal logic and strengths of the argument itself.

The interaction between reading and writing suggests two additional uses of writing in the teaching of reading: for instruction and evaluation. Lunzer and Gardner (1979) addressed the problem of promoting more reflective, thoughtful reading that would increase secondary students' ability to learn from assigned readings. One promising approach was through the use of group discussion activities involving collaborative prediction and selection, before and after reading, using such techniques as group cloze, SQ3R, sequencing, and reading for different purposes. Results indicated that the procedures were practical, the students enjoyed using them, "pupils revealed an ability to think about their reading in a way that is not evident when only the written outcomes of reading are considered," and teachers noted improvement in the quality of their students' reflection as confidence in using the procedures increased (pp. 309-310). Indeed, "One advantage of the discussion activities is the information they provide for teachers about thinking, knowledge, level of conceptualization, and reading difficulties of their pupils. They are diagnostic as well as teaching procedures" (p.311).

The closed questions, written or oral, that typically follow a reading assignment do not serve well either to reveal students' full understanding of a text or to stimulate the thoughtful reflection that might improve their subsequent reading. Just as group discussion appears to improve both assessment and subsequent performance, so a wider range of open-ended writing assignments, using informal, expressive writing (Britton et al, 1975), student questions, and tasks that require attention to text elements and varied reading purposes might also contribute to reading improvement.

Discussing the NAEP findings (1981) that American adolescents tend to be superficial in their assessment and interpretation of what they read, Anthony Petrosky (1982) stressed the importance of reading and writing in schools:

When multiple-choice testing and quick easy discussions dominate the curriculum, how can we expect anything but·the most basic performance from students? When reading and writing are separated in the curriculum and when students are not encouraged to discuss or write about their reading in any extended, reasoned way, is·it such a surprise that they then lack the more comprehensive thinking and analytic skills?

Sophisticated skills such as analysis, inference, generalizing, evaluating, and theorizing are best, and perhaps only assessed and taught through extended discourse—speaking and writing. It seems clear that speaking and writing tasks are necessary for the development of these critical thinking skills so absent from students' performance on this [NAEP] assessment. (p. 16)

The identification of a problem does not guarantee its easy solution. A recognition that reading and writing influence each other, and that the integration of writing and reading is essential to the development of critical reading skills does not tell us how this integration is to be achieved in practical ways, or what writing and discussion techniques will best work to the desired ends. But we do have some evidence from Lunzer and Gardner, Church and Bereiter, and others, that some very promising and practical techniques are in fact available. Perhaps the only essential element missing is our recognition of the need for integration, and our willingness to give practical classroom expression to the common sense realization that reading and writing cannot effectively be learned or taught in isolation from each other or from learning and thinking.

Reading, Writing, Learning, and School Language Policies

The similarities and relationship of reading and writing are perhaps most clearly seen in the role of language in learning and cognitive development. In the view of cognitive psychology and most contemporary language theory, learning occurs when experience and information result in a change in our cognitive structures—the combination of skills, knowledge, and beliefs that Frank Smith characterizes as the brain's "theory of what the world is like" (1982, p.30). Such changes in our mental representations of the world do not result from the passive accumulation of ready-made knowledge, but from an active processing that reformulates incoming information in terms of our prior experience, assimilating it into our existing theory or altering the theory to accommodate it. The role of language in this process has been explored by James Britton (1970; 1982, pp. 79–93), among others, and is concisely described in the Bullock Report's chapter on language and learning:

It is a confusion of everyday thought that we tend to regard 'knowledge' as something that exists independently of someone who knows. 'What is known' must in fact be brought to life afresh within every 'knower' by his own efforts. To bring knowledge into being is a formulating process, and language is its ordinary means, whether in speaking or writing or in the inner monologue of thought. Once it is understood that talking and writing are means to learning, those more obvious truths that we learn also from other people by listening and reading will take on a fuller meaning and fall into a proper perspective. . . . Something approximating to 'finding out for ourselves' needs . . . to take place if we are to be successfully told. The development of this individual context for a new piece of information, the forging of the links that give it meaning, is a task that we customarily tackle by talking to other people. (1975, p.50)

This notion that the active processing of language plays a part in most learning is a key concept in the "language across the curriculum" movement, which places great stress on the heuristic function of students' talk and writing (Bullock Report, pp.188–193) and raises serious questions about the place of students' language in today's classrooms. If talk and writing, and similar processes during reading, are important parts of learning, how are we to interpret the findings of research indicating a dearth of student talk, composing, and thoughtful reading in our schools?

This present situation is certainly understandable, given traditional teacher roles as dispensers of information, the pressure to cover extensive bodies of subject matter, and students' problems with reading and writing. At least in the secondary schools, content coverage leaves little time for student discussion and writing, especially if students can't be trusted to learn from assigned readings and must therefore have the material presented orally by the teacher. However, the price of bypassing students' active use of language may be unacceptably high. As Applebee (1981) notes, when a teacher substitutes multiple-choice and fill-in-the-blank exercises for actual student composing, "the teacher takes over all of the difficulties inherent in using language appropriate to a subject area—including much of the specialized vocabulary and rules of procedures which are embedded in the text—and leaves the student only the task of mechanically 'slotting-in' the missing information." What teachers may not realize, however, is that "the part of the task which they have taken over also involves important skills that are as relevant to the students' subject-area learning as to their writing instruction" (pp. 99–100).

Similarly, when teachers fail to demand and help students to achieve thoughtful, reflective reading, there is an apparent loss in cognitive skill development. As Lunzer and Gardner (1979) conclude:

Reading to answer [teachers'] questions can result in a passive absorption of facts rather than reflection or evaluation . . . teachers need to balance 'getting information' with genuine inquiry . . .
Instead of being passive recipients of information, students can be taught to approach the material in the role of interrogators and discussants. Reading for learning then becomes a 'conversation' with the text in which the students ask their own questions, and make their own comment. (pp. 301, 303)

The importance of questioning is also emphasized by Frank Smith (1979), who defines reading as "asking questions of printed text" and comprehension as "getting your questions answered" (p. 105). "One of the most important skills of reading—which we certainly do not teach to any extent—is knowing the right kinds of questions to ask for different kinds of text" (p. 107).

In England and Canada, language across the curriculum has become associated with a concern for schools' "language policies," the often unstated beliefs and procedures that determine how students are expected to learn language and how they use language to learn. Although schools usually attempt to produce an explicit, written statement of policy to which teachers can subscribe, the most useful starting point is an examination of present policies embodied in the implicit rules of the classroom game: how students are encouraged, required, or permitted to use language in the classroom; what happens as a result of their language use, and what they are taught—directly or indirectly—about language. A school's operational language policy reveals the way that theory, research, and general notions about reading, writing, language, and learning are translated into actual classroom practices: practices that often contradict even the knowledge and beliefs held by teachers and stated explicitly in the school's general philosophy.

Given our present understanding of language development, learning, and cognitive development, what would an effective school language policy look like in action? As we observe and reflect on our classroom practices, what would we accept as evidence that the school environment is consistent with current theory and research about reading and writing and is promoting development and learning in and through language? The following list is a compilation of teachers' responses to those questions. Although each item is little more than a straw in the wind, when taken together a theoretically sound picture begins to emerge.

In schools with effective language policies,

Students:

● frequently read, write, and talk for a variety of purposes, including their own

- have frequent conferences with their teachers
- do genuine authoring and problem-solving through writing
- see some of their writing published, or shared with their peers
- question and discuss what they read, rather than just answer questions from the teacher or textbook
- use a variety of written forms, formal and informal, to respond to their reading
- read for a variety of purposes, including pleasure
- use the library frequently and voluntarily
- talk voluntarily about their reading, considering its personal significance and its relationship to other reading and learning.
- play and experiment with language
- notice and question language variations and effects
- identify and accept ownership of problems in various subjects
- write and talk using expressive and exploratory (as well as formal or technical) language in all subjects
- include their own questions, predictions, hypotheses, speculations, and personal experiences in discussions of subject matter
- work productively in groups
- display increasing awareness of their own processes of reading, writing, and learning

Teachers:

- are readers, writers and learners who share experiences with their own students
- occasionally model their own reading, writing, and learning processes for their students
- are aware of their students' classroom uses of language and what it reveals about the students' language development and learning
- examine and reflect on their own classroom language: explanations, assignments, questions, examinations, interactions with students, and written comments
- know the amount and kind of reading and writing their students do
- give primary stress to students' intentions, composing, and ideas in writing and secondary stress to transcribing skills and correctness
- teach writing conventions and mechanics as students need them
- have frequent writing and reading conferences with individuals and groups
- provide assignments and reading materials that pose solvable problems for students, and encourage students to identify the problems
- provide a wide range of reading and learning materials in all subjects

- encourage student consideration of purposes and processes: how and why tasks are to be done
- inform parents about their methods
- use pre- and post-measures to evaluate students' development and progress.

Active, involved learning—largely revealed through students' uses of language—is at the center of an effective language policy, and it is no doubt easier to imagine than to obtain. Assuredly, there is no item on the foregoing list that is not evident in some—perhaps many—classrooms today. But research evidence suggests that they are the exception rather than the norm, and perhaps taken together they are rare exceptions indeed. Can we make them the rule? Can we give practical expression to the theories that emerge from examining the reading, writing, learning relationship? I believe we can overcome the distance between today's classroom practices and more effective language policies, but we must first look carefully at where we are, and the problems in our present locations. Before we begin a journey, we must agree that movement is warranted, and that the destination is desirable. In the light of present knowledge clear evidence of the continued isolation of reading and writing from each other and from their significant use may provide the needed impetus for simple but significant movement toward a more effective pedagogy that integrates reading, writing, and learning in the classroom, as well as in theory.

References

Applebee, A.N. (1981). *Writing in the secondary school: English and the content areas.* (NCTE Research Report No. 21). Urbana, IL: National Council of the Teachers of English.

Britton, J. (1970). *Language and learning.* Harmondsworth, England: Penguin Books.

Britton, J. (1982). *Prospect and retrospect: Selected essays of James Britton.* (Gordon Pradl, Ed.). Montclair, NJ: Boynton/Cook Publishers.

Britton, J., Burgess, T., Martin, N., McLeod, A. & Rosen, H. (1975). *The development of writing abilities.* London: Macmillan Education.

Bullock, Sir Alan. (1975). Chairman of the Committee of Inquiry appointed by the Secretary of State for Education and Science (U.K.) *A language for life.* London: Her Majesty's Stationery Office.

Cazden, C.B. (1977, October). Language, literacy and literature: Putting it all together. *National Elementary Principal, 57,* 40–42.

Church, E. & Bereiter, C. (1983, April). Reading for style. *Language Arts, 60* 470–476.

Emig, J. (1971). *The Composing Processes of Twelfth Graders* (NCTE Research Report No. 13). Urbana, IL: National Council of Teachers of English.

Emig, J. (1977, May). Writing as a mode of learning. *College Composition and Communication, 28,* 122–128.

Fillion, B. (1979, Winter). Language across the curriculum: Examining the place of language in our schools. *McGill Journal of Education*, 14, 47–60.

Fillion, B., & Henderson, J. (1980). *Inquiry into literature 1* (First in a four book textbook series). Toronto: Collier MacMillan Canada.

Flower, L., Hayes, J.R. (1981, December). A cognitive process theory of writing. *College Composition and Communication*, 32, 365–387.

Graves, D. (1978). *Balance the basics, let them write.* New York: The Ford Foundation.

Heath, S.B. (1981). Toward an ethnohistory of writing in American education. In M.F. Whitemanam (Ed.), *Writing: The nature, development, and teaching of written communication. (Vol. I. Variations in Writing* (pp. 25–45). Hillsdale, NJ: Erlbaum.

Koch, K. (1970). *Wishes, Lies and Dreams.* New York: Vintage Books.

Koch, K. (1973). *Rose, Where Did You Get That Red? Teaching Great Poetry to Children.* New York: Vintage Books.

Lunzer, E., & Gardner, K. (Eds.). (1979) *The effective use of reading.* London: Heinemann Educational Books for the Schools Council.

Maeroff, G.I. (1984, January 8). Teaching of writing gets a new push. *The New York Times/Education*, pp. 1, 36 + .

Moffett, J. (1968). *Teaching the universe of discourse.* Boston: Houghton Mifflin.

National Assessment of Educational Progress. (1981). *Reading, thinking and writing: Results from the 1979–80 National Assessment of Reading and Literature* (Report No. 11–L–01). Denver: NAEP.

Petrosky, A.R. (1982). Reading achievement. In A. Berger & H.A. Robinson (Eds.), *Secondary school reading: What research reveals for classroom practice.* (pp. 7–9). Urbana, IL: ERIC Clearinghouse on Reading and Communication Skills.

Rosenblatt, L. (1978). *The reader, the text, the poem.* Carbondale: Southern Illinois University Press.

Scardamalia, M., Bereiter, C. and Fillion, B. (1981). *Writing for results: A sourcebook of consequential composing activities.* Toronto: OISE Press.

Scribner, S., & Cole, M. Unpackaging literacy. In M.F. Whiteman (Ed.), *Writing: The nature, development, and teaching of written communication. Vol I. Variations in Writing.* (pp. 71–87). Hillsdale, NJ: Erlbaum.

Smith, F. (1978). *Understanding reading* (2nd ed.). New York: Holt Rinehart and Winston.

Smith, F. (1979). *Reading without nonsense.* New York: Teachers College Press.

Smith, F. (1982). *Writing and the writer.* New York: Holt Rinehart and Winston.

Smith, F. (1983, May). Reading like a writer. *Language Arts*, 60, pp. 558–567.

Torbe, M., & Medway, P. (1981). *The climate for learning.* London: Ward Lock Educational.

Chapter 6
The Curriculum As Language

Carolyn N. Hedley
Fordham University

The concepts dealt with in *Language Across The Curriculum* (Marland, 1977) and *From Communication to Curriculum* (Barnes 1976) could well form a point of departure for this chapter. Each of these volumes support the notion of dealing with curriculum content as a language activity. These authors point out that when content is presented through the integrative activities of talking, reading, and writing, many children achieve much better not only in the knowledge of subject content, but in these language processes as well. Marland (1977), responding to the Bullock Report, recommends a language policy across the school to be implemented by teachers in the subject areas, with less isolation of the subjects and greater integration of knowledge fostered by such language policy. Clearly, these authors feel that language development, including the development of reading and writing abilities can be integrated and can be an integrating force for the bridging distinctions in the content of the curriculum areas.

In this chapter, another perspective of the curriculum as language is developed—that is, the distinctiveness of the language of each of the curriculum areas is discussed. Each of the content areas of the curriculum uses a common language, in this case, the English language, to govern its functions. Yet, the convenience of having a common language to discuss all of the subject areas, should not disguise the phenomena that in each of the subjects, the English language is used in a very distinctive way. To overstate the case, the fact that language is used so differently in each of the disciplines is covered over by the superficial appearance of familiarity given the the use of a common language (English); we might see the difference of language and language function better if we used a discrete language in which to couch the discussion. I am not suggesting that we separate the disciplines to a greater degree by creating new languages—a phenomena which occurs in limited degree by use of the professional idiom and its jargon. What I propose here is that we look at the distinctive functions of each of the disciplines and treat the teaching of that discipline as primarily a language which reflects the functions that are unique in that discipline. Several current philosophical perspectives suggest that the distinctiveness of the language of each of the disciplines is directly related to the distinctiveness of the discipline itself. What is *common* among the language of the disciplines is that:

1. They reflect social activities inherent in the behaviors relevant to the discipline.
2. They create their own linguistic forms and regularities.
3. The use of these distinctive social activities, language forms, and regularities occur in order to achieve the acknowledged goals of the discipline.

The function of language across the disciplinary areas share the above principles. But these very principles create the functional language distinctions that we find in teaching subject matter. Bloom's taxonomy and other analyses of knowledge in the disciplines—Goodlad's conceptual system and Adler's course of study (Goodlad, 1979; Adler, 1982) make the case for the language regularities and conventions within each of the disciplines. These curriculum hierarchies provide a kind of metacognitive scheme for looking at the curriculum and the distinctions among the disciplines. A first demand using such analyses is that the teacher must master the language of the content that she is teaching—including the concepts, the conventions, the means of analysis and synthesis, and the ways in which one evaluates the knowledge that one is teaching. Thus, if one looks at the symbolic forms in any subject area and masters these forms and conventions, grammars, and rules, then one virtually has command of the discipline itself. Literacy becomes a key objective and a unifying concept for the various schema that organize the curriculum areas.

Students of language and cognitive process see the necessity for schematizing, elaborating, restructuring, and developing strategies in terms of the content, contexts, and activities called for in higher level language and thought (McNeil, 1984; Goelman, Oberg, & Smith, 1984). Researchers of reading and language comprehension and process do not simply apply language and reading "skills" to the content areas. Rather the context of the material presented, the goals of the lesson, and the interactive nature of language use is considered. Strategies are developed which promote active, participatory, and creative approaches to knowledge. The student as teacher and peer tutor, often under the guidance of a teacher, is helped to accommodate tasks by virtue of development of his own schema, his own questions, his own strategies, his own restructuring of knowledge, and his own method of sharing and participating in the scholarly community.

Philosophical Perspectives about Language

In passing, it is worth noting that there are several twentieth century philosophies which accommodate the notion of curriculum as language or the curriculum as comprised of a variety of language activities. Three major philosophies support the notion of a distinctive language base of each of the subject areas: *pragmatism, existentialism,* and *ordinary language analysis.* These contemporary theoretical philosophies analyze language and symbolic activity as a way of viewing man's experience, and man's study of himself and his world. Common to the three views is the idea that language is necesssary to community or necessary for personal definition within community. The notion that all disciplines rightly deserve to be taught as humanities is endorsed by such a position. If what students read and talk about is not related to human activities, conduct, and behavior, then learners are bound to lose their perspective of and purpose for disciplined knowledge. The study of even the most esoteric subject reflects its human and social functions. Greater knowledge in any discipline should enthrall the learner, because the student sees it as a social and civilizing activity.

Pragmatic View of Language and Curriculum

Many of us, have had a basic course dealing with Dewey's pragmatism and we will briefly discuss his theory of language as it relates to curriculum, simply because it is the most familiar. According to Dewey (1916), language came into being in primitive times, when man found that he could benefit by acting with others, in other words, by functioning together (hunting, or protecting himself as examples) or in community. Thus, spoken language and later, heiroglyphics and written language came into being when man discovered he had common needs with others like himself. From this basic need to gather together—from community—came the need for better communication in order to improve organization, control, and cooperation. Thus, the various disciplines emerged—the study of one's own and other cultures (sociology, geography, and cross-cultural anthropology), the study of man in time (history), man in his environment (geography), man in the marketplace (economics), and man as a personal and social entity (psychology, anthropology, sociology)—as human beings sought to understand themselves and their world and to progress in a more complex society. Simultaneously, the need to quantify experience and develop mathematical concepts became essential. Language and the written forms of language were the means of pursuing studies leading to increased understanding of community. For thousands of years, before the development of alternative recording devices, written language was one of the few ways in which man could preserve and view his past. Language became the means of anticipating and planning a future predicated on past, and sometimes, vicarious experiences. Thus, the view of the pragmatists presents us with a view of language that is accutely basic to man's humane and social life. Moreover, his knowledge and rationalization of his life experience (now retitled the disciplines) cannot accrue nor develop without a language.

Existential Use of Language

A second philosophy which analyzes symbolism uniquely is existentialism. Existentialism as a philosophy is concerned with the individual in his present circumstance. How the individual interprets and uses his present experience includes his interpretation of the past and his anticipation and conceptualization of the future. The interpretation of the past and an anticipation of a future can only occur symbolically. The present is all that one can experience in any concrete sense. What happened an hour ago, or what may happen tonight, are created by language and symbolism for one's immediate and created existence. For the existentialist, the only limit to the freedom of an individual is the individual himself. Limits are self-imposed by the individual's ability to recognize his possibilities; that is, all the alternatives and options that are open to him. These limits and their options are functions of language and thought in the creation of present existence. For the existentialist, man exists only in the present; he interprets the past in terms of his present needs and circumstance. He has a future only in that he is able to create it in his present condition. His very existence—that he knows he has a past and future—lies in what he is able to create for himself in the present, and that is founded in symbolic thought, language, and action. Thus language and thought are critical to man's being in the here and now.

Ordinary Language Analysis

At about the same time as existentialism was coming into its own, another group of philosophers was getting some attention. These were the ordinary language analysts. At the same time as the ordinary language analysts were the *logical positivists*, led by Ayer, Russell, and others. The logical positivists tried to devise a logical language with which to deal with the knowledge of the disciplines. This kind of language analysis was attempted by the men of the Vienna Circle in order to restructure knowledge with a more exact linguistic system.

In part as a reaction to the logical positivists, the ordinary language analysts felt that one could not ignore meaning as it was found in ordinary language. It is the thinking of the ordinary language analysts which is having an impact on much sociolinguistic study today. Britton and others (Pradl, 1982; Marland, 1977; Barnes, 1976; Shafer, Staab, & Smith, 1983) owe their philosophic perspective and ethnographic approach to language study to this school of philosophy, and acknowledge them in their work (see references to Austin and Wittgenstein). Hedley (1968) writes:

> Ordinary language analysis—referring to those philosophers who follow the kind of concern evidenced by the later work of Ludwig Wittgenstein—represents a philosophic activity which seeks to reveal the source and function of ordinary language. While such philosophic activity focuses upon the perplexities arising within philosophy itself, this activity bears directly upon the problems that arise from the increasing demands of language in dealing with the complexities of modern society and the increasing dependency of society upon symbolic forms. The need to refine the distinctions among the various functions of language has never been more pressing. Or perhaps, the need still exists just to recognize that ordinary language has more than one function—a matter that has escaped the attention of earlier philosophers. (p. 3)

What all of these philosophies indicate is a concern for oversimplification of the role of symbolic forms and for language as it influences our lives. Using the ideas of the ordinary language analysts, we see that language must be looked at in terms of its usefulness or function. In other words, language meaning, even word meaning, changes according to its context and its function or use. If we deal with the distinctive use of language in each of the content areas, we have to see what it is that makes each of the subject areas (disciplines) unique. Why do we study physics? Math? Art? English literature? Why do we who teach in schools tend to sort them out as separate? Does each of these subject areas have a unique function? What is the origin of distinct subjects or disciplines?

Implications

What is implied about language in all of these philosophies? A point made in all three philosophic views of language is that language is primarily a *social* activity. Language is critical to community and for personal definition within a community. We may ask what is social about the sometimes lonely work of a scientist or a forestry specialist. Each discipline forms its own "community of discourse" by means of which each member is recognized, his work evaluated, and the discipline progresses.

If we view all disciplines as rightfully belonging to the humanities, much of subject area study will provide stimulation for the learner who taught math and other subjects as being intimately related to the human enterprise. He studies math to know how to better quantify and judge experience, to see relationships between entities. Collectively, we study science, because we need to know enough about our health and the physical world about us to make decisions and carry on in a way that will benefit ourselves individually and the society as a whole. It is the contention here that if the teaching of the disciplines included their particular social activities, language forms and regularities, and their goals or aims—all reflected in the language peculiar to that discipline—we might have a more participatory and responsible student body. The learning environment would focus on the language transaction, with students teaching and learning from one another.

A second point found in these philosophies and growing out of the discussion above is that language is dynamic—a changing and vital force that influences human behavior even more than the actual events and experiences that are described in language. Language meanings change depending on contexts and personalities, even within a language. Pragmatic thought indicates that language developed along with the need for community—implicit in this notion is the idea that new forms evolve when the needs of the community alter or expand. Existentialism indicates that we create symbolic constructions to accommodate a present existence, a present need. Ordinary language analysis uses the analogy of the game, as a way of looking at language activity. The goals, the behavioral rules, and the social activity are what determine language behavior. Language has meaning as a function of its use in transaction; obviously, it can be viewed only as a dynamic. When second languages and other cultures within a larger culture are involved, the possibilities for symbolic meaning and for its confusion are increased enormously.

Finally, pragmatism, existentialism, and ordinary language analysis support and allow that language is rule-governed, that there is grammar and consistency, a predictability about language behavior that allows humans to understand one another. Nowhere is this more evident than in subject area study, where each discipline calls for a unique use of language for the purpose of understanding how knowledge in the subject area must be acquired and go forward. Understanding the regularities and the rules of a discipline as well as the higher levels of thought and language processes in the discipline allows us to master the discipline. It is the same understanding that indicates when the rules are restrictive and should be broken for greater creativity to take place. Axiomatically, the use of language is restrictive at the same time that it allows us to create.

Like language itself, the disciplines and their languages are *functional, social,* and *rule-governed,* involving procedures and regularities, knowledge frameworks, concepts, and methods of inquiry that are basic to further study. In order to be considered knowledgeable in a discipline, one must master these conventions that are social, functional, and rule-governed and use them in acceptable, appropriate ways. The study of any subject is not simply a mastery of facts, but a developing awareness of how to function in the area in a participatory way.

In times past, particularly at the elementary level, texts were often so poorly organized that the knowledge frameworks and the procedural niceties of functioning as a student amateur in a discipline were not readily obtained by reading the book. This phenomena was aggravated by the fact that teachers often followed the books as an orderly way of presenting the subject. In science and math as well as literature, students got bits and pieces of applicational activity without understanding the conceptual whole from which such activity derives. Again, in what may seem a contradiction, the integrated curriculum should occur by virtue of knowledgeable teachers interacting with students. The textbook should be rather straightforward and clear, building concept upon concept and developing conventions through procedures. By pointing out relationships, by questioning, and by other interactive techniques, the teacher can move to higher level thought processes and integrative activity.

The Distinctiveness of the Language of the Content Areas

Now we move to looking at the distinctiveness of the language of each of the content areas. First, we must acknowledge the fact that reading, writing, listening, and speaking are abilities, or cognitively-based processes, which have no content in themselves. They are the processes by which we communicate socially and symbolically. The content for these processes derives from life experiences and from the disciplines as life experiences, usually abstract by virtue of rationalization, and therefore removed somewhat from the actual experience. This kind of language content and process is reflected in the school curriculum. The following sections will deal with the content areas of social studies, science, math, and art and will indicate how, in each subject, language functions in a discrete and unique manner.

The Social Studies

The social sciences deal chiefly with how man organizes himself in relation to his community (or society) and to the members of the same society as well as to others in other communities and societies. Language is the basis of community, according to Dewey and other philosophers. The social disciplines—history, geography, sociology, economics, anthropology, and psychology—are studies of man as he relates to his fellow man. Clearly language as the basis for community is the basis for the study of community. Therefore, it would follow that the teaching of social studies involves the teaching of particular language activities. This involves two distinct considerations.

The first consideration lies outside the concern of this present chapter. It involves the effects of language on the social development of the child and upon his integration into society. This is a continuous process that proceeds with or without formal instruction, in and out of schools, and continues throughout the life of an individual. Schools can offer formal and positive direction to this process only if a "language policy" is clearly and formally articulated on a school-wide basis and given wide support by the community.

The second consideration is that of the specialized activities that constitute the various disciplines that contribute to our understanding of our present "community" or society, and is the concern of this chapter. Students can gain an increased understanding and appreciation of history, for example, by being involved in the "doing" of history. In this case, students would be using language to create a story in the past tense which would be consistent with the facts presented, complete in the sense of covering a particular time frame, and plausible in the context of human behavior.

Sociology will serve as our second example. Including sociology in the curriculum would provide an opportunity for students to understand the ways and methods that sociologists attempt to study in the phenomenon of community and, in particular, the role played by symbolic forms in the creation and preservation of a society. Educational activities in the teaching of sociology need not be restricted to textbook materials. Educational simulations dealing with all varieties of social behavior as symbolic and language-dependent activity are available in increasing numbers.

As a final example, the introduction of economics into the curriculum could only lead to the further appreciation of the overwhelming importance of symbolic forms in the maintainance of "community" or society. The history of man's economic activities will provide the student with a deeper understanding of the language of economics, its vocabulary, and its symbolic forms. This understanding will include not only the role of the language of economics in describing man's economic activities, but how the prediction of economic behavior is possible only to the extent that the language, the symbolic forms themselves, determine that behavior.

Thus, whenever language becomes the focus of the social science curriculum, the student is not only made aware of the many social functions of language, but also of language as a valuable tool for the study of society. He is then able to pursue his own social inquiries while at the same time becoming an ever more effective participant in that society.

Mathematics

Mathematics seems to be an intellectual and abstract exercise, once removed from experience. And it is. The language of math does not use conversational or ordinary English. It is a language unto itself. One begins to realize that the language of math is somewhat cross-cultural, since persons who speak a foreign language can frequently handle mathematical concepts in another language, even though they do not understand the language in which the concepts are being taught. The means of *measuring* the human experience seems to have a kind of universality; quantification of experience seems to be a human necessity.

What is the nature of the language of mathematics? First, it is highly abstracted and symbolic language, not in the sense that all language is symbolism, but that figures and letters often stand for complex things and processes. Much is said in the shorthand of formulas that does not have a visible counterpart in the real world. One would never speak in the manner in which an algebraic problem is written. Excepting the seasoned and enthusiastic mathematician, most persons do not have a schema for math—often neither a knowledge schema nor an experiential base. Often mathematics does not seem to be connected with experience. The learner will say, when one asks him why he is studying math, that he needs to be able to make change or to handle money. We do not use mathematical constructs and information, because we do not have a schema for them. Yet the basic concept which is used to justify the mathematics curriculum is that math quantifies and qualifies experience and makes it possible to see relationships that may not be revealed in the routine of daily living.

Not only is mathematical logic highly symbolic, dealing with esoteric forms of the language, it is highly compacted language. Think of all of the operations and concepts that are included in the notion of radical 9 ($\sqrt{9}$). One must know square root, how to divide, multiply, subtract, and add; one must understand powers of numbers and notational subscripts and superscripts in order to ascribe meaning to the symbol. Thus the constructions in the language of mathematics derive from one another; one cannot proceed with greater knowledge or operations in the mathematical hierarchy until the constructs which underlie the operation are understood. The language of mathematics is a derived, contrived and artificial symbolic process when contrasted with conversational English. Its language is abstract and dependent upon an internal mathematical logic, not easily apparent to the casual or novice learner. One does not deal with speculation, hypothesis, or analysis, but one is restricted by these conventions in dealing with math concepts.

Mathematics is difficult for many teachers to teach and children to learn because we lack schema. We use *realia* to make concepts and schema plausible. We use counters and measures; graphics and tables, so that students can see some of the logic inherent in the process, but for many children the beauty of the logic is lost by the lack of experiential contexts with which to bring these concepts to life. When reading math books and problems, we must teach children to read and reread, to graphically portray the ideas in the book. Often the teacher must disregard the math book and simply go to the language of daily living in order to explain what the book is trying to say. Many times, subject matter may be presented in a rote and formula-like way, on the assumption that if the knowledge of math progresses, comprehension will follow.

Most of all, students should understand that mathematics is a distinctive form of language. It has its rules (grammar), it has its purposes (uses), and it has its social value (the quantification of experience). For many reasons, math must be recognized as having distinctive language forms and distinctive language functions and therefore be taught as a unique language activity. An understanding of mathematical learning as an arduous language mastery task is but a beginning for the teacher. She must build an experience background for each concept, and provide strategies for accomplishing understanding along with graphic demonstrations of how to arrive at closure in the problem-solving process. Without such an understanding, we will surely produce another generation of defeatists among able persons, who have the same difficulties that many of us have had while dealing with math concepts.

Science

The language of science, whether biology, chemistry, physics, botany, or any other of the life sciences, is distinctive in that it seems to deal with facts, to be expository, and to be used for inquiry and rationalization of natural experiences. Usually scientific language deals with natural phenomena using nonemotional and exact description for precise analyis. Science, like all of the curriculum areas, has its epistomological beginnings in experience, yet it goes beyond experience to the explanation of experience to theories of experience. The nature of science is not merely to tell what happened, but why. The language of science is oriented to inquiry and rationalization, functioning less and less like social discourse for its own sake. The language of science is related to the distinct pursuit of the scientist, which is to rationalize and control natural phenonema. The language of science has a social function among scientists, but the language of the scientist may seem less than social to the uninstructed observer. Science and math are highly socialized activities and if we as educators do not see and teach for their social relevance, we lose students' interest. Science, like math, is a humanity. We lack the basic knowledge today to make the most fundamental decisions about life on our planet—pesticides, the atom bomb, nuclear reactors, space programs, jogging, and aerobics are activities where one needs basic science in order to know how to make judgments.

Science is an activity, not a passive reception of facts; moreover, it is a process that should be part of the thinking of daily living. Natural and social events about us should enjoy the application of rational thought through problem-solving techniques that give us some control over our own behavior and our existence. Whether we are viewing a softball game, watching the autumn leaves, eating an orange, or managing to get home in a rainstorm, scientific thought and vocabulary should enable us to look beyond the manifestation of an event and see the scientific principles involved. In a ball game, for example, one could note the movement and velocity of the ball, the angle and power of the strike, and diagram and simulate a model of some of the functions of the game.

To teach scientific method in the activities of daily life, the science teacher needs: (1) scientific knowledge, (2) knowledge of the history of science, (3) experience in scientific discovery, (4) training in linguistic inquiry techniques, (5) a strong functional knowledge of the higher level thought processes and (6) knowledge of scientific-social-process behaviors that model the life of scientific communities. The often premature social consciousness about scientific knowledge is a much more advanced and later kind of social knowledge.

The scientific community is a group of learners at any level from amateur to acknowledged authority—the bird watcher, the leaf gatherer, the computer hacker, or the poet—who need to solve problems in imaginative ways. In order to be proficient in science, one needs to understand the knowledge and conventions of science, particularly of the discipline in which one is most engaged. Science is not social in the way that a party or a softball game is, but it becomes more of social activity as the learner understands the rules of the game, the conventions, and the procedures as well as the limitations of what those conventions are.

Children must learn to do what scientists do. From the rock hound to the geologist, from the camera freak to the biologist or naturalist, or the anthropologist, the conventions of rational process as they contribute to social good should be made evident. Science is one of the humanities. Its purposes are profoundly linked with human progress. Emotions and interests regarding natural and social phenomena can be translated into knowledge. When science builds on natural interests, motivation occurs; when we stay with textbook explanations unrelated to human endeavor, we miss the dynamism and humanism of science.

Art

Art is an interpretation of reality—not by concepts but by intuitions. According to Cassirer (1944), art is both dialogue and dialectical. Building on stored experience, art is like language in that it is not a passive experience, but one that profoundly stirs the emotions. The unity of perception and thought is once again realized in the artistic experience, for visual and aesthetic perception lay the foundation for concept formation and lead us to generalities about our world and ourselves. To this degree, art and science are alike.

Productive thinking is perceptual thinking; thus we see that art and artistic symbolism as a kind of organizer of experience is critical to the educative process. Every artistic statement may be considered a declaration about the human experience. Both art and science are dedicated to the study of the forces that shape existence. Both are subject to the criteria of truth and both are dependent upon precision, order, and convention. Art utilizes perceptual abstraction and there is much in this perception that must be explained and abstracted for the learner. Thus art precedes conceptual development, in some ways it precedes language, although it attends to perceptual and symbolic forms. Art utilizes many conventions, but it is always inventive, fostering new ideas and new language forms. Writes Cassirer (1944): "The two views of truth (art and science) are in contrast with one another, but not in conflict or contradiction. Since art and science move in entirely different planes they cannot contradict or thwart one another. The conceptual interpretation of science does not preclude the intuitive interpretation of art. . . . The depth of human experience in the same sense depends on the fact that we are able to vary our modes of seeing, that we can alternate our views of reality. . . . Art gives us a richer, more vivid and colorful image of reality, and a more profound insight into its formal structure" (p. 169–170).

Thus, art precedes language and carries us beyond it, giving us another perspective with which to view reality.

Conclusion

Language as Curriculum

Researchers have looked for schema in subject area presentation in the same way that they have looked for schema in, say, a narrative or a folk tale. So far, schema within the subject areas has not emerged, except as knowledge schema. In other words, the student may understand the parameters of the discipline, the structure of the knowledge presented, or he may have a knowledge background in an content area. To the degree that the student is knowledgeable in an area of study (for instance, algebra) he has a knowledge schema. But there are not forms, as with the historical novel, the mystery the adventure story, where we can say, "Here is where you have been and now what do you anticipate?" Beyond describing the written text as expository, the student must command a knowledge of the subject in order to function well. McNeil (1984), when describing comprehension of expository text, asks the the student for a hierarchy of ideas first and then asks for background knowledge, preconceptions, task knowledge, points of view, organizational pattern, classification and order of content, augmentation of knowledge structure, restructuring schemata, and evaluation. Such an analysis of the expository reading task is brilliant, but it presumes a knowledge of the subject matter and its conventions before comprehension occurs.

When the student reads a science lesson or a social studies assignment, he may assume that he is reading expository information and attempt to apply the comprehension procedures above, but he has no other guidelines. He starts fresh and determines what the author is trying to say. He must learn strategies and procedures predicated upon a knowledge schema which he does not yet possess. Unlike the mystery writer who writes by formula, the author of a content area text does not have a schema apart from that which the knowledge itself creates. The lesson is often novel information, not reinforced by personal or classroom experience. Thus, most content information is data-driven; the student cannot bring the knowledge he has to bear on that which he is learning. What we as teachers must try to do is more in-house modeling of behaviors that lead students to see that the study of subjects in the curriculum is not merely an exercise, it is a distinctive language task in each discipline involving knowledge mastery. Further, it involves a knowledge of the purposes, the processes, and the social function of subject matter study for real meaning to occur. However, the rational and artistic life involving such symbolic mastery is not alien to enjoyment and good living. Indeed, we are hardly civilized persons if we do not embrace such knowledges-seeking processes and strategies that are both predictable and social.

References

Adler, M.J. (1982). *The paidaia proposal.* New York: Macmillan.
Anderson, J.C., Osborn, J. & Tierney, R. (1984). Learning to read in American schools. Hillsdale, NJ: Erlbaum.
Barnes, D. (1976). *From communication to curriculum.* New York: Penguin Books.
Cassirer, E. (1984). *An essay on man.* New Haven, CT: Yale University Press.
Dewey, J. (1916). *Democracy and education.* New York: Macmillan.
Goelman, H., Oberg, A., & Smith, F. (1984). *Awakening to literacy.* Exeter, NH: Heinemann.
Goodlad, J.I., and associates. (1977). Curriculum inquiry: The study of curriculum practice. New York: McGraw-Hill.
Goodlad, J.I. (1983). *A place called school.* New York: McGraw-Hill.
Hedley, W.E. (1968). *Freedom, inquiry and language.* Scranton, PA: International Textbook Co.
Marland, M. (1977). *Language across the curriculum.* Exeter, NH: Heinemann Books.
McNeil, J.D. (1984). *Reading comprehension.* Glenview, IL: Scott Foresman.
Pradl, Gordon (Ed.). (1982). *Prospect and retrospect: Selected essays of James Britton.* Montclair, NJ: Boynton Cook.
Shafer, R.E., Staub, C. & Smith, K. (1983). *Language function and school success,* Glenview, IL: Scott Foresman and Company. Wilkinson, L.C. (1982). Communicating in the classroom. New York: Academic Press.

Additional References

Dewey, J. (1929). *Democracy and education.* New York: Liveright Press.
Gardener, D.P. (chairman). (1983). *A nation at risk: The imperative for educational reform.* Washington, D.C.: U.S. Department of Education.
Hosford, P.L. (1984). *Using what we know about teaching.* Alexandria, VA : Association for Suprvision and Curriculum Development.
Ringler, L.H., Weber, C.K. (1984). *A language-thinking approach to reading.* New York: Harcout Brace Jovanovich.
Roloff, M.E., Berger, C.R. (1982). *Social cognition and communication.* Beverly Hills. CA: Sage.
Seiler, W.J., Schuelke, L.D., Lieb-Brilhart, B. (1984). *Communication for the contemporary classroom.* New York: Holt Rinehart and Winston.

Chapter 7
Achieving Cognitive Synthesis Of Separate Language Skills: Implications For Improving Literacy

Roy O. Freedle
Educational Testing Service

In this chapter, there are several points about language which I will weave together. One is that there is a pervasive phenomenon which indicates that special reports of language use (such as those skills involved in literacy) seem to occur exclusively in very restrictive settings. That is, there appears to be no automatic transfer of skills from one skilled domain to another similar domain. Primarily the work of Ferguson (in press) on language registers and the results of Scribner's and Cole's work (1981) on Vai literacy will illustrate this point for us. Diverse language systems for various and special occasions and different audiences were described by both of these researchers. There appears to be no monolithic system of rules for automatically transferring language skills from one language mode to another. One way to conceptualize these facts is to assume that a cognitive barrier exists across language varieties and across language modes. As a consequence, language skills of the home may not transfer easily to the school; abilities in one language mode may not transfer to another—from reading to writing, for example.

A second point to be made is the cognitive inevitability of this phenomenon. That is, given our limited information processing capabilities and our limited ability to merge information, it is inevitable that language and the cognitive skills associated with it will show a certain degree of nongeneralizability across what appear to be similar situations and similar tasks. The cognitive basis for our limited representations of reality may lie in the very efficiency of the cognitive process—the need to schematize, to develop various kinds of automaticity, and to chunk information for rehearsal in various physical and social environments. Situations must be set up which explicitly lead a person to consciously make structural or pragmatic comparisons across these similar domains if a higher-order functional capability is to emerge.

This leads us to our next point. Here we suggest a procedure that has potential for reducing some of this boundedness or a language skill with a given situation or task. Methods of transfer require us to create situations in which the learner can compare underlying similarities or develop a cross classification of skills, or where higher-order organizational skills, dependent on semantic content, may aid transfer of lower-level signals across situations and modes. Two examples of a generalization procedure are presented which appear to rapidly merge the skills of one language domain with the skills of another language domain. The first example illustrates how children rapidly acquire competence in a special expository form after implicitly comparing it with a similar expository form and with a similar narrative form. The second example shows how some features of explicitness associated with written language can be transferred to the oral language mode. Both examples together lead us to speculate about the possibility of isolating what is called a supra-literacy skill which appears to exist within the Western school system. This supra-literacy skill appears to exist as a more generalized phenomenon over and above literacy skills alone.

My final point will be that while a simple transfer of knowledge of function and procedure might appear to hold promise for encouraging the flow of knowledge from current areas of competence to areas where the learner is less competent, and hence hold promise for encouraging the growth of literacy skills, nevertheless, there is reason to suppose that there are more powerful variables (supra-literacy phenomena) at work that may well be crucial for the rapid growth of literacy.

The Fragmentary Nature of the Language System: The Cognitive Separation of Language Skills

Ferguson (1981) has reviewed a number of linguistic phenomena dealing with simplified registers such as the language which we use in so-called "baby" talk. His review shows that simplification occurs at many levels of language including phonetic, lexical, and syntactic. What is most important for us, though, is his discussion of the apparent ignorance which speakers show in using this language skill across apparently similar language domains. For example, in baby-talk Moroccan Arabs use a voiceless labial stop /p/, yet their adult form has no /p/ in its phonemic inventory. Furthermore, these Moroccans tend to have trouble with p's when learning other language. Typically they substitute voiced b's for them. The puzzle is, how can they use /p/ correctly when speaking to children but fail to perceive and produce it appropriately when asked to learn another language which employs /p/. Is there some cognitive barrier between the phonemic inventory of baby-talk language and the phonemic inventory of adult usage? Apparently so. It is as though at some point in time and for different occasions they learned separate language systems for talking to babies versus talking to adults. What makes the puzzle more profound is that even though there is great overlap in the phonemic inventories, this single occurrence of voiceless labial /p/ and the cognitive opaqueness that surrounds it suggests a much deeper phenomenon is at work in language use.

As an example closer to home, Ferguson (1981) shows that speakers of American English find it difficult to perceive and produce glottal stops in learning another language such as Syrian Arabic. Yet they produce glottal stops regularly and easily in such expressions as *uh-oh* (or *oh-oh*) signaling unpleasant surprise or in *uh-uh* /ʔmʔm/ signalling an informal negative response. Again we are faced with a perplexing puzzle. Is there a cognitive barrier between a language system used for special occasions and for a special audience and a similar language system used more generally to other adults? If so, what is the source of the barrier? Have we in fact learned different language systems for special occasions even though one can find many linguistic similarities across these systems? Ferguson points out that examples of this type occur not only at the phoneme inventory level, but occur as well at the intonational level, pronoun use level, and basic word order constraints. Apparently language is not the monolithic unified system of "rules" that we have generally supposed it to be.

The main point to draw here is that the language system that we use in some situations need not be cognitively accessible in another apparently similar situation in terms of literacy. The skilled use of language in a home situation using the oral mode need not spontaneously transfer to skill in using the written mode at home or at school. The apparently large overlap in language structures used in home and school supported by a single memory system may only be an apparency and not a reality—we may in fact be using two cognitively separate language systems. This is the strongest possible statement of the cognitive barrier hypothesis concerning language varieties and language registers and later we will seek examples which will allow for any number of intermediate gradations of this hypothesis.

Some recent findings of Scribner and Cole (1981) can be said to support this strong hypothesis. To quote:

> This experimental essay . . . helped lay to rest some misconceptions about the psychology of literacy that went unchallenged in the past for lack of empirical data. First, it is clear from the evidence . . . that nonschooled literacy, as we found and tested it among the Vai, does not produce general

cognitive effects as we have defined them. The small and selective nature of Vai script and Arabic influences on cognitive performance precludes any sweeping generalizations about literacy and cognitive change. At best we can say that there are several localized literacy-specific effects on certain task specific skills.

Implicit in the foregoing discussion, but worth stating explicitly, is the fact that there is no evidence in these data to support the construct of a general "literacy" phemenon. Although many writers discuss literacy and its social and psychological implications as though literacy entails the same knowledge and skills whenever people read or write, our experimental outcomes support our social analysis in demonstrating that literacies are highly differentiated. Arabic and Vai script do not trade off for each other in predicting cognitive performance, nor do they (singly or in combination) substitute for English literacy. (Scribner & Cole, 1981, p. 132)

Let me reframe these results so that it will be clear how they are similar to some of the patterns observed by Ferguson.

The cognitive skills that come into play in order to use one language register would seem to have to be the same cognitive skills involved in using what appears to be a structurally similar language register. Yet the fact that one can find examples, a la Ferguson, that show the existence of a cognitive barrier between language use across situations must mean that these underlying cognitive skills cannot be identical across these purportedly *similar* language registers.

Being literate in Vai script would seem to imply the existence of some cognitive skills having to do with the coordination of language knowledge, eye-hand coordination, and the fine-motor skills associated with translating these symbols into writing. On the face of it these cognitive skills would appear to be virtually identical to those needed to use the Arabic script and would appear to be identical to those needed to be competent in both Vai and Arabic scripts, and would appear to be identical to those needed to be literate in English. Yet the Scribner and Cole results suggests that, in spite of these similarities, the cognitive skills underlying these literacy skills appear to be not identical. Neither Vai script nor Qur'anic-learning and Arabic-script act as surrogates for schooling. They do not produce the range of cognitive effects that schooling does, nor do they always act on the same tasks. Discrepancies between effects of these literacies and schooling challenge the hypothesis that schooling affects thinking by equipping children with a "written language."

We are at a perplexing crossroads. Our intuition tells us that we *cannot* really reinvent language for each and every situation in which we use these special language registers or language modes—be it baby-talk, speech to adults, or use of a special written script. Yet the specific results from Ferguson and the specific literacy results of Scribner and Cole suggests that something like that must be going on. It is useful to state the hypothesis in this bold form in order to jog us out of our presupposition about the unity and flexibility of the mind across all situations. Such a presupposition will not help us to understand the specific yoking of language skills to underlying cognitive skills. Ferguson has suggested a number of ways to represent the partial unity of knowledge across some situations and we shall return to his ideas later in this paper. For the time being we shall use the heuristic force of the strong hypothesis of a separate representation of language subsystems with its implied separate access to underlying cognitive skills in order to sketch the next several ideas.

The Cognitive Basis for Limited Representations of Reality

It is impossible for our brains to keep track of all the nuances that take place in the environment. Psychologists such as Miller (1956) have found that we can handle a small amount of information and can make only a few decisions per unit of time. How then do we manage to survive in this complex world? Part of the answer is that we do it by oversimplifying the world—we schematize it. Why should this be an effective strategy? It seems to work because the physical and social world is redundant and somewhat predictable; therefore, these schematizations very often lead to correct and workable interactions with the environment. The only decision we have to make is which schema appears to be in operation at any one time; when we find the apparently correct one that fits the current situation, all we then must do is follow out the familiar steps of the schema in ways which resemble our past strategy. This familiar strategy greatly reduces the new decisions that have to be made at any one time. Furthermore, with a great deal of experience, we discover that in recurrent situations all the nuances that could be noticed do not really have to be honored. This generalized strategic behavior simplifies the cognitive decision-making pressure still more. Also, we humans favor highly redundant sociocultural enviornments, possibly in order to make our world even more predictable and less threatening. Such organizations help to overcome our limited processing capabilities even more.

Thus far, I have emphasized our human *limitations* in processing complex information and argued that this must lead to schema formation when we interact with the physical and social realms. Obviously this constraint must apply to the schema associated with language use as well as it applies to perceptual-motor skills. The complexity of the goals which we are to accomplish in our cultural life forces us to adopt schematizations of language (or language routines). Some situations evoke or employ one language routine, and other situations evoke or employ other language routines.

Habitual use of these routines brings to the fore a unique strength that greatly offsets our inherent limited processing capabilities. With a great deal of practice we are able to convert very complex tasks that originally required hundreds of decisions—piano playing, for example—into virtually *automatic* tasks. Paul Fitts (1964) was an early explorer in this realm. He found that the early learning phases of complex task performance greatly depended upon the more analytic cognitive abilities, but the later phases of learning complex tasks tended to be uncorrelated with these analytic cognitive skills. That is, the well-rehearsed tasks tended to be characterized by unique variance that suggested that the task and its underlying cognitive components had separated away from the conscious analytic skills and was not functioning in an almost autonomous and holistic way. Furthermore one can continue to augment the complexity of these automated tasks by adding new subroutines to an already existing autonomous skill. This might be analogous to increasing the repertoire of piano pieces that one can perform—one might develop recitals that typically involve just the romantic literature while on other occasions one might perform just the preromantic literature. If done consistently, these recitals might themselves become *higher-order* automatic routines each consisting of subroutines or separately rehearsed individual piano pieces.

The analogy this bears to language routines is not so hard to establish. As we move through adulthood we encounter language varieties that initially may require conscious cognitive processing of the structure, but with a great deal of practice, this language variety probably comes to function in a fairly routine way. Structurally it may be similar to other language routines, but functionally it may operate in an almost automatic holistic manner.

Clearly two powerful forces are at work. One is our inherent limited processing ability and the second is our ability to automate large chunks of behavior which over time overcomes our inherent limitations. The result of the joint occurrences of these two forces is that behavior gets chunked into patterns that are suited to the needs of the physical and social environments, and that depending upon what chunks get rehearsed together, there need not be any simple set of rules that describe how one set of underlying skills comes to be correlated with another set of underlying skills. Further weakening of a correlational effect across skills is related to the degree to which the skills have become autonomous.

Thus far we have made two major points. A review of language registers suggests the existence of cognitive barriers between registers which limit our ability to discover and use a structural similarity across these registers. Two sources of the formation of these cognitive barriers seems to be the necessity for chunking behavior into schematized routines and the necessity for rehearsing these chunks of behavior so that they become automated leading to their being functionally separated from their common roots.

Experimental Methods for Achieving Transfer

Now I shall suggest a method which will create a condition by which a person is likely to bring together two previously separated but structurally similar language routines, so as to increase the chance that the person will discover their structural similarities. The consequence of this discovery will be the flow of competence from one realm to the other; the reverse flow may or may not occur, as we shall see.

The motivation for introducing this transfer method is that the ability to transfer competence from one domain of behavior to another domain of language behavior may in some cases improve the literacy level of individuals. For example, competencies in the oral mode for creating a coherent and logical string of events may possible be transferable to the written mode (or vice versa); and, competencies in one domain of one discourse genre may be transferable to a similar domain which just happens to be more closely identified with high literacy levels, namely, the expository mode.

In the world of language use some types of topics tend to occur with only certain kinds of language structure; for example, scientific topics tend to occur with expository text formats, although this need not always be so. For foreign science students studying in the United States, scientific topics may tend to have been experienced with the English language and the student may not have had many opportunities to read scientific articles in his/her native tongue. Other language structures tend to occur in written modes rather than oral modes, that is, certain parts of the lexicon tend to occur in oral speech (e.g., "you know," "sure") and other parts occur primarily written language (e.g., "notwithstanding," "inferentially").

Creating Situations Which Increase One's Chance to Compare Underlying Similarities of Structure with the Consequence that Transfer of Skills Across Previously Separate Domains Can Occur

Our first example of transfer across structurally similar domains comes from a study of how well kindergarteners and fourth graders can recall two kinds of expository texts and one kind of narrative text. Examples of these three kinds of texts is given in Table 7-1.

An earlier study reported by Freedle and Hale (1979) suggested that it may be possible to increase the competence of kindergarteners' comprehenson and recall of expository text (E-1 texts) by first having the youngsters recall a familiar narrative form and have this followed after a brief delay by an expository form which mimics the semantic flow of information in the narrative. A more elaborate version of this study has been completed (Freedle, 1980). The results show a much more complex process at work than the one originally studied by Freedle and Hale. The new study used two kinds of expository texts—called E-1 and E-2 (see Table 7-1 for examples).

E-2 type texts are somewhat close to a string of commands (politely and indirectly phrased) that a parent might deliver to a child. For example, "if you want to help dad, you can first clean the car. Then you can go wash the basement walls, and help Mom do the grocery shopping." As such, one might say that E-2-type expositions have some *familiarity* to youngsters. In contrast our intuition suggests that expositions of the E-1 type involving a third person are somewhat less familiar. Narratives are, of course, familiar structures from a very early age (Mandler & Johnson, 1977; Stein & Glenn, 1979).

If we scan the structural differences of the three texts in Table 7-1 we see that both expositions use a hypothetical type verb structure (modals) along with conditional (if) statements. The narrative structure uses simple past tense. The other dimension of structural similarity between these three texts is whether it is written from one third person or second person perspective.

Of the three studies completed, one primarily sheds the most light on transfer across these text types. Seventy-five kindergartners and 79 fourth-graders—all from white middle-class backgrounds—were studied. In all cases children were assigned to severe experimental conditions. We were primarily concerned with comparison among conditions which changed the order in which the children were exposed to the different genres. In one condition the narrative was presented first, then E-1, then E-2; in another we presented E-2 first, followed by E-1 and finally the narrative, and so on. Of these seven, we used three conditions which presented the same type of text over all trials in order to assess practice effects.

Table 7-2 presents the main findings regarding transfer effects. When E-1 is preceded by E-2 we get the maximum improvement in percent of correct verb types used for E-1 text types. This improvement is significantly greater than one would expect due to practice alone as the

Table 7-1. Two kinds of expository texts and one kind of narrative text using the same semantic content

Expository (3rd person) "farmer" passage	Expository (2nd person) "you" passage	Narrative (story)* "farmer" passage	Semantic Category label for story information
Here's how a farmer can get his stubborn horse into the barn.	Here's how you can get your stubborn horse into the barn	Once there was a farmer	Setting
		who wanted to get his stubborn horse into the barn.	Response-Goal
The farmer can go into the barn and hold out some sugar to get the horse to come and eat.	You can go into the barn and hold out some sugar to get the horse to come and eat.	The farmer went into the barn and held out some sugar	Beginning
		to get the horse to come and eat.	Attempt
But if the horse does not like sugar, he will not come.	But if the horse does not like sugar he will not come.	But the horse did not like sugar	Response
		and he did not come.	Outcome
Here's another thing he can do.	Here's another thing you can do.	The farmer tried something else.	Beginning
Suppose the farmer has a dog.	Suppose you have a dog.	The farmer had a dog.	Setting
He can get the dog to bark at the horse.	You can get the dog to bark at the horse.	He got the dog to bark at the horse.	Attempt
This may frighten the horse	This may frighten the horse	This frightened the horse	Response
and make him run into the barn.	and make him run into the barn	and made him run into the barn.	Ending
(E-1)	(E-2)	(N)	

*Notice that there is something anomalous about trying to write the narrative from the 2nd person perspective. There is something odd in writing "You wanted to get your horse into the barn. You went into the barn and held out some sugar . . . You tried something else. You had a dog . . ." Because of the oddity of this, we did not study how such a structure would interact with the two kinds of expositions listed herein; future studies may pursue this comparison, however.

115

Table 7-2. Task orders which facilitate transfer compared with task orders which do not lead to transfer

Type of Score used	Grade Level	E-1 Mean for cond. A	E-1 Mean for cond. B	Signif. A vs. B	E-1 (task 2) Mean for cond. C	Signif. C vs. B
Percent correct verb structures	K	56.1	90.6	$p < .05$	56.1	$p < .05$
"	4th	77.3	91.9	ns	88.0	ns
No. Semantic	K	3.5	3.8	ns	4.0	ns
Categories Recalled	4th	5.2	6.7	$p < .05$	6.0	ns
Subjective Cohesion	K	4.5	2.5*	$p < .05$	4.0	ns
	4th	2.5	1.5*	$p < .01$	2.0	ns
		Cond. X	Cond. Y	X vs. Y	E-2 (task 2) Cond. Z	Z vs. Y
Percent correct verb structure	K	75.6	98.9	ns	76.9	ns
	4th	88.9	100.0	ns	97.9	ns
No. Semantic	K	4.1	.6	ns	4.4	ns
Categories Recalled	4th	6.4	7.0	ns	5.6	ns
Subjective Cohesion	K	3.0	3.2	ns	3.0	ns
	4th	2.0	1.8	ns	2.0	ns

Key:

	1st Task	2nd Task
Condition A:	E	E-1
Condition B:	E-2	E-1
Condition C:	E-2	E-1

	1st task	2nd task
Condition X:	N	E-2
Condition Y:	E-1	E-2
Condition Z?	E-2	E-2

Comment: The top half of this table compares the effect of E-1 performance for three performance scores when E-1 is preceded by either narrative or E-2 structure. There is a clear facilitation in performance for E-1 when it is preceded by E-2 (column called "A vs. B") for both age groups; the right-most column suggests though that some of the improvements might be attributable to practice effects or task position effects, except for the row indicating that kindergarteners still show an overall facilitation effect for percent correct verbs used, regardless of practice or position effects. The lower part of this table shows that there is not a reverse facilitation for E-2 when it is preceded by either narrative or E-1 tasks.

significant result as the right-most column indicates. While other significant effects also are shown for scores which deal with number or semantic categories recalled and subjective cohesion of the recalled passage, nevertheless the most critical results—and the most stable, with respect to ruling out practice effects—comes from the examination of verb structures used in E-1 following prior exposure to E-2.

As the lower half of Table 7-2 shows, there is no evidence that a reverse effect occurs which facilitates E-2 performance following a prior presentation of a type E-1 text.

Because of the importance of verb types as being reflective of the transfer effects, we focused on a further analysis of the sequence with which the two main types of verb types occurred during a student's recall of E-1 passages. In Table 7-3, we present the main results of this sequential analysis. The first set of results for condition A in the table shows that on 19 occasions the students persisted in using a past or present tense verb given that they had already used it in the preceding clause. On four occasions they switched from a past-present type verb to a hypothetical modal verb which we have identified here as signaling the expository frame. The degree to which the off-diagonals have large numerical entries is the degree to which the students fail to appreciate the psychological reality of a narrative versus a hypothetical-type framework for the text. While both diagonal entries are large (19 and 40), there still are substantial entries in the off-diagonal. Thus compared with the next set of conditional entries (from condition B), we can say that prior presentation of the narrative may in fact have contributed to some confusion in isolating the critical structural characteristics of expositions. Condition B however presents a very clean effect; here, we get a pure use of just the hypothetical modal verb structures throughout the entire transfer condition, while condition C, which represents performance on E-1 as a result of mere practice, still shows a residual type of confusion about the underlying structure of E-1

As a comparison with these transfer effects, the three transitional matrices listed on the right-hand side of Table 7-3 tend to reveal a somewhat similar pattern of results. Students who respond to an E-2 type text following an E-1 type text tend to reveal fewer confusions with a narrative type structure. Because of this, we should be cautious about claiming that the sequential analysis necessarily tells us that the effects of transfer have necessarily clarified for the student the critical distinction between narrative and expository type structures. Another type of analysis for exploring the details of cognitive merging (transfer) can be found by examining pauses, filled pauses, and false starts.

The results of this study, and projected studies based on this transfer model, seem to hold promise for evolution of a technology which will

Table 7-3. Transition matrix for verb type sequences to reveal the specific effects of transfer on the psychological reality of genre structure (for kindergarteners only)

Condition A:
N, E-1

trial n	trial n + 1	
	past/present	modals
past/present	19	4
modals	5	40

Condition B:
E-2, E-1

trial n		
	pp	modals
past/Present	9	0
modals	9	31

Condition C:
E-1, E-1

	pp	modals
past present	12	1
modals	0	22

Condition X:
N, E-2

	trial N + 1	
	pp	modals
past/present	7	1
modals	2	24

Condition Y:
E-1, E-2

	pp	modals
past/present	0	2
modals	1	48

Condition Z:
E-2, E-2

	pp	modals
past/present	6	4
modals	3	40

encourage rapid acquisition of expository text comprehension. This is important because these text types play a prominent role in the school system as one progresses through the grades. As such, mastery of expository form is probably correlated with our notions of literacy skills, and for that reason deserves special attention in future work on transfer.

Cross-classification of Skills which Promotes Transfer from the Written Mode to the Oral Mode

A second type of transfer study—cross classification of skills—comes from our noticing that college students do not appear to be very coherent in their oral recall of expository passages of moderate difficulty. Since we expected most of these students to be excellent writers we wondered whether it wasn't possible to set up an experimental paradigm where we could encourage the transfer of the students' organization skills in the written mode over to their oral mode so as to improve their oral coherence scores. This brief pilot study is now presented.

We shall demonstrate that one way to transfer competence across modes (e.g., from written mode to the oral mode) is to first present a passage for recall in the oral mode—this is expected to show poor coherence. But suppose we then ask the student to follow the oral recall with a written version of the passage (without any additional exposure to the original passage). If our earlier arguments are correct, the student should suddenly exhibit greater coherence in the written version (because the school system does provide more opportunity to exercise the written skills as opposed to the oral skills). The coup de grace, now, is to suddenly ask the student to again recall the passage in the oral mode without further recourse to the original passage. Since the same content is being requested, the student is more likely to use structural elements from the more coherent written mode and incorporate them in the final oral recall. If the student does incorporate such elements, his coherence rating for the oral mode is likely to dramatically improve. Further practice with this triad (first an oral recall, then a written recall, then a final oral recall of the same material) is likely to lead to dramatic improvement in oral coherence over a very short time period.

Example of Possible Effects of a Written Recall upon the Form of a Subsequent Oral Recall

We shall now present evidence that this transfer from written to oral modes does occur, leading to great oral coherence in a very short period of time. The following passages lend substance to our claim that certain features of oral recall, *in the absence of a written recall,* tend to have less cohesion, less clarity, and less high level structuring than a corresponding oral passage which followed directly after a written production of a passage presented for recall.

The following passage was read to a subject:

> A landlord must, no matter what the lease says, maintain the premises in a good state of repair, and fit for habitation, and must observe all housing, health and safety standards required by law. You can check at your municipal office to find out what these minimum standards are. It does not matter that the premises were in a bad state of repair when you moved in. A landlord must also repair damage caused by vandals or strangers. A tenant must keep the place reasonably clean and repair any damage caused deliberately or carelessly by the tenant, the tenant's family or guests.

The subject was first asked to recall orally as much of the passage as he could remember. His recall consisted of the following:

> A landlord must (I'm terrible) keep the premises clean and in good shape (laughter) at all times. If he is not sure what the details are, he can go to his municipal (laughter) to check on the code for landlord and tenants. A landlord is responsible for repairing tenants' damage.

Next the subject was asked to *write out* his recall without further recourse to the text that he had originally heard. He wrote the following:

> Here are some rules and regulations concerning the obligations and liability of the landlord and/or tenant. First I will consider the obligations of the landlord. A landlord must keep the utilities of tenant-premises in good functioning order and be responsible for keeping the premises safe and comfortable for the tenant at all times. A tenant in turn is responsible for paying for damages to the premises after or upon vacating said premise. The landlord however is responsible for making these necessary repairs.

Immediately following this written statement, the subject was asked for a second oral recall, again without recourse to the original text, and without recourse to the written passage which he just completed. Here is his second oral recall:

> This material concerns itself with the duties and obligations of a landlord and his or her tenants. First the landlord's obligation to the tenant are that he or she must keep the utilities of the premises in good working order at all times. The tenants' obligations on the other hand involve paying for damages that are made to the property upon vacating the property with the understanding that the landlord will actually *do* the repairs.

Coherence in a text can be achieved by a number of different structural organizers or signaling devices. These devices may join units of text at different levels. At the highest level the coherence markers join units of a text at the sentence or paragraph level. At a lower level, the markers typically equate phrases or associate local units with each other. At the lowest level lexical repetition, pronominal reference and a synonymy create links between specific lexical items. Any text will likely show a combination of these markers in achieving coherence.

The most striking organizational feature of the written and second oral recall compared to the first oral recall, ignoring the accuracy of the subject's recall, is the presence of high level structural organizers. In the written version, the first word "here" is a cataphoric reference indicating *what is to come*. The first word of the second sentence in the second oral recall, "first" picks up on the organization suggested by the first sentence, and similarly in the written paragraph "in turn" continues and completes the organization. These features are clearly *not present in the first oral recall* but were transferred or carried forward to the second oral recall. The cataphoric "here" in the written is represented by "this material" in the first words of the second oral recall. The organizing word "first" from the written is repeated exactly in the second oral recall, and the organizing words "in turn" of the written version correspond to the phrase "on the other hand" from the second oral recall. It is important to note that none of these high level organizers are present in the first oral recall. This already suggests that some skills that make for competent writing may be transferable directly to the oral mode. The results thus far further suggest that these organizing skills (at least the overt markers of them—not the underlying skills themselves) are not initially present in the oral mode, but can be readily elicited under the proper task formats.

Table 7-4A summarizes the results.

A second interesting example which contrasts these oral and written recalls has to do with what we shall call intermediate-level text organization. For the first oral task there is only one main "actor" or point of view represented—that of the landlord; grammatically this results in "landlord" being the subject of each of the three sentences. In the written passage the point of view of the writer as actor is introduced by the word "here" (as in pointing) and later in the phrase "I will consider. . . ." This is followed by a shift in "actors" from first the landlord *and* tenant, to landlord alone, and finally to tenant as the sole actor. This complexity of shifting points of view is carried into the structure of the second oral recall with the following results: "this material" indicates the point of view of the speaker; then we have the landlord as actor, followed by the tenant as actor. It is obvious that the written version is the most highly structured with respect to shifts in point of view, while the simplest is

Table 7-4a. A List of Coherence Markers in Two Oral Recalls Separated by a Written Recall

Coherence	First Oral Recall	Written Recall	Second Oral Recall
HIGH LEVEL Signals		Here are . . . (cataphora) First . . . . (cataphora) in turn	This material . . . (cataphora) First . . . (cataphora) on the other hand
MIDDLE LEVEL signals	clean and in good shape	rules and regulations obligations and liability landlord and/or tenant safe and comfortable after or upon however	duties and obligations
LOW LEVEL Signals	he→landlord the details→(assumed rules) he→landlord he→landlord his→landlord landlord landlord	obligations = liability obligations landlord landlord responsible = obligation tenant premises safe = comfortable tenant/tenant responsible premises said→premises premises landlord responsible these→(assumes damages) repairs	itself→material his or her→landlord landlord obligation the tenant→tenant he or she→landlord the premises→(assumed) tenants obligations the property→premises landlord the repairs→(assumes damages)

In the list of low level signals: 1. equal signs (=) indicate lexical cohesion of synonymy; 2. arrows (→) indicate anaphoric reference to material earlier in the text; 3. words listed without annotation are instances of lexical repetition. (I am very indebted to Dr. Jonathan Fine for his help in analyzing these pilot data which appear in the Table 7-4a as well as Table 7-4b).

the first oral recall in which there is but one point of view. It seems reasonable to suggest that the superiority of the last oral recall is a reflection of the increased structuring of the *written* recall. This result along with the earlier materials presented suggests to us that orally recalled texts *will* be more skillfully organized if there is either (1) an overt instruction to think through or plan what the main idea of a passage is prior to speaking, or (2) elicitation of higher level skills, by preceding the oral recall with a written version—where the written passage appears to elicit by itself the higher level skill, without explicit instructions to do so.

In terms of the number of words elicited, the first oral is the shortest, while the written is the longest. While length differences pose some problems of interpretation for our next set of observations, there seem to be the following traits observable at the low level of text organization

Table 7-4b. A visual display of how three levels of coherence organizers interconnect for the written recall*

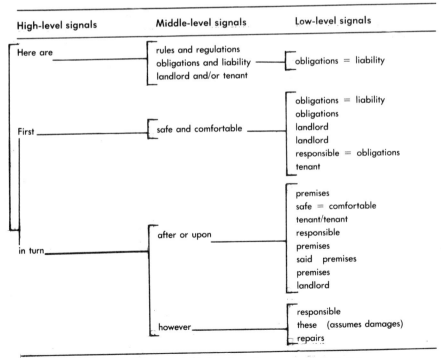

High-level signals	Middle-level signals	Low-level signals
Here are	rules and regulations obligations and liability landlord and/or tenant	obligations = liability
First	safe and comfortable	obligations = liability obligations landlord landlord responsible = obligations tenant
in turn	after or upon	premises safe = comfortable tenant/tenant responsible premises said premises premises landlord
	however	responsible these (assumes damages) repairs

*This table represents another way to present the information contained in Table 7-4a.

which we shall call the level of simple cohesion. The first oral recall has very little lexical repetition (note the repetition, though, of "landlord") but does make use of anaphoric reference (e.g., "he" "he" "his"). In the written recall there is repetition of a number of different lexical-terms, for example, "landlord" is used four times across sentences, "tenants" is used three times across sentences, "obligations" is used twice, "premises" is used three times).

As well as lexical repetition there is cohesion by use of synonyms (e.g., obligation-liabilities-responsible are close synonyms). Other kinds of links include the anaphoric links of "said" (said premises) and "these" (in "these necessary repairs"). Both these items refer to earlier chunks of the text and so create coherence. The second oral recall also retains the anaphoric reference cohesion of the written recall but uses less formal cohesive markers—for example, "the" in the phrases "the property" and "the repairs." This suggests that the written recall has helped organize the material at this low level yet the subject is sensitive to the change to a spoken mode, and moves from the rather formal anaphoric reference of "*said* premises" to the less formal use of "the" as in the examples above.

In conclusion, the examples suggest a ready transfer of the higher-level organization from the written mode directly to the oral mode and a less direct transfer of several of the lower level signals from the written to the oral mode.

Individual differences

Some cautionary statements are in order now. It is likely that there may be three categories of students with respect to contrasting their relative oral and written text skills. The first group might be classified as possessing strong organizing skills in the written mode, but not in the spontaneous oral mode. A second group might be classified as having strong organizing skills in the oral mode, but lack them in the written mode. Finally, there is a residual group which is poor in both written and oral skills to begin with. While transfer could flow from high competence to low, for two particular project our focus of concern will be promoting the skills of transfer for the first group of students as we have reason to believe they demonstrate the predominant pattern.

In conclusion, the examples suggest a ready transfer of the higher-level organization from the written directly to the oral mode and a less direct transfer of several of the lower-level signals from the written to the oral mode.

Conclusion

The simple techniques which I have just presented all seem to help focus the individual's attention on underlying structural similarities and almost invites him/her to try out some of the structural features from one domain to another. Part of this strategy for increasing structural awareness of similarities seems to depend on presenting identical semantic content (as in the oral to written study). There probably are other techniques which will be discovered to increase the awareness of structural similarity.

By implication, if a person notices the similarity in the experimental situation, they must not really have noticed it before. So this might be taken as indirect evidence of the cognitive barrier that may exist between language registers and language variants which on the face of it "should" have been noticed to be similar, but for some reason had not been noticed to be similar. Thus indirectly, our experimental results provide another avenue of evidence for the types of observations made by Ferguson on strictly linguistic observation grounds.

In his paper, Ferguson (1981) suggests that earlier he had conceived of these special set of modifications in phonology and so on as "a supplementary set of rules applied after all the normal rules." Now he prefers, however, the metaphor of plugging in a supplementary system which ordinarily remains unplugged and does not affect the working of the system unless plugged in. The supplementary unit may be a minor attachment which affects only a small part of the total system or it may be a much more substantial unit or even a whole system that rivals the primary system or serves as an alternative to it" (p. 7).

Psychologists of language would do well to explore the behavioral consequences of these several types of variations considered by Ferguson in order to choose the system of widest explanatory adequacy. The few empirical results I have presented today may play some role in bringing the naturalistic observations of the linguist into a laboratory situation, narrowing down the many theoretical possibilities regarding cognition and language processes, especially as these processes relate to the difficult issue of the gradual automatization of subsystems of literacy skills as a function of use.

One final point. When we treat students like machines by immersing them with lock-step curricula for laborious growth in literacy skills (usually by a bottom-up assumption as the basis guiding the structure and sequencing of these curricula), we get machine-like responses back from the students. It isn't really surprising, is it? By paying a little more attention to the humanistic side of learning (which might be captured more by a top-down processing approach) we begin focusing upon the most general basis for motivating literacy—the desire to communicate with others. Establishing skill in communication first requires establishing a sound relationship between teacher and student. Without this relationship there is precious little possibility for communication and hence precious little need for honing the tools of communication, namely, learning the skills of literacy.

Isn't it curious that when we treat students like machines, we have the same problem communicating with them that we have in trying to get computers and machines to understand human language?

References

Ferguson, C. (in press). Simplified registers and linguistic theory. In L. Menn & L. Obler (Eds.), *Exceptional language and linguistic theory.*

Fitts, P. (1964). Perceptual-motor skills learning. In A.W. Melton (Ed.). *Categories of human learning.* New York: Academic Press.

Freedle, R. (1980). Final report on NIE project: acquisition of a new comprehension schema for expository prose based on trasfer from related schemata. Unpublished.

Freedle, R., & Hale, G. (1979). Acquisition of new comprehension schemata for expository prose by transfer of a narrative schema. In R. Freedle (Ed.), *New directions in discourse processing.* Norwood, NJ: Ablex.

Mandler, & Johnson, N.S. (1977). Remembrance of things parsed: story structure and recall. *Cognitive psychology, 9*, 111-151.

Miller, G.A. (1956). The magic number seven, plus or minus two. *Psychological Review, 63*, 81-97.

Scribner, S., & Cole, M. (1981). *Psychology of literacy.* Cambridge, MA: Harvard University Press.

Stein, N., & Glenn, D. (1979). An analysis of story comprehension in elementary school children. In R. Freedle (Ed.), *New direction in discourse processing.* Norwood, NJ: Ablex.

Chapter 8
Reading And Writing With Computers

Brian D. Monahan
Yonkers Public School District, New York

Until very recently, computer hardware and software that were purchased by schools and school districts went to one of two places. One alternative was to put it in a computer lab and use it for a course in computer science or for a program in computer literacy. While such activities are admirable, they treat computing as an end in itself. The second alternative for placement of computer hardware and software was the mathematics department. It seemed an unwritten rule that mathematics teachers knew about computers and that they should have access to them. In recent years, educators have become aware that the computer can be a useful tool in all areas of the school. Not only is it educationally sound to use computers in all areas of the curriculum, it is also cost-efficient. Computers are rather expensive, but they don't wear out from overuse. This article will discuss how computers can be invaluable in reading and writing instruction.

Christopher Wells, a computer scientist at the University of California, recently compared the invention of computers to the invention of the alphabet (Thomas, 1983). Just as the alphabet was originally developed as a counting mechanism, so computers were first thought of as counting machines. Today, people are coming to realize that the computer is a language as well as a numbers machine, and the computer in the English classroom has moved beyond typically computational tasks such as computing readability formulas.

The ability of the microcomputer to do word processing is the capability of the computer that is receiving the most attention from language arts teachers. Although offices have used word processors for several years, their use in teaching is quite new. In fact, the use of the computer for word processing developed almost accidently in some schools. Many schools had already purchased microcomputers for purposes other than word processing when they discovered that relatively inexpensive software could turn those machines into word processors. Now, many individuals and organizations purchase microcomputers solely for their word processing capabilities, probably because micro-computers tend to be considerably less expensive than dedicated word processors (machines that are designed specifically for word processing and perform no other tasks).

When the microcomputer functions as a word processor, the user types in much the same way as on a traditional typewriter, except that the text appears on the screen as it is typed. The text is also temporarily stored in the memory of the computer. The great advantage of the word processor is that the typist can make revisions easily at any point. When the user is satisfied with the document, it may be saved on a disk or on tape. Finally, the user may print out as many "original" copies of the text as are needed.

By itself, the word processing capability of the microcomputer is prob-ably significant enough to justify the purchase of one or more micro-computers for use in English and language arts classes. Suttles (1983) paraphrases Taylor (1980) in stating that the word processor can "act as a tutor when it offers suggestions based upon what a student has written, as a tool simplifying the student's attempt to write and as a tutor when the computer is corrected by the student and 'taught' to write" (p.33).

While no conclusive body of research yet exists to answer the question of whether the use of a word processor improves student writing, the research does seem to suggest that students enjoy using the machines, and that they are likely to write longer papers and revise them more when using a word processor (Colburn, 1982; Daiute, 1982; Monahan, 1982). Favorable student response to word processing is not surprising since word processors make it fun to enter text and easy to revise it. John Jerome (1983), a professional writer, suggests what is perhaps the greatest potential value of the word processor. Jerome claims that "the computer shortens the distance between the idea and the word" (p. 173).

Despite the promise of word processing for the teaching and learning of composition, the word processor has certainly yet to revolutionize writing in schools. The research on the use of word processing to improve the writing skills of younger children must be considered tentative. Bro-zan (1983) cites Karen Sheingold, director of the Center for Children and Technology at the Bank Street College of Education. She used word processors with eighth graders: "We assumed that if the capability was in the technology, children would take advantage of it. But they did not do significantly more revising than with a pencil" (p. 3).

To some extent, the failure of word processing to significantly change the way writing is taught and learned is a function of a lack of widely available word processing software available for precollege students. In addition, as ironic as it may seem, word processing in elementary and secondary classrooms may be negatively influenced by the enthusiasm of the teachers. There is an ever-growing number of educators who have learned what a wonderful tool the computer can be for helping us with our work. Many of us have learned about the text processing capabilities of the computer while writing and revising manuscripts and theses. We have found the computer to be so helpful for us that we have decided to use it to help our students. Unfortunately, most educators are adults and most word processing software is designed for use in business and industry and the home, by adults. What is probably needed is a word processing program appropriate for younger students. At first, the *Bank Street Writer* was hailed as the answer to the word processing needs of younger students, but the results of using the program have been mixed. First, *Bank Street Writer* is not available for all computers. Second, the program suffers from some severe limitations. As one reviewer pointed out, *Bank Street Writer* may be easy to use, but it is not easy to learn (Chan, 1983). Despite the limitations of the program, it is reasonable to assume that there are more and better programs coming soon, since *Bank Street Writer* was the first word processing program designed for student use. Assuming that a word processor can be developed which is powerful, yet easy to use by elementary and secondary students, there is reason for optimism about the impact that word processing will have on the composing process.

The fact is that word processing has been more successful in improving the writing of college-age students who are older and better able to follow the procedures necessary to use most word processing programs. Based upon an experiment with 12 writing instructors and four freshman composition students, Bran (1983) suggested that the computer can help beginning writers to revise their initial drafts with less emphasis on lexical substitution and grammatical correctness and with more emphasis on reshaping ideas through successive drafts. Keefer and Smith (1983), in a study of freshman composition students using a computer programmed with software from Bell Labs, found that textual analysis with computers intrigues college writers and speeds the learning of editing skills by offering immediate reliable and consistent attention to the surface features of their prose.

One of the advantages to having students write their compositions on a word processor is that it facilitates interaction among students. If an entire class is familiar with the editing functions of the word processor, students can suggest revisions in one another's papers. In addition, the fact that a portion of a text can be displayed on a screen makes it easy for students to work in groups. Seymour Papert (1983) suggested that at the present time in the United States there is approximately one computer available for each ten children. He suggests that the ratio be reduced to approximately one in three. If such a time comes, a promising area for research in language arts and other educational areas will be the interaction that takes place as students work together on computers.

Despite the promise of word processing for writing, it is not likely that it will cure all the problems that students have with writing. Some writers will never learn to compose at a keyboard. (This writer does all his best work with yellow legal pages.) If the word processor is to fulfill its potential, two major changes seem to be required. First, fully equipped computer labs must be provided for composition classes—students must have access to these labs at a variety of times. Second, schools must begin to teach typing earlier. Doing so will help students, not only with word processing for their English class, but also with all of their subjects. Lawrence Schwartz (1983) has said "that it is now possible, both technologically and financially, to give every student free access to these powerful writing instruments and to end the so called crisis in basic writing."

When students use the word processing function of the computer, they are essentially using the computer as a tool. In language arts, the computer can also be used to provide drill and practice, tutorials and simulations in both language and literature. The computer can be used to provide drill and practice in areas of the curriculum in which the teacher feels students are weak. While drill and practice programs are not difficult to write, many graphically attractive ones are currently available at reasonable prices from the various software houses. Among the areas of language arts which are covered are spelling, rules of English grammar, and punctuation. While such programs may benefit from their novelty, they are often little more effective than the traditional teacher-made ditto sheets. Their ineffectiveness is consistent with the current research which suggests that the teaching of traditional grammar does not improve student writing.

It is in the use of tutorials that some of the most exciting work in language arts is being done. When a computer is functioning in the tutorial mode to help students write, the machine is serving as a "friendly editor." One type of tutorial that is used successfully in language arts is the "story starter." The story starter is a technique that has been used successfully in language arts instruction for years; the computer simply makes the procedure more efficient. A relatively simple story starter called "Story Time" (Monahan & Monahan, 1982) prompts the students for their names and asks them to give a title to their story. It then allows them to input a story, one line at a time, until they decide that their story is long enough. At that time, the story can either be printed out immediately or saved on a disk. The individual student or class can build up a library of stories. More sophisticated "story starter" programs are available from commercial publishers. Those programs include graphics and usually prompt the student by providing the opening of the story. They also ask periodic questions to help the students along as they compose their stories. One particular program, *Story Machine* (1982), assists students in composing stories by providing them with nouns, verbs, and articles. The program then graphically demonstrates action appropriate to the action described in the sentence. Thus, if a student composes "The boy ate the fence," the screen will show a boy moving across the screen and proceeding to devour a fence. With the help of IBM, a school district in Burlington, North Carolina (IBM, 1983) took the concept of the helpful editor for young children even further. The concept that students can and should begin composing even before they begin reading is not a new one (Chomsky, 1971). IBM developed software which teaches students 42 phonemes which allow them to spell any English word. The computer is programmed to accept those "words" as input as the children write their stories.

Tutorials can also help students to understand literature. "Understanding Mood in Literature" (Monahan & Fowkes, 1983) is a program which uses selections, such as Browning's "Meeting at Night" and the opening section of Steinbeck's *Of Mice and Men*, to help students learn to analyze the mood of a literary work. The program shows the students the opening section of the literary work and prompts them with questions to point them toward specific details which the author uses to create the mood. Ultimately, the students are tested on their understanding of the mood through the use of a multiple-choice question, but before being given the question, students are provided with printouts of their open-ended responses to the earlier questions. Those printouts can also be used later as "notes" to help the students complete the final task: the completion of an essay which analyzes the moods of the literary works.

A closely related area in which the computer can be helpful in language arts and English instruction is providing heuristics to help students in composing. Programs which help students to develop heuristics for composing extend the word processing function of the computer. To establish the heuristics the computer engages in a dialogue with the user. In such a situation, the computer is functioning as a tool because the students use the computer as a device on which to compose. It is functioning as a tutor because it is providing the students with a plan to help them compose. Finally, it is functioning as a tutee because the students are actually instructing the computer about how the composition should be composed.

An example of a computer program that makes use of the heuristic approach that is described above was developed by Schwartz (1982), who set out to write a computer program that would provide a heuristic for invention and audience feedback. She developed SEEN, The Seeing Eye Elephant Network. The program works in two modes, the solo mode and the network mode. In the solo mode the computer prompts students to "see" what they have already observed. In the network mode, the program allows the students to compare their work with the work of others. Schwartz admitted that the students in her program did not write papers that received higher grades, but she did report that the students in her group spent more time on their papers. She suggested that there may have been qualitative differences which did not show up immediately.

Woodruff (1982) used a computerized "editor" to help sixth-grade students with their composing and examined the reactions of the students. The results indicated that the students perceived the computer as helpful. Seventy-five percent of the sixth graders participating claimed that their computer-assisted compositions were superior to those written without the aid of the computer. One of the disadvantages of using the computer as such an aid is that it may lead to an oversimplified "what next" view of composing, rather than a more realistic, highly recursive view.

A compromise is suggested by Cronnell (1981). He developed a system in which students choose a topic and are presented with a set of heuristic questions about the topic. The students' answers are stored and presented to them when they begin writing. In this case, the computer serves as something of an electronic notepad. Obviously, this type of notetaking can be valuable in all subject areas, not just in language arts. In addition, heuristics need not only be helpful in the expository mode. Marcus (1982) developed a program called "Compupoem." Students who use the program respond to questions and, often to the students' initial surprise, produce a poem.

The use of computers in English and language arts classrooms is not likely to produce the utopia that some envision. Zaharias (1983) suggests that "At least at present, it appears that the utility of the microcomputer as a primary delivery unit system is relatively limited" (p. 992). Although most students and teachers enjoy using computers, studies thus far have shown little or no improvement in student performance over that produced by conventional teaching methods. Wresch (1982) reports that an Educational Testing Service study in 1975–76 to examine the effectiveness of PLATO, perhaps the largest collection of drill and practice programs available anywhere, found no significant impact on either achievement or attrition. Robertson (1978) found no significant difference between the achievement of computer users and a control group in a study of a program for poor third-grade spellers. Anandam (1979) studied RSVP, a program designed to provide individual analysis of writing problems for remedial students at five community colleges and found that it produced no significant improvement in writing skills. In each case, however, the computer work did no harm, and the students liked working with the machines. Many of the above-mentioned programs are or will soon become obsolete and will be replaced by new technology.

The problems faced by those involved in linguistic computing are similar to the problems of those artifical intelligence researchers who are involved in natural language processing. Often it is the sheer number of linguistic alternatives that makes it impossible to develop solutions to language-related problems. Computers are adept at selecting the "right" answer from among a group of answers that includes some wrong answers. In linguistic computing, the computer must find a way of selecting *the* right answer from among a group of "right" answers. As computer memory becomes less expensive, the possibilities for dealing with linguistic problems will become greater. As hardware and software become less expensive, computers will become more and more useful in the dissemination of linguistic information. Horn (1983) suggests that ideographs are in the future. (An ideograph is a publication which is written and specifically printed for an individual.) Thus we are approaching the day when we will read newspapers and magazines which contain stories and ads aimed at our own needs and interests.

Recently, Lawler (1980) introduced his 6-year-old daughter to writing on the computer—by the time she grows up, computer-assisted-instruction in English will have too. Many of the promises of CAI in English will be fulfilled at the same time that the problems are being solved.

References

Anandam, K., et al. (1979). *RSVP: Feedback program for individualized analysis of writing.* Research Report, Miami: Computer based instructional development and research. (ERIC Document Reproduction Service No. ED 191511)

Bran, J. C. (1983). Computerized word processing as an aid to revision. *College Composition and Communication, 34*, 146-148.

Brozan, N. (1983, July 2). Computers as a learning tool. *New York Times*, p. C1.

Chan, J. (1983). The Bank Street Writer. *Computers, Reading and Language Arts, 1*(2), 40-41.

Chomsky, C. (1971). Write first, read later. *Childhood Education, 47*, 296-299.

Colburn, P., et al. (1982). *Practical guide to computers in education.* Reading, MA: Addison-Wesley.

Cronnell, B. (1981). *Using microcomputers for composition instruction.* Washington, DC: National Institute of Education. (ERIC Document Reproduction Service No. 203872)

Daiute, C. A. (1982, March/April). Word processing. *Electronic learning, 2*, 29-31.

Horn, W. (1983). The computerized text and its reader. *The Kentucky English Bulletin, 33*, 38-41.

IBM. (1983). *Viewpoint.* Atlanta, GA.

Jerome, J. (1983, June). Making the leap: A creative writer muses on the word processor. *PC, 3,* 167-176.

Keefer, K., & Smith, C. R. (1983). Textual analysis with computers: Tests of Bell Laboratories Computer Software. *Research in the Teaching of English, 17,* 201-214.

Lawler, R. (1980). One child's learning: Introducing writing with a computer. A.I. Memo No. 575. Cambridge, MA: MIT. (ERIC Document Reproduction Service No. ED 208 415)

Marcus, S. (1982). Compupoem: A computer-assisted writing activity. *English Journal, 71*(2), 96-98.

Monahan, B. (1982). Computing and revising. *English Journal, 71*(7), 93-94.

Monahan, B., & Fowkes, R. (1983). *Understanding mood in literature.* Yonkers, NY: Yonkers Public Schools.

Monahan, B., & Monahan, T. (1982). *Computer first: Read and write later.* (ERIC Document Reproduction Service No. ED 226 357)

Papert, S. (1983). *Beyond the personal computer.* Paper presented at the annual conference of the Association for Computing Machinery, New York, NY.

Robertson, G. (1978). *A comparison of meaningful and nonmeaningful content in computer-assisted spelling programs.* (Report No. 51). Regina: Saskatchewan School Trustees Association Research Centre. (ERIC Document Reproduction Service No. ED 184 128)

Schwartz, H. J. (1982). *A computer program for invention and feedback.* Paper presented at the annual meeting of the Conference on College Composition and Communication, San Francisco, CA.

Schwartz, L. (1983). Teaching writing in the age of the word processor and personal computer. *Educational Technology, 23*(6), 33-35.

Schwartz, M. (1982). Computers and the teaching of writing. *Educational Technology, 22*(11), 27-28.

Story Machine, (1982). Cambridge, MA: Spinaker.

Suttles, A. L. (1983). Computers and writing: Contemporary research and innovative programs. *Computers, Reeading, and Language Arts, 1,* 33-37.

Taylor, R. E. (1980). *The computer in the school: Tutor, tool, tutee.* New York: Teachers College Press.

Thomas, O. (1983). The alphabet and the computer: Artificial intelligence and syllable recognition. *Computers, Reading and Language Arts, 1,* 23-26.

Woodruff, E., et al. (1982). On the road to computer assisted composition. *Journal of Educational Technology Systems, 10*(2), 133-144.

Wresch, W. (1982) Computers in English class: Finally beyond grammar and spelling drills. *College English, 44,* 483-490.

Zaharias, J. A. (1983). Microcomputers in the language arts classroom: Promises and pitfalls. *Language Arts, 60,* 990-994.

PART III
PERSONAL CONTEXTS OF READING: VARIATIONS IN LANGUAGE AND READING DEVELOPMENT

Chapter 9
Reading And The Special Learner: Variations In Language And Reading Development

Rosa A. Hagin

Fordham University

Consideration of the context of reading must inevitably focus on the individual child as the primary context in which learning occurs. Implicit in this focus is the splendid variety that can be found as one examines special learners and the processes by which they deal with the task of learning to read. Of all of the accomplishments we expect of young children, reading may be one of the most difficult. It draws upon a complex of biological, sensory, perceptual, cognitive, linguistic, experiential, social, and motivational processes, the exact mix of which has not yet been clearly delineated, although it has engaged the attention of investigators from a broad range of disciplines for decades (Morgan, 1896; Hinshelwood, 1917; Monroe, 1932; Robinson, 1946; Money, 1962; Critchley, 1964; Benton and Pearl, 1978; Gaddes, 1980).

Identifying Unsuccessful Learners

There is much concern for identifying children who do not learn to read well, despite adequate intelligence, normal sensory acuity, conventional educational opportunity, and appropriate motivation. Much of this research has been directed toward differentiating between the successful and unsuccessful learners with the hope of increasing the size of the former group and diminishing the size of the latter. This approach has served to emphasize the contrast between the groups and to obscure within-group variations. Thus, the unsuccessful learners came to be regarded as a homogenous group in which the members had much in common with each other. Descriptions of both assessment and remediation practices would refer to "the learning disabled child" as if the problem were a clinical entity.

This easy dichotomy does not make for conceptual clarity, for one cannot assume that the conditions associated with learning failure in one child are the same as those in any other child who fails to learn. In reality, within the group of children designated as learning disabled, there are marked individual differences in strengths and deficits. For the researcher the importance of these variations is that, in any study of large numbers of children, these individual differences may cancel each other out. The resultant balancing effect may cause one to dismiss as unimportant some variables that may indeed be crucial to understanding some of the children in the sample. However, the very multidimensionality that invites confusion, frustration, and failure of replication for the researcher provides for intriguing and challenging variety for the teacher.

Techniques of Classification

It is in the instructional context that the diagnostic pieces come together. In the classroom, the children can be seen, not from the single dimensions that comprise the mosaic of the assessment process, but as living, breathing individuals. There they can be viewed not only in terms of the needs they present, but also in terms of their strengths, their compensatory resources, and most significantly of all their differential responses to remediation.

A 10-year follow-up study of intervention results first highlighted differences in the outcomes of remediation among the youngsters we worked with (Silver & Hagin, 1964). When we related these findings to our original clinical data, we found that common characteristics in both diagnostic data and educational outcomes could be used to identify subgroups within the heterogeneous sample we studied.

A number of investigators have used intuitive methods for identifying instructionally relevant subgroups, using such methods as analysis of spelling patterns (Boder, 1973), sorting of neurological and pychological data (Mattis, French, & Rapin, 1975), comparing patterns of academic performance (Johnson & Myklebust, 1967; Rourke & Finlayson, 1978). As multivariate statistical methods came into general use, the number of subtype studies increased. Developments in computer technology made it possible to apply methods such as the Q-technique of factor analysis (Doehring & Hoshko, 1977), cluster analysis (Lyon, Stewart, & Freedman, 1982; and Rourke & Strang, 1983) and multidimensional scaling (Stokes, 1983) to the mass of data that previously could only be handled in limited segments. The availability of multivariate methods also made it possible to cross-validate inferences based on intuitive interpretation of clinical and educational data.

Background for Subgroup Studies

Clinical experience at the Learning Disorders Unit of the Department of Psychiatry at New York University Medical Center suggested to us intuitive groupings of children with special learning problems. Continuing work with children made us aware of similarities among them. We would observe that a given child was, for example, "an Eileen," or that another was "a Virginia" or a "Lennie," groupings named for children in our follow-up study sample. While these informal classifications were useful in our clinical work, they left something to be desired in scientific rigor.

The school-based preventive projects conducted by the Learning Disorders Unit in cooperation with Community School District 2 offered an opportunity for more rigorous study of subgrouping within the broad group of special learners. From 1969 to 1983 our work in these projects involved scanning intact grade samples of children in kindergarten and first grade to locate children who were vulnerable to learning failure, providing interdisciplinary diagnosis to clarify the reasons for their vulnerability, and supervising educational intervention by teachers and educational assistants. Developed as a model program with funding from the Bureau of Education for the Handicapped, this preventive program was validated in 1979 by the Joint Dissemination Review Panel of the U.S. Department of Education on the basis of its educational impact, replicability, and cost-effectiveness. As a validated program model, it became part of the National Diffusion Network.

Along with provision of diagnostic and intervention services, the preventive projects generated multidisciplinary, longitudinal data from intact grade samples of children who participated in the program. These data, drawn from the natural context of the school, had a number of advantages over clinical data: (1) the school samples were not subject to the biases of selectivity implicit in the referral process, (2) data permitted longitudinal study of the learning trajectory of the special children who were served by the program, and (3) comparisons with achieving children of the same age and school background were possible.

Our data consisted of the results of the scanning test SEARCH (Silver & Hagin, 1976) and the multidisciplinary diagnostic examination. SEARCH is a 20-minute individual test which was administered to all children enrolled in the grade in order to locate those who are at risk for learning failure. The ten components are utilized as a total score to identify vulnerability and as individual scores to yield a profile of assets and needs to guide educational intervention. The multidisciplinary examination consisted of neuropsychiatric and psychological examinations, achievement testing, and developmental histories obtained from parents and school and hospital records. Our diagnostic procedures, including rating procedures for the neurological and psychiatric examinations and the diagnostic use of the Wechsler Preschool and Primary Scale of Intelligence (WPPSI), have been described in previous publications. (Hagin, Silver, & Corwin, 1972; Silver & Hagin, 1972).

Results of these examinations for one sample, children born in 1971, (BD 1971) were used to identify subgroups of children with special learning needs. The sample, numbering 494, represents all the children enrolled in the first grades of seven elementary schools located in the Lower East Side or midtown areas of Manhattan. There were slightly more boys (52%) than girls (48%) in the group. The ethnic census for these schools showed that there were 11.5% black, 35% Oriental, 53.5% white, including 34% Hispanic. Thirteen children were found to have insufficient English for valid testing on SEARCH and were dropped from the sample. Otherwise, the group represented the intact enrollment of beginning first graders of seven schools.

By the end of first grade, 25.4% of the sample were found to be vulnerable to learning failure. The sex distribution was relatively even: 60% boys, 40% girls. The ethnic distribution in the vulnerable group closely paralleled the ethnic distribution of the schools from which the sample was drawn. WPPSI IQ scores for the vulnerable group ranged from 61 to 124, with a mean of 93.39 ± 12.43. Scanning and diagnostic data from this sample were used to identify subgroups.

Subgroups of Special Learners

Children with specific language disabilities comprise the largest subgroup identified. These children had associative learning problems that affected every aspect of their learning in reading and the language arts. On SEARCH they demonstrated problems in the orientation of symbols in space and sounds in time. Neurological examination showed evidence that cerebral dominance for language had not been established and the body image concept and right–left discrimination were immature. Otherwise there was no evidence of structural defect of the central nervous system or of the peripheral sensory apparatus, either on examination or in the developmental histories. Histories suggested that the origin of this kind of learning problems might be familial, (i.e. that the child's inherited pattern of development is one in which language specialization develops more slowly than other brain functions.) In the BD 1971 sample, 83 or 17% of the children were diagnosed as having specific language disabilities. The proportions of boys and girls were not significantly different, with percentages of 58% and 48% respectively. Sam is an example of the youngsters in this group:

The examiner found Sam to be a well-developed boy who was friendly, yet well-controlled during the sessions. He was self-confident to the point of presenting a macho image, which may mask subtle doubts and concerns about his abilities. There were definite immaturities in finger schema recognition, left-right discrimination, and spatial orientation. The remainder of the neurological examination was within normal limits. Sam's functioning of the WPPSI placed him within the average range, with a full scale score of 100, a verbal IQ of 107 and a performance IQ of 92. He worked slowly and deliberately. Verbal concepts were well developed and ideas were expressed easily. High point in the record occurred with a test of social judgment, on which he earned a superior score. The only significantly low point was with the Animal House subtest, which taps the ability to make associations of colors and animal names. Sam did the task slowly, naming colors as he worked, but he did not learn the code.

Children with neurological deviations presented the common characteristics of vulnerable children: problems in spatial orientation and temporal organization. However, in addition they showed deviations on one or more areas of the neurological examination. This examination included assessment of muscle tone, power, and synergy; gross and fine motor coordination; cranial nerve functioning; maintenance of posture and equilibrium; deep, superficial, and pathological reflexes. Rarely do the findings with children in this group point to focal brain damage and rarely can specific causal factors be found in their histories. Children with neurological deviations numbered 23 or 5% of the BD 1971 group. Of these 23 youngsters, 16 were boys and 7 were girls, a proportion significantly different from the relatively equal sex distribution in the total sample.

Even within this small subgroup, some variation is seen. On the basis of the neurological data, this group can be subdivided according to three clusters of symptoms: children with attention deficit disorders, children with problems in motor coordination, and children with deviations on the classical neurological examination.

Children with attention deficits presented a restless, driven quality in their behavior. Their quick, impulsive movements resulted in difficulties with many aspects of the examination, particularly because of the uneven nature of their responses. Yolanda is an example of this group:

On the psychological examination Yolanda earned scores in the low average to borderline ranges. However, because the scores for individual subtests of the WPPSI varied from a low of 4 to a high of 14, these scores could be regarded as minimal estimates of her potential. The psychologist commented that she was an extremely difficult child to test because of her poor attention and impulsive behavior. She had to be refocused many times so that she would attend to the task at hand. Enroute to the testing room, she had to be physically restrained from plunging down the stairs.

She said she occasionally brought herself to school, but the psychologist reported that her responses to the Comprehension subtest of the WPPSI did not reflect the type of judgment and impulse control that are necessary for such independence.

Children with motor problems contrasted with the children with attention deficit disorders in their response to the diagnostic examination. Joe is typical of the children in this subgroup:

Joe was described by the examiner as social and affectionate. He was verbally fluent, despite some oral inaccuracies persisting in his speech. Few positive findings appeared on the neurological examination, except for difficulties with fine motor coordination, adventitious movements, and convergence of the outstretch arms. He was not restless; indeed, he was somewhat hypoactive. Uncertain line quality and distortions of the drawing of the human figure and geometric designs reflected his difficulties in fine motor coordination. On the WPPSI Joe earned an average verbal score, while his performance scale score fell somewhat below average. Good reasoning abilities were seen in his superior scores on the Similarities subtest of the WPPSI, but there were gaps in his vocabulary. Joe worked very slowly on the Animal House subtest. He had difficulty keeping his place in the rows on the board and remembering to refer to the code sample in dealing with the test.

Children with findings on the classical neurological examination were characterized by their variability, both among children comprising the subgroup and in the day-to-day functioning within the individuals themselves. Because of this variation, children in the subgroup generally require provision for overlearning in any teaching plans, not only because of the wide range of symptoms, but also because of their predisposition to anxiety. Al is an example of this group:

For Al there were positive findings on the neurological examination of cranial nerves, reflexes, and cerebellar signs. Muscle tone was decreased and myoclonic activity was present. He had difficulty with patterned motor behavior and fine motor coordination. Signs of dysfunction of the autonomic nervous system were also present. Al related to the examiners in a shy and inhibited fashion. He seemed fussy, insecure, and easily overwhelmed. As his anxiety increased, he attempted to avoid difficulties by responding in a clowning, humorous manner. His scores on the WPPSI placed in the average range for the verbal scale and in the dull normal range for the performance scale. He earned superior scores with items tapping social awareness and vocabulary, but he had difficulty with rote memory items. The psychologist commented on his sluggish articulation and clumsiness with fine motor tasks. Al was strikingly aware of his problems and tended to respond defensively when he felt overwhelmed.

Children with general immaturity comprise a small part of the sample, less than 1%. They were children with nonspecific learning problems. Although there is no historical or clinical evidence of structural defect of the central nervous system, slowness was reported in reaching most developmental landmarks. This uniformly low curve of maturation was apparent in their physical appearance, as well. They tend to be small in size for their ages. In gross and fine motor development, in language, and in social awareness, they appear to be younger than their ages would suggest. Although these children function below average in psychological studies, no evidence of currently described syndromes of mental retardation was present. Nora is typical of this group:

> Nora was a small delicately built youngster who seemed younger than the other first graders. Although she was shy at first, this faded rapidly into candid expression of feelings. She discussed her concerns about her difficulties in learning to read. The neurological examination was within normal limits, with the exception of immaturity in left-right orientation, finger schema, and auditory memory. She earned a full scale score of 81 on the WPPSI, with the verbal score at 84 and the performance score at 82. Subtest scores were relatively even, ranging from 5 to 9. During the testing session Nora seemed at ease, initiating conversation with the examiner. Her response to difficult items was to withdraw, although she could be encouraged to try some items. She tended to respond in a global manner, in the manner of a younger child. Some verbal concepts were present, but she tended to be concrete in her approach to conceptual tasks.

Other children identified as vulnerable consisted of a group of 15 youngsters whose neurological examinations were found to be within normal limits. Of these, 6 children (5 boys and 1 girl) demonstrated on psychiatric examination the presence of emotional problems serious enough to impair learning. Some of these children were reacting to pathological conditions within the family and the resulting disruption in the home. Others presented severe neurotic and behavior problems reflected in every aspect of their lives, including school learning. This emotional subgroup accounted for less than 2% of the sample.

There were four children for whom diagnosis was deferred. Of these, two children were found to have mild hearing losses which needed evaluation and possible medical treatment. There were, in addition, two children who were newly arrived in the United States. Although they had adequate English to communicate during the assessments, it was felt that cultural differences prevented valid use of the diagnostic tests with them.

Finally there were five children who had been identified as vulnerable on scanning, but who proved on diagnosis to be normal learners. This represents a 1% rate of false positives on our predication measure. The rate of false negatives was found at the end-of-year achievement testing to be 8.5%.

Cross Validation of the Subgroups

After the foregoing subgroups had been identified through the sorting of multidisciplinary clinical data, the groupings were cross-validated by Stokes (1983) using multivariate statistical techniques. A separate sample of 141 cases was drawn from the same data pool from which the original clinical study had been drawn. Profiles of perceptual and cognitive functioning were analyzed using hierarchical, agglomerative average-linkage cluster analysis. The cluster analytic solution was checked by a k-means iterative partitioning procedure. Then multidimensional scaling procedures were used to confirm the adequacy of the cluster solution and to establish the number and consistency of dimensions necessary to conceptualize intersubject differences.

Cluster analysis identified seven statistically homogeneous subgroups: three specific language disability groups, a motor organic group, a group characterized by significant neurological impairment, a developmentally immature group, and a group characterized by family disorganization and personality disturbance. The subgroups thus identified show considerable similarity to the subgroups previously identified in clinical-inferential models. However, because this research approached the problem of classification through radically different techniques, it has provided quantitative verification of the subgroups that were identified through more subjective clinical procedures.

Implications for Education

The educational trajectory for each of the subgroups can be identified from our longitudinal studies of children with special learning problems. While each of the youngsters brings an individual pattern of strengths, needs, and resources for compensation, some common characteristics emerge as the subgroups move through the school years.

The specific language disabilities are often recognized early by their parents and nursery school teachers because of delays in language development. Even when they begin to talk within the usual time span, oral inaccuracies—"baby talk"—may persist in their speech. These language delays may contrast with their abilities in other areas. Mathematics is frequently a high point, and excellent nonverbal conceptual abilities may also be observed. Their social and emotional development will usually be unremarkable during the nursery years.

It is in elementary school that their difficulties begin to manifest themselves. Their associative learning problems interfere with the normal development of word attack skills in reading. Some immaturity in motor control will also be apparent in their pennmanship, particularly in relation to left-right orientation problems. Mathematics will continue to be a high point unless it is taught through a highly verbal approach. If the initial reading approach emphasizes visual memory for "sight words" they will have difficulty retaining the words from day to day. A phonic approach gives them better chances for success with beginning reading. Social and emotional development will be good provided these children succeed in school. If they begin to fail in school, reactive problems will appear; for, despite good nonverbal abilities, these youngsters frequently consider themselves to be less bright than their verbally fluent classmates.

Children with specific language disabilities carry these feelings of self-devaluation on into adolescence and adulthood. It is very important for people concerned with them—teachers, counselors, parents—to deal with these secondary effects of the learning problems. This may mean giving emphasis to compensatory activities and special abilities in nonverbal areas. For example, many of these youngsters have unusually good abilities in mathematics, art and graphics, computer programming, or athletics. Opportunities in these areas should be exploited to the fullest, in order that the youngsters do not lose faith in their ability to learn.

Development of skills in the language arts and reading should, with appropriate help in the earlier grades, now be at a "convalescent" stage. This means that the basic skills have generally been acquired, although they may not be automatic. Supportive help in such areas as planning compositions and research papers, note taking, and handling longer reading assignments is often helpful. Some high school and college students make use of the *Talking Books* tapes for the blind and physically handicapped in order to lighten the burden of extended reading assignments.

Youngsters with specific language disabilities usually do well in mathematics. However, the verbal components of algebra and geometry may give them trouble, so that they may require supportive help in those areas. In contrast, they are enchanted by computers and may in high school be found to spend a good deal of time in the Computer Lab.

Their motor control matures at about the age of nine or ten years. It sometimes finds expression in art, graphics, and design. Their conceptual abilities may also accelerate if they are well taught at school.

Their ideas will more often find expression in the visual media or in three-dimensional structures.

As adolescents their social judgment is usually good, although feelings of depression may trouble them because of their tendency toward self-devaluation. These feelings can be understood when one considers that these youngsters often must work very hard to achieve results at school, yet they see others who seem to handle the same academic tasks easily. This tendency toward depression calls into play two common defenses: withdrawal and overassertiveness. Some youngsters withdraw from competition, choosing not to invest efforts in tasks that they might not succeed with. The adults around them must learn how to encourage them without overwhelming them with praise that they might regard as insincere. The overassertiveness can best be handled by counseling directed toward better understanding of self and of the nature of specific language disability.

As adults these people are seldom eager readers. They continue to demonstrate good social judgement, although emotionally they continue to experience feelings of depression and sensitivity to what they perceive as criticisms reflecting on their intellectual abilities. They seek work usually in nonlanguage fields with their occupational choices often in the fields of art and design, art history, architecture, engineering, mathematics and finance, and business management.

Youngsters with attentional problems during preschool years may seem limited in cognitive abilities. They do not learn from experiences because their contact with the world around them is often fleeting and superficial. Their approach to motor tasks is hasty and primitive. Their poor organizational abilities produce lags in concept development. Their driven, self-centered quality makes socialization difficult. For all of these reasons, early cognitive assessments should be regarded as minimal estimates and should be rechecked as intervention plans are implemented.

During the elementary years, the schoolwork of these children is uneven. Teachers despairingly describe them as having "a short attention span" as if it were a concrete physical characteristic. Actually, they often can pay attention for extended periods of time to activities that they find interesting. Their motor control continues to develop slowly, so that their handwriting is frequently illegible. Their impulsivity produces lags in concept development and sometimes behavior problems as well. Their social contact is often poor and they tend to see themselves as isolated and misunderstood.

At high school age, these youngsters are usually less restless than during their early years, but stress may produce regression in this area of control. Some gaps in background skills will persist. When remediation is offered for these lags in secondary school, it may be rejected by the youngster who will cite some of the high points in his skills as indications that help is no longer needed. What *is* needed frequently is the integration of skills so that they can be applied to effective completion of school assignments. This kind of help in planning and organizing work is often more effective than continued emphasis on individual skill areas in reading the language arts for this group of youngsters. Motor control usually continues to be a problem area and the youngster is often impatient with the attempts adults make to offer assistance. Interpersonal problems may continue, because these youngsters may have difficulty in understanding cues in the behavior of others.

Children with motor problems also show slow language development at nursery school age, but it is usually in the form of motor inaccuracies in their speech rather than in semantic or syntactical deficiencies. These inaccuracies often disappear with maturation; otherwise, speech correction will be an effective intervention with them. They have difficulty with fine motor tasks, even with such things as matching finger to object when they are learning to count. At school they avoid drawing and painting activities. When they are asked to draw, they will produce weak, uncontrolled lines and scribbles like those of younger children.

In elementary school their language will accelerate and they often learn to read easily. Their concept development will be good and their participation in class discussions will be active. Written work will be difficult for them. They write illegibly, inconveniently, and as infrequently as possible. People often suggest that they learn to type. This is a premature suggestion that, if implemented, usually results in even more frustration because they have just as much difficulty with the fine motor control that typing requires. They are often popular, socially-aware youngsters who learn early to use clowning and humor to avoid difficult tasks. Adults need to protect them from taking on the role of class clown.

At high school age the youngsters with motor problems may acquire an unfortunate reputation among their teachers because of their failure to complete written work. They will be seen as bluffers who avoid getting down to the task at hand by talking. Because of their good reading, they will not be regarded as having learning problems. Their poor grades will be dismissed as the results of laziness and procrastination. They do badly on tests that require essay type answers because of organization and handwriting problems. Their notebooks are usually disorganized, messy, and nearly empty because they can't write well enough to take notes in class. At this age, their social adjustment will be endangered by their lack of success at school. They may begin to choose friends among the students who are not motivated to achieve at school. Gradually they drift from nonattendance to truancy to dropping out of school or college.

As adults, because of the limitations imposed by their limited education, these people are often employed below their intellectual level. They become fritterers, talkers who do not produce results with the projects they attempt. Their work is disorganized often because they can't write easily enough or fast enough to set up a work structure. Although their ingratiating manner and the early-learned interpersonal skills continue, their personal adjustment as adults may be marginal.

Children with findings on the classical neurological examination present a varied picture when considered from a longitudinal viewpoint. As young children their language development may be delayed or accelerated. They may be hyper- or hypoactive. All of these characteristics depend upon the individual pattern of strengths and deficits that may be elicited on neurological examination. As a group, however, they should be regarded as vulnerable to stress that is either physiological or psychological. Parents describe the extreme physical responses to common childhood illnesses which appear to result from the biological sensitivities associated with central nervous system dysfunctions. Their psychological status will also reflect these problems, but parental support and understanding are particularly important in helping these children to compensate for biological insults.

It is not easy to generalize about their work in elementary school, because this depends upon their strengths, needs and resources for compensation. Their progress may be uneven, with skills learned but not easily integrated into the behavioral repertoire. Problems in perception persist and will not disappear spontaneously. Work is done rapidly and erratically. Reading comprehension may be impaired by the lack of systematic encoding and decoding skills. Organization of all aspects of their lives is difficult. Teachers complain of their messy desks; mothers complain of their sloppy bedrooms.

Socialization may be difficult for these youngsters because they are often so caught up in their own concerns that they do not learn to "read" behavior cues in others. They may also be emotionally labile, given to mood swings and impulsive or explosive behavior.

At high school age, these characteristics continue. They learn best when there are opportunities for overlearning and structure available to them. Some of the characteristics of the youngsters with motor problems will appear here also. Conceptual difficulties may be apparent when highly abstract content is encountered in their studies at the secondary school level. Continued support with both academic assistance and counseling is important if these youngsters are to realize their potential. Continuing assessment of strengths and deficits is also important in delineating areas of strength and special skills that will serve to motivate further schooling and to provide appropriate vocational goals.

Children with general immaturity will be recognized in preschool years by their generally slow rate of development in all parameters. At elementary school age they will also be regarded as immature when compared with their classmates. Their patterns of growth do not synchronize with the expectancies on which the regular school curricula are based. Some adjustment in the rate of progression through school is needed. Often this takes the form of repetition of grades, although alternative class grouping such as multiple-grade organizational patterns would be a more enlightened way to handle this need.

These children are not mentally retarded, although this question may come up in school settings in which a rigid grade achievement requirement prevails. Placing these children in classes for retarded children represents a tragic misclassification because it may prevent these youngsters from learning what they are able to learn. They need, instead, the models of the children in regular classroom settings, the language stimulation provided in contacts with other children, and most important of all, the expectation of relatively normal functioning in adulthood.

Summary

Clinical study, statistical analysis, and longitudinal follow-up have identified within the broad, heterogeneous group of children with special learning problems specific subgroups that are more homogeneous in clinical characteristics and educational needs. However, all of these children can best be understood within a personal context, for outcomes depend not only upon the nature of the original problem, but also on individual capacities for change and the compensatory resources available to them.

References

Benton, A.L., & Pearl, D. (Eds.) (1978). *Dyslexia: An appraisal of current knowledge.* New York: Oxford University Press.

Boder, E. (1973). Developmental dyslexia: A diagnostic approach based on three atypical reading-spelling patterns. *Developmental Medicine and Child Neurology, 15,* 663–687.

Critchley, M. (1964). *Developmental dyslexia.* London: William Heinemann.

Doehring, D.G., & Hoshko, I.M. (1977). Classification of reading problems by Q technique of factor analysis. *Cortex, 13,* 281–94.

Gaddes, W.H. (1980). *Learning disabilities and brain function: A neuropsychological approach.* New York: Springer Verlag.

Hagin, R.A., Silver, A.A., & Corwin, C.G. (1972). Clinical diagnostic use of the WPPSI in predicting learning disabilities in grade one. *Journal of Special Education, 5,* 221–232.

Hinshelwood, J. (1917). *Congenital word-blindness.* London: H.K. Lewis.

Johnson, D.J., & Myklebust, H.B. (1967). *Learning disabilities*. New York: Grune & Stratton.

Lyon, G.R., Stewart N., & Freedman, D. (1982). Neuropsychological characteristics of empirically derived subgroups of learning-disabled readers. *Journal of Clinical Neuropsychology, 4*, 343–365.

Mattis, S., French, J.H., & Rapin, I. (1975). Dyslexia in children and young adults: Three independent neuropsychological syndromes. *Developmental Medicine and Child Neurology, 17*, 150–163.

Money, J. (Ed.) (1962). *Reading disability: Progress and research needs in dyslexia*. Baltimore: Johns Hopkins University Press.

Monroe, M. (1932). *Children who cannot read*. Chicago: University of Chicago Press.

Morgan, W.P., (1896). A case of congenital word-blindness. *British Medical Journal, 2*, 1378.

Robinson, H.M. (1946). *Why pupils fail in reading*. Chicago: University of Chicago Press.

Rourke, B.P., & Finlayson, M.A.J. (1978). Neuropsychological significance of variations in patterns of academic performance. *Journal of Abnormal Child Psychology, 6*, 121–33.

Rourke, B.P., & Strang, J.D. (1983). Subtypes of reading and arithmetic disabilities: A neuropsychological analysis. In M. Rutter (Ed.), *Developmental neuropsychiatry*. New York: Guilford.

Silver, A.A., & Hagin, R.A. (1964). Specific reading disability: Follow-up studies. *American Journal of Orthopsychiatry, 34*, 95–102.

Silver, A.A., & Hagin, R.A. (1972). Profile of a first grade: A basis for preventive psychiatry. *Journal of the Academy of Child Psychiatry. 11*, 645–674.

Silver, A.A., & Hagin, R.A. (1976). *Search: A scanning instrument for the identification of potential learning disability*. New York: Walker Educational Book Corportation.

Stokes, J. (1983). Children vulnerable to learning failure: Identification and description of identifiable subtypes. *Unpublished doctoral dissertation*, Graduate School of Education, Fordham University, New York.

Chapter 10
The ESL Reading Class: Reality Or Unreality

Carlos A. Yorio

Lehman College/Graduate Center
City University of New York

The purpose of this paper is twofold: first, to draw teachers' attention to the kinds of reading activities that take place in many ESL classrooms from kindergarten through university, and to compare these classroom activities with real-life situations in which people are reading for various purposes or reasons. These comparisons will show that in most cases the degree of "unreality" of the ESL reading classes is striking and worthy of further analysis. The second purpose is to show specific ways in which the ESL reading class can be brought closer to reality, an endeavor which, I will argue, is essential for the development of ESL literacy for academic as well as life purposes.

The following observations are the result of actual classroom visits that I made. It has become clear to me, and to other people engaged in classroom-centered research, that in order to understand what we actually do in the classroom, we must observe it and describe it in detail (Seliger & Long, 1983).

As Clarke (1984) puts it "If we are able to understand how learning takes place in classrooms, we have to eschew formulaic prescription, generic description, abstract references. We have to look at the minute-by-minute interaction of people in real, or at least believable classes. We have to adjust the frame of our vision so that we can examine a specific activity *as it is occurring*" (p. 583).

Because of the limitations imposed by the length of the chapter however, the amount of detail has been kept to a minimum. It is hoped that teachers will recognize the techniques and will appreciate the value of looking at classroom activities—their own and those of colleagues—from the outside, as an objective observer or a researcher would do.

The first class that we visit is in an elementary school; it is a first grade class. We see a teacher, or maybe a teacher-helper, sitting at a table next to a youngster. The teacher is reading a story from a book at which they are both looking. The teacher reads slowly, deliberately, and often points at the pictures; occasionally, she even points at the pictures and uses a Spanish word or two: "The cat jumps," "el gato da un salto." This goes on for some time, while other children are engaged in various other activities. It is clear that the child is both interested and amused and that he enjoys the company of the teacher.

The second class that we stop at is a fourth-grade class, but there are some older children too. This is a withdrawal class, where children from several classes meet with an ESL teacher for a couple of hours daily. In this class, the teacher is also reading out loud, but in this case, the children have the book in front of them and are following along. The teacher stops often and offers paraphrases or comments on what is being read. Sometimes, she asks students to repeat what she has read. Often students repeat without being asked; some even read along with her, more or less loudly. This activity is informal and the conversations or dialogues between the teacher and the students by and large deal with the content of the story and a commentary on the action, although every so often the teacher will remind students of words "they had seen before." The atmosphere in this class is relaxed. Although it appears as if all the children were engaged in one single activity, they are actually doing different things: reading aloud, reading silently, listening to a story, interacting with the teacher, and so on.

Our next class is in a secondary school. There is a box in one corner of the room. Students go to that box, select a colored card, and come back to their desks; they read for a while and then answer questions in a book. Then they go back to the box again, return the card they just read, and pick another card; then the process starts all over again. The teacher moves from desk to desk, observing, answering questions, giving brief explanations to individual students. We also notice that some students often refer to a dictionary which they have on their desks. Some of them, in fact, do this quite frequently. The mood in this class is very different from what we observed in the first two classes. These students appear to be "working," they are "busy," and there are no overt signs of joy or amusement.

The fourth class in an adult evening class, part of the continuing education program in a community college. Students had been asked to read a certain story from the book at home in order to discuss it in class. It is painfully obvious, however, that half of the class has not touched the book. Some students are looking at the story now, while the others are talking, in a vain attempt at finding out what the story is about. Finally, students end up reading out loud from the story and the teacher ends up correcting their pronunciation. Needless to say, this class is a bit of a failure; what is taking place in the class is not what the teacher had planned. Student reactions vary: some are participating eagerly, in fact, they are monopolizing the conversation; others appear very uninterested or maybe just tired—they seldom, if ever, contribute to the discussion.

Our next stop is at a university, at an intensive English language program. In this case, students appear to be having a great time. The classroom does not look like a class; in fact, there is a sign on the door that says: "Resource Centre/Activity Room". Two or three students are reading today's newspapers, other are reading magazines—*Sports Illustrated, Vogue, Newsweek, People*. The teacher is also reading a newspaper. Other students are writing letters, or playing Scrabble. After a while, about twenty minutes, the teacher moves around and asks the students "What are you reading?" She also makes comments about the topic and occasionally answers questions about words students do not know. The hour passes quickly and some students continue reading their magazines or playing Scrabble during recess.

In our last visit, we stop at a university class. Students are reading a science paragraph, a rather lengthy paragraph. When they finish, they have to do a number of exercises: choose one out of four statements which best expresses the overall meaning of the paragraph, infer the meaning of certain words from the context, answer certain questions about the content of the paragraph, and so on. These students are also "busy," but they do not seem to be bored or uninterested—the atmosphere is one of constant questioning, trying to understand, demanding explanations, clarifying doubts. It is clear that these students are "highly motivated" or at least show signs of interest, involvement, and commitment to their own learning.

These six classes are more or less typical. The activities that have been described are not unusual. They are not, obviously the only activities that students perform in an ESL reading class, nor do they constitute the only techniques that teachers use to teach reading. But I am certain that all of us find something familiar in some or all of these classes.

Let us now leave the world of the ESL classroom and venture into the *real* world of reading. Our first trip takes us to the New York City subway system. It is 8:30 in the morning. The subway car is jammed, it is noisy and not particularly well-lighted. From our vantage point, we see at least five people reading: three are reading newspapers, one is reading a magazine, and one is reading a long novel—*Shōgun*. The newspapers have been expertly folded into a size that makes good manipulation in a crowded subway car easy or at least possible. They are all deeply concentrating on their reading, undisturbed by the people around them, the noise, the poor lighting, and the swaying train.

Our second visit is to a city park; it is sunny and warm; it is the lunch hour and dozens of office workers are eating their lunch in the open

air—they are also reading. And what are they reading? Again, newspapers, magazines, and novels. If we look more closely we see that they
are reading Harlequin Romances, detective stories, and science fiction.
Now let us visit a home. It is 7:30 p.m. The 5-year-old girl has been
fed and bathed; she is now tucked in bed ready for the story that she
has already chosen from among her books. Her father sits on the bed
and starts reading. Every so often he distractedly skips a line, but she
corrects him—she knows the story by heart. Finally, she falls asleep, well
before the end of the story. The familiar ritual is over.

It is now two hours later, and the little girl's parents are relaxing in
the living room. The man is sitting in a comfortable armchair, with his
feet up. In one hand, he is holding a beer; in the other a book: *How to
Beat the Internal Revenue Service.* Every so often, he says: "Ah, listen to
this!", and reads out loud to his wife about a possible tax loophole he
had not been aware of before. The wife is also reading. Her book is
called *Automobile Repairs Made Easy.* In fact, that is the textbook for a
Continuing Education course she is taking. Every now and then, she
interrupts her husband with questions about sections she doesn't understand—he seldom knows the answers either. This couple is reading
and constantly sharing what they are reading. .

Our last visit is to a college library reading room. Students are sitting
around large tables studying and reading. Some are by themselves, others are in pairs or in small groups. We can hear hushed conversations
all over; sometimes they talk about what they are reading but most often
they're just talking—taking brief breaks. Many have taken their shoes
off, some are eating candy bars or sunflower seeds. They often get up
and go out for a cigarette, or to the rest rooms and then return to resume
their reading.

Once again, these scenes are not unique; they are examples of people
reading in real life. We could think of many other examples but these
will suffice to make the point. This point is that little, and in some cases
nothing, of what was going on in reading classes that we visited earlier
is found in real life. The settings are different, the circumstances are
different, the activities themselves are different and the materials being
read are also different. The only classes where there appeared to be
some evidence of realism were the elementary school class where the
teacher was reading a story to a child, and the university class in the
intensive program where the students were reading newspapers and
magazines in the Activity Room.

Every other class was "unreal," in the sense that what teachers and
students were doing bore little resemblance to what the same people
might be doing if they were reading outside of the classroom, performing
the reading activities that literate humans usually perform.

The questions that we must raise and try to answer is whether this discrepancy between the classroom and real life is good, bad, or indifferent. To what extent must the language class in general (and the reading class in particular) be like real life? Is it better to perform activities that are "real," in the language class? Or is it better to prepare learners in a slower-paced fashion, step by step, even if these steps, or typical classroom activities, bear little or no resemblance to real life activities? Is this lack of resemblance between classroom and real life serious or is it superficial? Is the apparent unreality of the reading class truly unreal?

By and large, schools are institutions designed to give people skills, knowledge, and theories which are to be tested and/or put to use outside of the institution, in real life. Some skills, like reading effectively in English, also serve a much more urgent need. They need to be mastered for school success *first*. In addition, students must be prepared for the time when they leave our institutions. As teachers, then, we have a double task: an immediate, academic one; and a long-range, life-oriented one.

If we are to do this, it is essential that we make school tasks real or at least realistic. The *unreality* of schools is an issue that has often been discussed by educators. Furthermore, we must see our task as continuing after our students have left our classrooms—that should be the ultimate test of our success or failure. As Britton (1970; p. 129) puts it: "It is not only that the classroom must more and more merge into the world outside it, but that the processes of school learning must merge into the processes of learning that begin at birth and are lifelong. We can no longer regard school learning as simply an interim phase, a period of instruction and apprenticeship that works the change from immaturity to maturity, from play in the nursery to work in the world. School learning must both build upon the learning of infancy and foster something that will continue and evolve throughout life."

Shirley Brice Heath (1983) claims that schools often make children forget the habits they bring to their first grade classroom—habits where life and learning are one. Britton (1970, p. 128) describes this situation as follows: "The idea that learning is something you do sitting in a seat is a highly sophisticated notion, and to a young child, a very peculiar one."

Our failure to see the discrepancy between classrooms and real life that we ourselves have created has produced widespread lack of faith in schools and complaints of irrelevance of education for the real world.

If we accept the notion that our ESL reading classes will have to become more realistic and relevant, we must first try to understand what it is that we mean when we say "reading is real life." In order to gain some perspective on real-life reading activities, a distinction must be made between: reading as a *public activity*, reading as a *private activity*, and reading as a *shared activity*.

Reading as a public activity is the least common kind of reading. Delivering a lecture from notes is public reading. News broadcasters, for example, are also public readers. They are neither reading to or for themselves, nor is there any reaction expected from the audience—it is clearly neither a private nor a shared activity. Public reading is even less common than public speaking, since we are often called upon to make oral presentations, arguments, or reports, or simply express our personal opinions. But how often do most of us have to read aloud in this public fashion?

The most common kind of reading is usually private. In the vast majority of cases, when we read, we read silently, for ourselves and by ourselves. Even when we are not by ourselves (in the train, in the library) we try to isolate ourselves by concentrating, by keeping everything and everyone outside. In private reading, the reader always has a specific personal or private reason or purpose for reading, it is done either for information or for pleasure. The same is not true in public reading where readers almost always know what they are reading and in many cases might have written the message themselves. Private reading is what we in language teaching have traditionally called *extensive reading*; that is, reading which is not directly associated with language study, but rather reading for information or for pleasure, reading done primarily outside of the classroom.

The third kind of reading activity is less common than private reading but not as esoteric as public reading—I call it shared reading. In this case, the reader or readers are interacting with each other or with people around them. There is constant or frequent information exchange or commentary on the part of the people involved. They may be reading the same material (as in the case of two people studying together) or they may be reading different materials (as in the case of people sharing information from different parts of the newspaper they are all reading at the breakfast table, or the case of the couple we visited earlier).

Notice that what we do in our reading classes does not usually fit very comfortably into any of these categories, although there may be some elements of one, some, or all of them. Reading out loud, a very common classroom activity whether we want to admit it or not, is, in spirit, close to what we have defined as public reading—reading to an audience without interaction or reaction expected except maybe the correction of pronunciation. We have also said that public reading is extremely rare—a skill that will seldom be called into play in real life.

Most other classroom activities that I can think of are neither private nor shared. Most of what we do appears to fall into some totally different category which I will call reading as a *training activity*. These training activities can be of two kinds: those that give students practice for the development of skills and strategies—*practice activities*—and those that test students to see whether those skills and strategies have been learned or whether the content of the material has been comprehended—*testing activities*.

In reality, testing activities—particularly those which test comprehension of content—are used much more widely than we might think. Many techniques that we do not normally associate with "testing" are precisely that. A typical example in reading are the traditional "comprehension questions" which, in fact, have little to do with the teaching of reading skills. This emphasis on testing activities is unfortunate. I am convinced that students would learn more if we practiced more and tested less.

Many of these common classroom activities, by the way—activities which seem to have been criticized above—do have redeeming qualities, but we must understand what the shortcomings of these activities are. Traditional comprehension questions and reading aloud are acceptable activities, if we understand that they are primarily *testing activities* (for content and pronunciation, respectively) rather than activities that will make a major contribution toward developing our students' actual reading skills. Another point that we must remember, as teachers, is that using a written text to teach language does not necessarily, in fact, seldom has anything to do with the teaching of reading skills. The history of language teaching (first and second) is full of examples of methods and techniques where reading as a part of language development is not taught or developed at all. There is reading going on, but it is incidental, secondary to the primary purpose which is the teaching of language, or more precisely, the dissemination of information about the language. In fact, this is what *intensive reading* is—the study of grammar and vocabulary through reading or more exactly, through written texts.

Let us go back for a brief recapitulation of the different kinds of reading activities:

1. Reading as a public activity
2. Reading as a private activity
3. Reading as a shared activity
4. Reading as a training activity

This last category includes all those educational activities which are designed to develop the linguistic and psycholinguistic skills necessary to read effectively. Of necessity, this category will include practice activities and testing activities. The testing activities will determine whether or not the skills taught are being learned and whether or not the written messages are being comprehended. It is essential, however, that teachers distinguish clearly between practice and testing activities—this hasn't always been done and has been detrimental to the effective teaching of reading.

Having made these distinctions, let us go back to our original question and answer it. How "realistic" does the classroom have to be? How much of the reading activities 1, 2, and 3, do we want in reading activity 4? And how do we do it?

In my view a second language reading class must, of necessity, contain training activities—this is what a reading class is! These educational activities, however, should, as much as possible, contain elements that bring the class closer to the ultimate tasks that are the objectives of instruction—reading in real life. In other words, private and shared reading activities, the two most common kinds, should be part of the reading class. Educational activity should be seen as a bridge to future use in real life. In a plenary address delivered at the 1984 TESOL conference in Houston, S. Brice Heath (1984) made a distinction between *literacy* skills and *literate* skills. She claimed that, contrary to what we often hear, our schools have not failed in developing literacy skills in the students they have trained—by and large, more or less well, students *can* read. Schools may have failed, however, to make students literate—they have not made them habitual readers, they have not taught them to enjoy the pleasures and to reap the more pragmatic benefits of a literate society. This gap must be closed.

Reading as a language skill presupposes two things: knowledge of the code and knowledge of literacy skills. In other words, for a person to be able to read effectively, he or she must know the language and must also be literate. Illiterates may know the language, but they lack reading skills. Conversely, one can know how to read and lack knowledge of the code. I am literate but I can't read *War and Peace* in the original because I don't know any Russian.

In a second language class, since both the code and the skills are being taught, the teaching and the learning tasks are extremely complicated. In a first language reading class, reading difficulties can be largely attributed to skill problems. In a second language class, reading problems can arise from insufficient (or insecure) knowledge of the language or from poor reading skills, or from a combination of both (Yorio, 1971).

If students are illiterate in their native language, the problems the teacher faces are obviously of two kinds: the code (the English *language* has to be taught) and decoding skills (literacy) have to be developed. This is why teaching someone to read in a second language is an enormous task; it is the reason that students often have problems—problems to which we must be both sensitive and sensible. We must move the second language classes closer to reality but we must never forget that they are still reading *classes* and that what our students are trying to learn is complex and difficult. By bringing realism to the ESL classes we will accomplish two things: we will enable students to learn ideas they will find useful after leaving our classes and we will make those classes more interesting and fun.

Now, how do we bring our reading classes closer to reality? Let us start by establishing in what specific ways the two sets of activities we described at the beginning of the chapter were actually different. We could classify these differences in four categories; the physical setting, the circumstances, the reading material, and the purpose.

Let us begin by discussing the last category—the purpose. Why do people read? The following is a list of the main purposes:

1. To obtain knowledge of content (textbooks, professional journals, and so on).
2. To understand instruction (recipes, rules of the game, manuals).
3. To understand correspondence (personal and business).
4. To keep in touch with the world (newspapers).
5. To obtain useful information about our immediate world (schedules, menus, programs).
6. To seek enjoyment (novels poems, stories) (Adapted from Rivers and Temperley, 1978, p. 187).

In a second language class, students do not seem to read for any of these purposes. Rather, it seems that they read for the following purposes:

1. To learn the language (reading is incidental).
2. To learn *how* to read.
3. To please the teacher who asks them to read.

Category 3, to please the teacher who asks them to read, is a reason rather than a purpose; it shows a lack of purpose, in fact. Purposes 1 and 2 are valid, but if we compare them to the purposes of reading in real life, there is an obvious mismatch. No one reads in real life in order to become a better reader—that happens only in school.

The ideal would be to integrate real life motivations with classroom motivations. They are not, after all, incompatible. Our students read for those very same purposes in their native language, and it is for those purposes (or at least some of them) that they want to learn how to read in English. This integration of motivations should be possible if we select carefully what we are reading in the second language class, or better yet, if we allow our students a certain amount of choice in selecting what they read.

This bring us to the second area of difference that we noticed: reading materials. It is in this particular area where significant changes are needed and where it is actually not too difficult to make changes. If we look at reading textbooks or reading passages in language books—particularly for secondary schools and adults—we find that, in general, they fall into two types: prose passages and dialogues. The prose passages vary in length, depending on the specific book or the specific task; they usually range between 100 words and 2,000 words. Although we may find different kinds of rhetorical organization in these passages, they are usually very simple narratives, or rather straightforward descriptions or arguments. The most serious problem with most of these is that everything has been simplified; not only the structures of the language (syntax and vocabulary), but also style and tone. These passages tend to be plain, simplistic and on the whole, boring.

The other kind of reading selection that we find are dialogues. These also vary in length from a few lines to a page. In general, they are stilted and rather formal; quite often, structural and vocabulary simplification or restrictions make these dialogues forced and unnatural.

And then there is the content: what are these passages or dialogues about? Again the range is broad: from descriptions of the small actions people perform every day (in low or medium level proficiency materials) to simplistic arguments about the morality (or lack of it) of the death penalty, pollution, euthanasia, and women's liberation (in materials for the more advanced and mature classes).

In principle, there is nothing wrong with these topics; they cover areas of vocabulary that students must become familiar with or they are issues that adults are supposed to be interested in discussing. The problem lies in the fact that these topics, as they are dealt with in class, don't have any immediacy, relevance, or reality for these students.

In real life we discuss these issues and any other issue when there is a reason for it. We saw a program on TV or an article in the newspaper, or something happened to us or to a friend. Then, and only then, the topic becomes relevant. In a second language class, topics are discussed because they are there, because it is the chapter that follows the previous chapter! Today we talk about the death penalty, tomorrow we talk about violence on television. In real life, we do not choose conversations or reading topics like this. There has to be a spark of personal or immediate interest. We are not all interested in the same issues, and if we are, we are not interested in them at the same time. *The point is that we must find ways to bring immediacy and relevance to the reading class.* P. Freire's whole philosophy for the development of literacy is based on this principle (Freire, 1970a, 1970b).

Depending on the age and proficiency level of our students, an effort must be made to deal with issues that are of interest to them. In an intensive English class, or in a secondary school class, for example, the first half-hour or 45 minutes of the day should be spent reading the newspaper. In such a class, students will read what interests them, and will share, and make comments, and ask questions when they do not understand. This will be a true communicative reading class. Teachers will be amazed at the number and range of topics that come up for discussion—not because they come next in the syllabus, but because they have become relevant and of real interest.

In what other ways can we make reading material more real in the second language classroom? Detective stories and science fiction constitute the largest part of the literary mass market. Close behind are "romances." Although for some people these genres are the object of serious study, for most of us they are escapist entertainment. Some of them are trash and some are superb—but that is not the point. The point is that when people want to read for entertainment, on the whole, they choose books of this nature. Not everybody, of course, reads these books. Some people do not read fiction at all; they prefer nonfiction—biographies, nature stories, books about seashells, or bird and bees. In every reading class, from elementary school through university, one of the projects of every course should be for the student to read any book of his or her choice in this "entertainment" category.

In a survey that I did at the University of Toronto, I asked students in an intensive language program if they thought that reading outside of class was important. Of the 711 students surveyed, 618 (87%) said that it was very important, 75 (10.5%) said that it was important but not essential, and only 11 of the 711 said that it was unimportant. It seems to me that these students would be very willing to undertake an enjoyable extensive reading task (Yorio, 1984).

As evaluation, if evaluation is needed, students can be required to write a short report, or present an oral report to the teacher about the book—not about the content necessarily (and this is important!) but rather about the kinds of issues that we talk about in real life when we talk about books: Did you like it or not? Why or why not? Do you recommend it? How does it compare with other books of its kind that you have read? Would you read another book of this kind, on this topic, by this author? Was it easy or difficult? These projects do not always have to be individualized. If you ask your students at the beginning of the course what they enjoy reading, or ask them to rank certain choices, you will find that many of them like the same things. This is neither surprising nor unexpected. You can then have small groups of students reading the same book. Final reports, or better yet, discussions can be held in small groups rather than individually. The idea of having ex-

tensive reading projects where students choose what they read is a technique that could be exploited much more extensively in our language
programs—it is learner-centered and it is real.

This technique of allowing students to choose what they read can also
be used as a springboard in the teaching of other skills—reading selections made by the students themselves can provide the content, the input
for oral presentations or reports, or for writing assignments. There is
no reason why we should all write about the same topic. These practices
are already in effect in many ESP (English for Special Purposes) classes
where people work with material that is of particular relevance or interest
to them. This is reality too.

In junior high and high school, the ESL teacher should use the manuals or textbooks that student need to read and understand for their
content courses—math, social sciences, biology, and the like. In order
to coordinate this enterprise, the ESL teachers will have to work closely
with regular classroom teachers. Again, such practices are occurring in
many schools. The more integration between language and curriculum
content, the more real those classes will be.

What else can we do to bring reality to the reading class in terms of
materials? It is clear that at certain proficiency levels and in certain
classes, some control is going to have to be exercised in order to develop
certain skills. If we want to teach our students to skim or scan, we are
going to have to use materials which are appropriate for doing this; this
is part of the *classroom reality*. We can, however, make these activities
more "realistic" if we select passages or dialogues or nonprose material
(maps, graphics, diagrams, as examples) which are, at least, well-written;
at best, we should find material that has style, that is original; material
that has some aesthetic or literary merit. Material that is stylistically or
linguistically hybrid should be avoided. Textbook writers are becoming
more conscious about style and genre; thus, it is possible to find reading
materials that are well-written and natural—even for low proficiency
levels.

Another way of bringing reality to the "unreal" educational tasks of
the reading class is to attempt to make these tasks more communicative.
We achieve this communicativeness by using slight twists or variations
in the ways in which we have traditionally done these types of exercises.
Let me illustrate with examples from my own book *Who Done/Did It?*
(Yorio & Morse, 1981). After each story, comprehension questions are
presented. These comprehension questions have a hidden agenda: they
are disguised scanning or skimming exercises. The instructions on the
exercises read: "Are the following sentences true or false? Support your
answers with evidence from the text." These exercises are no longer
content tests, they are skill-practicing exercises. If, in addition, you allow

your students to work in groups and/or check their answers with each other, you have a great communicative reading/speaking exercise—this is what people who study together actually do. What had been a boring test has become much more like real life.

The whole idea of having people working in pairs or small groups while doing the more traditional reading exercises adds an invaluable communicative dimension which we have exploited recently in speaking/talking classes, but not so much in reading and listening classes. We should do more small group activity. This is reading as a shared activity.

In classes for children, teachers have been doing small group shared activities for a long time; children in North America will not have it otherwise. In choosing reading materials for children, we must not forget that they have individual preferences. They have certain story books which they favor and certain others which they do not. These likes and dislikes should be respected as much as possible. Children are wonderful at producing their own stories too and these should be used as a source of reading materials.

These practices need not be restricted to the elementary school. Students at every level, including adults, should be writing at least some of the material that they read. This is particularly relevant in literacy classes. It is one of the foundations on which Paulo Freire's approach to the development of literacy in adults rests. These materials that the students themselves produce can take many shapes, such as newspapers, collections of folk-tales from their native countries, or reports on field trips. All of these become common property, part of the class library—an example of community language learning.

The other dimensions along which reading in real life and reading in the classroom differed were the physical setting and circumstances. These are, of course, difficult to manipulate at school. Classrooms can be made physically more like home, but one can only go so far. Allowing students to drink or eat in class would probably create problems that are less desirable than a homey atmosphere. Group work and the integration of several skills within one lesson, however, can go a long way toward creating a more relaxed social and physical environment, and this we certainly can and should promote.

To summarize: reading classes are, and have traditionally been, devoted to training activities, both practicing and testing. Little or no effort has been spent in promoting other activities which are more real or realistic. This we must do, without ever losing sight of the fact that these activities must be subordinated to the needs of the student as a language learner.

Reality can be brought into the reading class in a variety of ways: by allowing students to choose at least some of the materials they read; by promoting extensive reading activities (outside the classroom) and by integrating them with classroom work; by choosing material that is relevant and of interest to the learner; by allowing students to write some of their own reading material; by integrating reading tasks with other skills—listening, writing and talking; by using communicative teaching techniques which will make language use in the classroom meaningful and functional, and by using material that is well-written and as authentic as the proficiency level of the learners will permit.

Language classrooms are not "real life," but if we are to prepare our students for the world out there, we must make an effort to bring at least some reality to what we do as teachers and to what they do as learners.

References

Britton, J. (1970). *Language and learning.* Baltimore: Penguin Books.

Clarke, M. (1984). On the nature of technique: What do we owe the gurus? *TESOL Quarterly, 18*(4), 577-594.

Freire, P. (1970a). *Pedagogy of the oppressed.* New York: Seabury Press.

Freire, P. (1970b). The adult literary process as cultural action for freedom. *Harvard Educational Review, 40*,(2), 363-381.

Heath, S.B. (1983). *Ways with words; Language, life and work in communities and classrooms.* New York: Cambridge University Press.

Heath, S.B. (1984). Literacy or literate skills: Consideration for ESL/EFL learners. Plenary Address, 18th Annual TESOL Convention, Houston, Texas.

Rivers, W., & Temperley, M. (1978). *A practical guide to the teaching of english as a second or foreign language.* New York: Oxford University Press.

Seliger, H., & Long, M. (Ed.). (1983). *Classroom oriented research in second language acquisition.* Rowley, MA: Newbury House Publishers.

Yorio, Carlos A. (1971). Some sources of reading problems in foreign language learners. *Language Learning, 21*,(1), 107-115.

Yorio, C.A. (in press). Consumerism in ESL teaching and learning. *Canadian Modern Language Review.*

Yorio, C.A., & Morse, L. (1981). *Who done/did it? A crime reader for students of english.* Englewood Cliffs, NJ: Prentice-Hall.

PART IV
THE ASSESSMENT OF READING IN CONTEXT

Chapter 11
Looking At Reading Instruction: Sociolinguistic And Ethnographic Approaches

David Bloome
University of Michigan

Judith Green
Ohio State University

In the last decade a new direction in research on reading instruction has emerged that brings new insights into the nature of instruction and student participation. Research within this direction explores instructional activities from sociolinguistic and ethnographic perspectives (Bloome & Green, 1984). Researchers within this direction study reading instruction as it occurs as part of everyday interactions between teachers and students. They focus on describing instruction from the perspective of participants in the instructional activity. By identifying patterns in the ways in which teachers and students interact with each other, researchers are able to explore instruction as it unfolds and researchers are able to identify factors that support and/or constrain participation and learning.

The accumulation of knowledge about reading instruction based on sociolinguistic and ethnographic approaches derives from a comparative perspective (cf. Glasser & Strauss, 1967; Hymes 1974, 1977). Knowledge gained in one situation is compared with knowledge about the nature of reading instruction in other analogous and nonanalogous situations. Through comparison with and across specific instances of reading instruction, knowledge about reading is accumulated. Researchers within this perspective are concerned with the identification of both situation specific aspects of reading instruction and generic factors that cross instructional activities.

Reading Instruction: The Emerging Picture

The picture of reading instruction that is emerging from sociolinguistic and ethnographic studies of reading differs from definitions of reading instruction obtained from other perspectives. Reading instruction, from sociolinguistic and ethnographic perspectives, is a process that involves both academic tasks and social, interpersonal contexts. That is, during reading, students need to display the acquisition of reading strategies while simultaneously displaying appropriate group behavior (e.g., turn-taking). In other words, the academic task is embedded in the social tasks involved in appropriately participating in a group activity.

At least three types of relationships between academic and social, interpersonal contexts of reading have been identified to date. First, the *academic task is defined through the social, interpersonal context.* In this instance the academic task (e.g., silent reading, vocabulary development, story discussion) is produced during interactions among teacher, students, and texts; academic tasks are not the preset or explicitly stated tasks provided in curriculum guides, teacher guides, or lesson plans. One way to think about preset tasks in lesson plans and guides is as espoused or intended tasks. What actually constitutes the academic task depends on how it is delivered during the social and communicative interactions of teachers and students. The academic task is the *delivered* task. That is, the ways in which the task is delivered (e.g., what is done, to whom, for what purpose, in what ways) defines what is actually required of students. From this perspective, academic tasks are products of the social, inter-personal context of reading instruction (e.g., Bloome, in press; Cochran-Smith, 1984; Collins, 1981; Heap, 1984). For example, recent work has shown that two teachers may have the same materials, similar groups of students, similar training, and the same stated task (reading and dis-cussing a story) and not produce the same academic task. Differences in delivered task result from the ways in which the teacher distributes turns, the types of questions asked, the point at which questions are asked, the types of information to be discussed, the ways in which stu-dents respond, and so forth (Golden, in press; Green, in press; Harker, in press).

Second, *how students are evaluated on academic tasks is influenced by the social, interpersonal context.* The evaluation of academic tasks within and across classrooms and schools is, at least in part, based on social, inter-personal criteria. For example, the match or mismatch between teacher and student's interactional style has found to be related to teacher per-ception of student ability (e.g., Collins, 1981; DeStefano, Pepinsky & Sanders, 1982; Gilmore, in press; Scollon & Scollon, 1984). Collins (1981) found that reading ability was evaluated on students' narrative style and use of prosody. Students whose narrative style and use of prosody matched the teacher's implicit model of what reading "should sound like" were evaluated as more competent readers.

Third, the *academic task influences the nature of the social, interpersonal context.* The nature of a given task may require reformulating, either explicitly or implicitly, the nature of the social context. For example, a recitation task permits different types of interaction patterns from that of a task given to small group to complete. Bossert (1979) has shown that the type of task influences factors such as social relationships among peers and competition among students.

The different relationships presented above suggest that the social interpersonal context influences and may transform academic tasks, and academic tasks influence and may transform the social, interpersonal context. The purpose of this chapter is to examine issues involved in capturing simultaneously the academic and social, interpersonal context of reading instruction. The discussion will focus on studies and approaches found in recent work in sociolinguistic and ethnographic studies of classrooms. However, before turning to a discussion of approaches one last issue needs to be considered—the relationship between knowledge of process and approach.

The issues involved in simultaneously capturing the academic and social interpersonal dimensions of reading instruction derive, in part, from knowledge about the nature of reading instruction. Hence, how one looks at reading instruction is also informed by what is already known about the nature of reading instruction. However, how one looks at reading instruction is also informed by a set of principles from sociolinguistics and anthropology that are generic to descriptions of educational processes. As knowledge is gained about the nature of reading instruction, approaches for looking at reading instruction evolve and become refined. Reciprocally, as approaches for looking at reading instruction evolve and become refined, knowledge about the nature of reading instruction and instruction on a general level accumulates and becomes more explicit. Therefore, in the discussion below, both accumulated knowledge about the nature of reading instruction and generic processes for describing reading instruction are presented together in order to illustrate the relationship of knowledge and process in providing approaches for describing reading instruction. The discussion is organized around the three types of relationships between academic tasks and social, interpersonal contexts described previously.

The Social, Interpersonal Context Defines the Academic Task

The direction which researchers take in exploring how the social context defines the academic task depends, to a great extent, on how researchers define social context. The definitions of social context upon which the studies discussed in this chapter are based derive from recent work in the ethnography of communication (e.g., Erickson and Shultz, 1977;

Hymes, 1974; Gumperz & Hymes, 1972) and from definitions of culture within anthropology (e.g., Goodenough, 1971; Geertz, 1973). For heuristic purposes, the differences among the approaches can be described along two dimensions: a) emphasis on face-to-face interaction (e.g., teacher-student interaction) versus emphasis on broader, cultural units (e.g., community), and b) emphasis on participatory structure and standards versus emphasis on meaning and interpretation. These differences in underlying emphases provide the framework for the discussion below.

Face-to-Face Level: Emphasis on Participatory Structure and Standards

Erickson and Shultz (1981) focusing on the participatory nature of the social context define context as follows:

> Contexts are not simply given in the physical setting—kitchen, living room, sidewalk in front of the the drug store—nor in combination of personnel (two brothers, husband and wife, firemen). Rather contexts are constituted by what people are doing and where and when they are doing it. As McDermott (1976) puts it succinctly, people in interaction become environments for each other. Ultimately, social contexts consist of mutually shared and ratified definitions of situation and in the social interactions persons take on the basis of these definitions. (Mehan et al., 1976)

> These interactionally constituted environments are embedded in time and can change from moment to moment. With each context change, the role relationships among participants are redistributed to produce differing configurations of concerted action, e.g., two brothers can play together one moment and fight the next; firemen can play cards one moment and jump on the fire truck the next (Blom and Gumperz, 1972). Mutual rights and obligations of interactants are continually amenable to subtle readjustment (Cicourel, 1972) and redistribution into differing configurations of concerted action that can be called participant structures (cf. Philips, 1972, 1974) or coherently co-occurring sets (cf. Ervin-Tripp, 1972). These structures include ways of speaking, listening, getting the floor and holding it, and leading and following. (Erickson & Shultz, 1981, p. 148)

The participation structure—for example, who gets to speak, when, how and about what—of reading instruction may differ across reading events (e.g., Bloome, 1984) across reading groups (e.g., McDermott, 1976) and cross-cultural groups (e.g., Au, 1980).

Bloome and Green (1982) describe the participatory structure of reading events along a continuum from isolated reading to social reading. Isolated reading involves a single reader and a text. The reader interacts only with the text. Social reading involves several readers who interact with each other and a single text. In describing classroom reading at the middle school level, Bloome and Green (1982) found that the participatory structure of reading instruction moved in the direction of social reading when the teacher was removed from the situation. When teachers directed classroom reading, the participatory structure moved in the direction of isolated reading. Reading outside of the classroom in home and community situations primarily involved social reading configurations. Examples of social reading outside of school included parents reading a book to a child, teenagers sharing comic books, siblings sharing a book at night in bed, friends reading and discussing a note. Bloome and Green's (1982) descriptions of social reading and isolated reading are based primarily on nonverbal behavior (especially postural configurations, following the earlier work by McDermott, 1976) and on general, broad patterns of turn-taking behavior.

McDermott's (1976) descriptions of reading groups is also based on nonverbal behavior and on turn-taking behavior. McDermott described how the turn-taking routines of the top reading group allowed students to spend more time reading and in reading instruction than students in the bottom group. Although students in the bottom group met for as much time as the top group, they used a great deal of time in bidding for turns to talk and/or avoiding being called on to orally render the text. In addition, the bottom group provided opportunities for students outside the group to interrupt the group. Students, who were supposed to be working independently would call for the teacher's attention, disrupt the reading group, and use time that might have been spent on academic tasks. Differences in the postural configurations of the top and bottom reading groups were cues to differences in the participatory structures of the two groups. In a concerted manner, both students and teachers made use of nonverbal cues in order to realize the participatory agendas which defined, in part, the academic task. For the top group, the agenda was round robin practice of oral reading while for the bottom group the agenda was the avoidance of frustration, failure, and embarrassment associated with engaging academic tasks.

Turn-taking routines can also involve cultural differences between students and school. Building on the work of Erickson & Shultz (1977), Au (1980) shows how school turn-taking procedures may violate students' culturally-based expectations for appropriate behavior. For example, during narrative events like story telling, within some cultures, it is appropriate for several people to speak simultaneously to add to the narrative in specified ways and it may be inappropriate to compete for turns. In school, students may have to compete for turns and only talk one at a time. Cultural differences in turn-taking routines across school and nonschool settings may mask students' skills by not allowing students to adequately display what they know. Cultural differences in turn-taking may also prevent students from fully participating in academic tasks. By modifying turn-taking procedures during reading instruction in ways consistent with students' culturally-based expectations, students may be better able to display reading development and engage in academic tasks.

The studies by Bloome and Green (1982), McDermott (1976) and Au (1980), among others, suggest the need for looking at participatory structure across reading events. Capturing differences in participatory structure of reading events provides one means for describing reading instruction. However, research by DeStefano, Pepinsky, and Sanders (1982) and Bloome (1983) raise questions about the meaning of differences in participatory structure for learning to read. In looking at teacher-student interaction in a culturally diverse first grade classroom across the school year, DeStefano et al. (1982) found that students learned how to appropriately participate in reading instruction. However, learning to participate appropriately was not necessarily related to how effectively the students were learning to read. In brief, what students learned was how to participate in reading instruction. Bloome (1983) offers similar findings at the middle school level, suggesting that teachers and students often engage each other in procedural display. Procedural display involves the display of interactional routines and procedures whose accomplishment counts as accomplishment of the academic lesson. However, the accomplishment of procedural display may not necessarily involve substantive contact or engagement with the academic content of the lesson. In brief, teachers and students can go through the appropriate interactional motions without getting the academic meaning.

The studies above suggest that the relationship between the participatory structure of reading instruction and students' reading development is mediated by a broad range of factors and processes. Although further research is needed, among factors identified to date are content coverage (e.g., Barr, 1984), the intrapersonal context (e.g., Cazden, 1982), the nature of the academic tasks and texts provided (e.g., Collins, 1981; Harker, in press; Golden, in press; Moll and Diaz, in press), continuity or discontinuity with student's home culture (e.g., Heath, 1983; Gumperz, Cook-Gumperz & Simons, 1981) and access to academic tasks and resources (e.g., Michaels, 1981; Gilmore, in press).

Part of the difficulty in specifying a model of a relationship between participatory structure and reading development is that both social and academic meaning within reading instruction events evolve from the meaning created by teachers and students within those events. That is, neither social nor academic meaning is predetermined but rather is "situated." Issues and approaches emphasizing meaning and interpretation are discussed in the next section.

Face-to-Face Level: Emphasis on Meaning and Interpretation

When people interact, they need to construct an interpretive framework so that they can understand each other. The conversational inferences that people make are based not only on what they bring to the situation (e.g., their expectations, background knowledge, social role, and background) but primarily on the framework that evolves and is negotiated as they interact. Gumperz (1982) describes conversational meaning and interpretation as follows:

> Conversational inference . . . is the situated or context bound process of interpretation by which participants in exchange assess others' intentions, and on which they base their responses . . . [I]nterpretation [is] a function of the dynamic pattern of moves and countermoves as they follow one another in ongoing conversation . . . One indirectly or implicitly indicates how an utterance is to be interpreted and illustrates how one has interpreted another's utterance through verbal and nonverbal responses, and it is the nature of these responses rather than the independently determined meaning or truth value of individual utterances alone that governs evaluation of intent. (pp. 153–154)

The conversational use of verbal and nonverbal cues to construct an interpretive context can be called contextualization and the cues themselves are called contextualization cues. Contextualization cues consist of verbal, nonverbal, and prosodic signals (see Table 11-1). By looking at patterns of contextualization cues, insights can be gained into the meanings intended and interpreted in face-to-face events such as reading instruction.

For example, Gumperz & Tannen (1979) describe a classroom situ-

TABLE 11-1 PARTIAL LIST OF CONTEXTUALIZATION CUES

NONVERBAL CUES	PROSODIC CUES	VERBAL CUES
Kinesic shifts (body movement)	Volume shifts	Verbal shifts (changes in the
Parakinesic shifts (style of	Tone shifts (changes in the	general syntactic and
body movement)	pitch of a message)	lexical patterns—e.g., a
Proxemic shifts (changes in	Rhythmic shifts (changes in the	shift from active to passive
interpersonal distance)	pattern of stresses)	voice)
Postural shifts (changes in eye	Stress	Register shifts (change in the
and facial direction)	Velocity shifts (changes in the	set of words associated with
Posturing (changes in	speed with which a message	particular situations and
positioning of the back and	is spoken)	status)
shoulders)	Pausing and the use of silence	
Postural configuration	Intonation shifts (changes in	
(changes in group	the pattern of prosodic	
proxemics and posturing)	cues)	

ation in which several Black girls consistently asked for the teacher's
help. On the surface level, one might assume that the girls' requests for
help were an indication of their inability to complete classroom assignments. However, closer examination of the ways in which the girls' contextualized their utterances, especially how they prosodically rendered
their requests, showed that what the girls wanted was for the teacher to
be near. Assumptions about the girls' reading ability based on their
requests for help would be inaccurate.

In the last two decades, researchers have described cross-cultural
miscommunication in classroom reading events involving Black students
(e.g., Heath, 1982a, 1982b; Bloome & Green, 1982; Michaels, 1981;
Gumperz & Herasimchuk, 1973), Native American students (e.g., Philips, 1972, 1974; Scollon & Scollon, 1981, 1982; Erickson & Mohatt, 1982;
Au, 1980), Latino students (e.g., Moll and Diaz, 1983), among others.
Further discussion and review of research on cross-cultural miscommunication in the classroom can be found in Bloome & Green, 1984;
Cazden, John and Hymes, 1972; Cook-Gumperz, Gumperz, & Simons,
1981; and Trueba, Guthrie & Au, 1981.

Beyond the occurrence of cross-cultural miscommunication, is the
question of how cross-cultural miscommunication affects or defines classroom reading tasks. Michaels' (1981) study of sharing time in a kindergarten classroom illustrates one way in which cross-cultural
miscommunication can affect classroom reading tasks. Sharing time can
be viewed as an instructional situation that prepares students for literate
behavior. Students get opportunities to produce narratives in a "literate"
style. The teacher expects students to produce narratives that "stick to
the point." Further, the teacher expects the structures of students' narratives to be revealed explicitly through verbal means or implicitly
through prosodic cues used in a manner consistent with the teacher's
expectations and culture. In brief, during sharing time, students are to
produce what Michaels (1981) labels topic-centered narratives. Students
who did not produce topic-centered narratives were provided less opportunity to practice literate-like narratives. These students were viewed
by the teacher as not sticking to the topic and as producing structurally
incoherent narratives. Michaels (1981) suggests that rather than producing incoherent narratives, the students narratives were structured in
a way consistent with narratives students were producing in a style found
in their "home" culture, a style unfamiliar to the teacher. Further, also
consistent with their "home" culture, students used prosodic cues to
indicate the structure of the narrative, but used the prosodic cues in
ways unfamiliar to the teacher. As a consequence of producing narratives
in a way unfamiliar to the teacher, students received fewer opportunities
to practice literate-like behavior duing sharing time.

Collins (1981) research also illustrates how cross-cultural miscommunication can affect academic tasks. Based on an ethnographic study of an elementary classroom, Collins (1981) has suggested that teachers, at least in some cases, may be making decisions about what academic tasks to provide students based on students' narrative performance. Students whose narrative performance was prosodically inconsistent with what the teacher expected were assigned reading tasks emphasizing words and oral rendition. Yet, the prosodic nature of the students' narrative performances was consistent with narrative performance in their "home" culture. Further, the students' prosodic style was unrelated to their ability to comprehend connected discourse. Students' whose prosodic style was consistent with the teacher's expectations for narrative performance were provided comprehension-based tasks and larger units of text with which to work. Collins (1981) suggests (1) that teachers may have implicit models of "what reading looks and sounds like" that are culturally based; (2) that teachers may have implicit models of different kinds of tasks to provide students who do not meet their expectations for what reading should look and/or sound like; and (3) that these implicit models may be unrelated to reading development.

The research on cross-cultural miscommunication in the classroom suggests a need for looking across classroom and nonclassroom settings. For both teacher and students, reading instruction is embedded not only in the context of the classroom but also in broader cultural contexts including "home" culture and the culture of the dominant society. Issues related to broader cultural contexts and reading instruction tasks are discussed in the next section.

Cultural Contexts of Reading Beyond Face-to-Face Interaction

Descriptions linking reading to the broader cultural context show how reading is embedded in the ways people have of thinking, feeling, believing, perceiving, and acting (cf., Goodenough's, 1971, definition of culture). Following Szwed (1977, 1981), researchers have described (1) the roles that reading and writing play in social life; (2) the varieties of reading and writing available for choice; (3) the contexts for the performance of the varieties of reading and writing available; and (4) the manner in which reading and writing performance is evaluated by ordinary people in ordinary activities.

For example, Heath's (1983) description of reading in three communities shows how reading is embedded in the cultural doings of each community. Reading is not viewed as separable from daily activities but rather an extension of the ways in which people logically do things. Consider Heath's (1983) description of early reading in Trackton, one of the communities she studied:

The children of Tracton *read to learn* before they go to school to *learn to read*. The modification of old or broken toys and their incorporation with other times to create a new toy is a common event. One mastermind, usually Tony, announces the idea, and all the children help collect items and contribute ideas. On some occasions, such as when one of the boys wants to modify his bicycle for a unique effect, he has to read selectively portions of brochures on bicycles and instructions for tool sets. Reading is almost always set within the context of immediate action: one needs to read a letter's address to prove to the mailman that one should be given the envelope; one must read the price of a bag of coal at Mr. Dugan's store to make the decision to purchase or not . . . As early as age four, Teggie Lem, Gary and Gary B. could scan the price tag, which might contain several pieces of information, on familiar items and pick out the price. (pp. 191–192, original emphases)

Reading is not viewed separate from playing with toys, speaking, shopping, listening, getting letters, going to church, writing, people's beliefs about growing and learning, and so on. Reading and writing are part of the social "doings" of people, and understanding reading and writing requires understanding its social contexts. Consider Heath's description of reading among Trackton adults:

For Trackton adults, reading is a social activity; when something is read in Trackton, it almost always provokes narratives, jokes, sidetracking talk, and active negotiation of the meaning of written texts among listeners. Authority in the written word does not rest in the words themselves, but in the meanings which are negotiated through the experiences of the group . . . One day when Lillie Mae had received a letter about a daycare program, several neighbors were sitting on porches, working on cars nearby, or sweeping their front yards. Lillie Mae came out on her front porch [and read the letter] . . . Conversation on various parts of the letter continued for nearly an hour, while neighbors and Lillie Mae pooled their knowledge of the pros and cons of such a program. The question "What does this mean?" was answered not only from the information in print, but from the group's bringing of experiences to the text. (pp. 196–197)

Heath (1983) also describes differences across communities in the cultural context of reading and literacy:

Roadville parents believe it is their task to praise and practice reading with their young children; Trackton adults believe the young have to learn to be and do, and if reading is necessary for this learning, that will come . . [In Roadville]. Behind the written word is an authority, and the text is a message which can be taken apart only insofar as its analysis does not extend too far beyond the text and commonly agreed-upon experiences.

> New syntheses and multiple interpretations create alternatives which challenge fixed roles, rules and "rightness." In Trackton, the written word is for negotiation and manipulation—both serious and playful. (pp. 234–235)

It is through what Hymes (1974, 1977) has called comparative generalization—looking across situations and events—that Heath (1983) is able to illustrate general principles of the relationship of reading and writing to people's culture.

> Roadville and Trackton residents have a variety of literate traditions and in each community these are interwoven in different ways with oral uses of language, ways of negotiating meaning, deciding on action, and achieving status. Patterns of using reading and writing in each community are interdependent with ways of using space (having bookshelves, decorating walls, displaying telephone numbers), and using time (bedtime, meal hours, and homework sessions). Habits of using the written word also develop as they help individuals fulfill self-perceived roles of caregiving and preparing children for school. (p. 234)

Heath's (1983) description of reading emphasized the social organization, goals, and participatory nature of reading events. Taylor (1983), in describing reading and writing among middle-class families with preschool children, emphasizes the personal meanings and social interpretations that reading activities have for the family. For example, Taylor describes story reading as the juxtaposition of learning to read processes, social processes, and the development of intimate and emotive parent-child relationships.

> Story sharing was intricately woven into the social processes of family life, with a broad panoply of purposes, faciliating communication between parents and children and forming one medium for the development of shared social heritage. In addition, story sharing developed into a routine that was highly dependent upon the individual educative styles of the participants. It was an occasion with a cumulative context, and one in which distinctly original family agendas evolved. More important, reading and telling stories and talking about pictures and texts were initially woven together as the parents endeavored to impart to the child the appropriate strategies and procedures necessary for the story to ultimately make sense. (p. 67)

Story reading is important not only because children are introduced to print and have opportunities to experiment with text but perhaps more importantly because story reading brings parents and children together. That is, story reading helps create the family as a social entity.

For example, consider the story reading event below described by the parent:

The other night Ellie [daughter] and I [mother] bought a copy of *Peter Rabbit* in French for Hannah [daughter] . . . Hannah has always loved *Peter Rabbit*, so we had it out here and we were looking at it trying to decide whether Ellie should have it because she just started French or whether we should have really give it to Hannah. Hannah came in from dancing class and said, "Oh my goodness, French Peter Rabbit" and picked it up and we both said to her, "Well Merry Christmas to you." Everyone was tired. Hannah has decided she's old enough to date; we've decided she isn't. Great constant conflict and very few close moments; it's a real pulling away. And she sat down with it and she opened it up and began looking through it and she said, "Look the pictures are exactly the same." We always keep *Peter Rabbit* right here so we got the English and we read a page and then she read a page and the next thing we knew were going through all the *Peter Rabbit* books, and when we looked up Dan [father] had gone to bed hours ago. It was twenty minutes to eleven and were reading *Peter Rabbit*, curled up on the couch the three of us. What a marvelous evening that was, to go all the way back to the age of three or four, and it was just a wonderful time. (pp. 82–83)

In terms of reading development and reading instruction, Taylor (1983) following Vygotsky (1962) suggests that the interpersonal context of reading precedes and provides the base for the intrapersonal reading processes. When children go to school, the intrapersonal processes they learn—such as metalinguistic awareness—are added onto the interpersonal processes of reading already developed.

Both Taylor's (1983) and Heath's (1983) descriptions of the cultural context of reading raise questions about reading instruction and the need to build on what children bring to school. Heath (1983) suggests that the culturally-based experiences many young children have with reading and literacy may not prepare them for reading in school. Since school reading is often based upon implicit and ethnocentric cultural assumptions about what reading is, and how reading is constituted, children whose cultural background experiences differ from those assumed by the school may find themselves at a disadvantage in school. It is not that children's "home" cultures are inadequate or lacking in literacy experiences, but rather that children's background and experience with reading may be negated or denied by the school's inability to see beyond its own cultural assumptions about the nature of reading.

The consequences of cultural differences in the organization and meaning of reading events between "home" and school—especially when cultural differences are not perceived and accommodated—may be the misevaluation of students' reading performance and ability.

Evaluation of Students' Academic Tasks

In order to evaluate student reading, teachers must make inferences about student reading from academic and social behavior that students display. For example, in scanning a class, a teacher may decide to view those students who are leaning over and looking at their books as actually engaged in reading. That is, the students look like they are reading. Of course, some of the students may be faking or engaged in what Bloome and Green (1982) have called mock participation. With mock participation, students may participate in the classroom activity in every way except that they are not engaging the substantive academic content of the lesson. A student may flip through textbook pages, raise his hand to answer questions (to which he does not know the answer), take notes, and so on—but the substance of the participation is void of academic content.

Heap (1980) describes three problems inherent in evaluating the occurrence of reading from displays of student social and academic behavior. The first problem is a source problem. When teachers ask questions of students about a given text they cannot be certain that the student has answered the question based upon reading the text. For example, if a student is asked to retell a story like *Rumplestiltskin*, the student may respond based on seeing the story on television or having heard the story from parents. Source problems not only involve confounding from television and books read outside of school, students may also pick up information and answers from other students or from teacher-student interaction.

A second problem is a barrier problem. When a student does not respond to a teacher question, or when a student does not give an expected answer, the teacher may infer that the student has not read or has not read adequately. However, a barrier may exist that prevents the student from adequately displaying that the student has adequately read. For example, consider a student who reads and understands a story but who does not understand the teacher's question. Also, consider a student who reads and understands but is unable to respond adequately in writing. In both cases, the student may be inaccurately viewed as not having read or as being unable to read.

A third problem is a frame problem. Reading requires interpretation. However, the framework with which students interpret a text may differ from the framework used by the teacher. Differences in interpretive frames may be the result of cultural differences, economic differences, personal experience differences, and so on. For example, consider the passage and question below taken from a reading workbook.

Bill Benson looked only once at his homework assignment. Immediately, he started moaning to his seatmate, Candy Caries, about its length. As he shuffled out of the room after the bell, he couldn't help but remark to his teacher that the room was too stuffy to work in. The teacher only smiled and shook her head at Bill's complaints.

3. Faced with the possibility of running an errand for his parents, Bill is likely to say ———.

A. "Do I have to go? Why don't you ask Uncle Joe this time?"
B. "Sure I'll go! Should I walk or take the bus?"
C. "Okay, Dad. I'll go right after I finish my homework."
D. I'm way ahead of you, Pop! I took care of it already." (*Reading House Series*, 1980, p. 71)

The answer designated correct in the teacher's guide is *A*. However, one ninth grade student who was given the task chose *C*. On the surface, his wrong answer would suggest that he either did not read the passage or did not understand it. However, he explained his answer by pointing out that the protagonist had no intention of doing his homework or going to the store and that the protagonist was procrastinating and deceiving his father. Confronting his father—which is the situation with answer *A*—would probably result in punishment. In answering the question, the student used his own background knowledge as a frame for interpreting the story and the question. However, when high-achieving students from the same grade, school, and background were given the same passage and questions, they gave the answer designated correct by the teacher's guide. In brief, one of the strategies some students may need to learn in reading instruction is to suppress their own background knowledge and assume the interpretive frame of the school.

The three problems Heap (1980) lists in evaluating the occurrence of reading emphasize that the evaluation of student reading behavior is based to great degree on the social and communicative display of "having read." Simply put, during reading instruction, students must produce social and communicative displays that match the explicit or implicit models of social and communicative behavior that teachers expect.

What counts as reading in one situation may or may not count as reading in another. For example, in classrooms the oral rendition of a text during reading group instruction may count as "reading" but reading directions to do a science worksheet may not be viewed as "reading." That is, only reading events formally recognized by the written curriculum may get counted as being reading or as being reading instruction (cf., Griffin, 1977). Further, Gilmore (1981, 1983) has shown how some peer activities which involve sophisticated literacy-related behavior may be discounted by teachers and other adults because of the social context of the peer activity. Gilmore (1981, 1983) describes a game played by

Black adolescent women that involves sophisticated and creative knowledge of spelling and word play. The same young women had a great deal of difficulty with less complex spelling and literacy-related tasks in the classroom. Yet, because the game involved taboo words and sexual allusions, the game was discounted as a literacy-related activity (whereas classroom spelling was viewed as a literacy-related activity).

The research by Heap (1980), Gilmore (1981, 1983), and Griffin (1977) among others, shows that definitions of reading—that is, what counts as reading—are situation-specific and determined, to a large extent, by social and communicative criteria. In breif, what counts as reading depends on the social context.

Influences of the Academic Task on Social Context

So far, the discussion has focused on how the social context influences and defines academic tasks during reading instruction. However, the relationship between academic tasks and social context is a reciprocal relationship, each influencing the other. That is, the nature of the academic task also influences the social context. There are, of course, many classroom factors that influence social context. For example, Bossert (1979) has shown how classroom structure can affect student social relationships.

Of specific concern here is how academic tasks mediate relationships between students and texts. For example, consider how the following academic task separates and distances students from a story and creates a passive orientation to both text and knowledge (reported in detail in Bloome, in press). The eighth grade students had read Pritchett's "The Saint"; —a story about a young man's questioning of authority and his subsequent loss of religion. Many of the students were in a situation similar to the young man. Several belonged to evangelical and fundamentalist religious organizations, and almost all of the students had recently been confirmed or just completed religious school training. The questioning of authority was a routine occurrence in the classroom. However, the discussion of the story focused on vocabulary words, the cataloging of character descriptions, and story structure. The discussion and assigned written tasks never allowed an active interpretation of the story based on students' personal or cultural experience. Student oral and written responses to the classroom tasks were extremely brief. The responses students did make were primarily reproductions of portions of the text or teacher comments. The relationship between text and student can perhaps best be described as "alienated"—students and text not really having much to do with the other.

While not all academic tasks produce "alienated" relationships between students and text, the example above illustrates how an academic task can influence the social task within which the academic task itself is completed. As implied in the example above, in order to explore the influence of the academic task on the social context, one must explore student's cultural background, the nature of text, and the academic task as they relate to each other.

Summary

In this chapter, we have examined issues involved in capturing simultaneously the academic and social, interpersonal dimensions of reading instruction. Of specific concern were approaches based on recent work in sociolinguistics and anthropology. The issues explored involved both knowledge about the nature of reading instruction and principles for looking at reading instruction. Special attention was given to how the social context defines the nature of the academic task, how the evaluation of academic tasks is influenced by the social context, and how the social context is influenced by academic tasks.

The approaches described in this chapter emphasize the importance of capturing the participatory structure, social meaning, and participants' interpretation of classroom reading instruction at the leve of face-to-face interaction and at broader cultural levels.

References

Au, K., (1980). Participation structures in a reading lesson with Hawaiian children. *Anthropology and Education Quarterly*, 11(2), 91–115.

Barr, R. (in press). *Classroom interaction and curricular content*. In D. Bloome (Ed.), *Literacy and schooling*. Norwood, NJ: Ablex.

Blom, J., & Gumperz, J. (1972). Social meaning in linguistic structures: Code switching in Norway. In J. Gumperz & D. Hymes (Eds.), *Directions in sociolinguistics*. New York: Holt, Rinehart & Winston.

Bloome, D., (1983). Classroom reading instruction: A sociocommunicative analysis of time on task. In J. Niles (Ed.), *32nd Yearbook of the National Reading Conference*. Rochester, NY: National Reading Conference.

Bloome, D., (in press). Reading as a social process in a middle school classroom. In D. Bloome (Ed.), *Literacy ands schooling*. Norwood, NJ: Ablex.

Bloome, D., & Green, J. (1982). *Capturing social contexts of reading for urban junior high school youth in home, school and community settings*. Final report to the National Institute of Education. Washington, DC: U.S. Dept. of Education.

Bloome, D. & Green, J. (1984). Directions in the sociolinguistic study of reading. In P. Pearson, R. Barr, M. Kamil & P. Mosenthal (Eds.), *Handbook of research on reading*. New York: Longman.

Bossert, S. (1979). *Social relationships and classroom tasks*. New York: Cambridge University Press.

Cazden, C. (1982). Contexts for literacy: In the mind and in the classroom. *Journal of Reading Behavior*, 14, 413–427.

Cazden, C., John, V., & Hymes D. (Eds.) (1972). *Functions of language in the classroom.* New York: Teachers College Press.

Cicourel, A. (1972). Basic and normative rules in the negotiation of status and role. In D. Sudnow (Ed.), *Studies in social interaction.* New York: Free Press.

Cochran-Smith, M. (1984). *The making of a reader.* Norwood, NJ: Ablex.

Collins, J. (1981). Differential treatment in reading instruction. In, J. Cook-Gumperz, J. Gumperz, & H. Simons. *School-home ethnography project.* Final report to the National Institute of Education. Washington, DC: U.S. Dept. of Education.

DeStefano, J., Pepinsky, H., & Sanders, T. (1982). Discourse rules for literacy learning in a first grade classroom. In L. C. Wilkinson (Ed.), *Communicating in the classroom.* NY: Academic Press.

Erickson, F., & Mohatt, B. (1982). Cultural organization of participation structures in two classrooms of Indian students. In G. Spindler (Ed.), *Doing the ethnography of schooling: Educational anthropology in action.* New York: Holt, Rinehart, and Winston.

Erickson, F., & Shultz, J. (1977). When is a context? Some issues and methods in the analysis of social competence. *Quarterly Newsletter of the Institute for Comparative Human Development.* 1(2), 5–12.

Erickson, F., & Shultz, J. (1981). When is a context? Some issues and methods in the analysis of social competence. In J. Green & C. Wallat (Eds.), *Ethnography and language in educational settings.* Norwood, NJ: Ablex.

Ervin-Tripp, S. (1972). On sociolinguistic rules: Alternation and co-occurrence. In J. Gumperz & D. Hymes (Eds.), *Directions in sociolinguistics: The ethnography of communication.* New York: Holt, Rinehart & Winston.

Geertz, C. (1973). *The interpretation of cultures.* New York: Random House.

Gilmore, P. (in press). Sulking, stepping and tracking: The effects of attitude assessment on access to literacy. In D. Bloome (Ed.), *Literacy and schooling.* Norwood, NJ: Ablex.

Gilmore, P. (1983). Spelling 'Mississippi': Recontextualizing a literacy-related speech event. *Anthropology and Education Quarterly.* 14(4) 235–256.

Gilmore, P. (1981). Shortridge school and community: Attitudes and admission to literacy. In D. Hymes (project director), *Ethnographic monitoring of children's acquisition of reading/language arts skills in and out of the classroom.* Final report to the National Institute of Education. Washington, DC: U.S. Dept. of Education.

Glaser, B., & Strauss, A. (1967). *The discovery of grounded theory: Strategies for qualitative research.* Chicago: Aldine.

Golden, J. (in press). Structuring and restructuring text. In J. Green & J. Harker (Eds.), *Multiple perspective analysis of classroom discourse.* Norwood, NJ: Ablex.

Goodenough, W. (1971). *Culture, language, and society.* Reading, MA: Addison-Wesley.

Green, J. (in press). Lesson construction and student participation. In J. Green, J. Harker, & C. Wallat (Eds.). *Multiple perspective analysis of classroom discourse.* Norwood, NJ: Ablex.

Griffin, P. (1977). How and when does reading occur in the classroom? *Theory into Practice.* 16()5), 376–383.

Gumperz, J. (1982). *Discourse strategies.* London: Cambridge University Press.

Gumperz, J., Cook-Gumperz, J., & Simons, H. (1981). *School-home ethnography project.* Final report to the National Institute of Education. Washington, DC: U.S. Dept. of Education.

Gumperz, J. & Herasimchuk, E. (1973). The conversational analysis of social meaning: A study of classroom interaction. In R. Shuy (Ed.), *Monograph series on language and linguistics 23rd annual roundtable, sociolinguistics: Current trends and prospects, 25.* Washington DC: Georgetown University Press.

Gumperz, J., & Hymes, D. (Eds.) (1972). *Directions in sociolinguistics.* NY: Holt, Rinehart, & Winston.

Gumperz, J., & Tannen, D. (1979). Individual and social differences in language use. In C. Filmore et al. (Eds.), *Individual differences in language ability and language behavior.* New York: Academic Press.

Harker, J.O. (in press). Constrasting the content of two story reading lessons: A propositional analysis. In J. Green, J. Harker, & C. Wallat (Eds.), *Multiple perspective analysis of classroom discourse.* Norwood, NJ: Ablex.

Heap, J. (1980). What counts as reading? Limits to certainty in assessment. *Curriculum Inquiry,* 10(3), 265–292.

Heath, S. (1982). Questioning at home and at school: A comparative study. In G. Spindler (Ed.). *The ethnography of schooling.* New York: Holt, Rinehart & Winston.

Heath, S. (1983). *Ways with words.* New York: Cambridge University Press.

Heath, S. (1982). What no bedtime story means: Narrative skills at home and school. *Language in Society.* 11(1), 49–76.

Hymes, D. (1974). *Foundations in sociolinguistics: An ethnographic approach.* Philadelphia: University of Pennsylvania Press.

Hymes, D. (1977). Critique. *Anthropology and Education Quarterly.* 8(2), 91–93.

McDermott, R. (1976). *Kids make sense: An ethnographic account of the interactional management of success and failure in one first-grade classroom.* Doctoral dissertation, Stanford University.

Mehan, H., Cazden, C., Fisher, S., & Maroules, N. (1976). *The social organization of classroom lessons.* A technical report submitted to the Ford Foundation.

Michaels, S. (1981). "Sharing time": Children's narrative styles and differential access to literacy. *Language in Society.* 10(3), 423–442.

Moll, L., & Diaz, S. (1983). *Towards an interactional pedagogical psychology: A bilingual case study.* Center for Human Information Processing, University of California, San Diego.

Moll, L., & Diaz, R. (in press). Teaching writing as communication: The use of ethnographic findings in classroom practice. In D. Bloome (Ed.), *Literacy and schooling: Beyond beginning school.* Norwood, NJ: Ablex.

Philips, S. (1972). Participant structures and communicative competence: Warm Springs children in community and classroom. In C. Cazden, V. John & D. Hymes (Eds.), *Functions of language in the classroom.* New York: Teachers College Press.

Philips, S. (1974). *The invisible culture: Communication in classroom and community on the Warm Springs Indian reservations.* Unpublished doctoral dissertation, University of Pennsylvania, Philadelphia.

Reading house series: Comprehension and Vocabulary. (1980) New York: Random House.

Scollon, R., & Scollon, S. (1980). *Narrative, literacy, and face in interethnic communication.* Norwood, NJ: Ablex.

Scollon, R., & Scollon, S. (1982). Cooking it up and boiling it down. In D. Tannen (Ed.), *Spoken and written language.* Norwood, NJ: Ablex.

Szwed, J. (1977). *The ethnography of literacy.* Paper presented to the National Institute of Education Conference on Writing, Los Angeles.

Szwed, J. (1981). The ethnography of literacy. In M. Whiteman (Ed.), *Variation in writing: Functional and linguistic-cultural differences.* Hillsdale, NJ: Erlbaum.

Taylor, D. (1983). *Family literacy: Young children learning to read and write.* Exeter, NH: Heinemann Educational Books.

Trueba, H., Guthrie, G., Au., K. (1981). *Culture and the bilingual classroom: Studies in classroom ethnography.* Rowley, MA: Newbury House.

Vygotsky, L. (1962). *Thought and language.* Cambridge, MA: MIT Press.

Chapter 12
Teachers As Reading Researchers*

Donald R. Gallo
Central Connecticut State University

The topic for our discussion is "Teachers as Reading Researchers." It will help me to know something about your background in this subject. First let me do a very brief and very informal diagnosis of your knowledge of research.

On a piece of note paper, write your answers to the following five questions:

1. What do the letters ANOVA stand for?
2. What is the difference between an ANOVA and a MANOVA?
3. Write down the formula for determing the Pearson Product Moment Correlation Coefficient.
4. Can you explain the difference between a Curvilinear Regression and a Multiple Regression equation? (yes/no)
5. Do you know the difference between a Chi square and a T-square? (yes/no)

Do you feel that you have *all* the answers correct (or three right and the last two "yes")?

How many of you have *four* positive responses?

Three? Two? One?

In a way, I suppose that I am an ideal person to be addressing you on this subject, though I'm not sure the people who selected me for this role would interpret my credentials the way that I do. It is true that I have done several pieces of research that some people have viewed as being important as well as informative. My doctoral research was regarded as a noteworthy (but failed) attempt to formulate a device for assessing teacher knowledge and competence. I have been invited to participate in several national conference sessions devoted to research

---

*A speech given at the Fordham Reading Institute, July 12, 1983.

in teaching English as well as reading skills. I was a member of the Board of Trustees of the Research Foundation of the National Council of Teachers of English. And for the past year and a half, I have been engaged in a somewhat ambitious study of the reading habits and interests of Connecticut students in grades 4 through 12.

I do not intend this abbreviated listing of my accomplishments to be bragging. I present them only to show you that *in spite of* those research activities, I do not consider myself a researcher. In fact, I do not rank even second best to the real Researchers (with a capital *R*) in the fields of reading or English. I consider myself *a teacher*, first and foremost.

And I must confess, here publicly today, that were I sitting in the audience with you, I would not have scored well on that little diagnostic test I gave you. I *do* know what the letters ANOVA and MANOVA stand for, and I *do* know what a T-square is, of course. I can't write down the formula for the Pearson Product Moment Correlation Coefficient, but I do know where to look it up when I need to use it. But I have only the vaguest idea of the difference between a Curvilinear and a Multiple Regression equation; I cannot do Rao's cannonical factoring to compensate for factoring errors; and I'm about as comfortable with Chi square as I am with Times Square or Columbus Circle.

I am not fearful of statistical manipulation. I am not a mathematical dummy. (I even balance my checkbook perfectly, to the penny, each month). It is just that as a classroom teacher I do not usually *need* to use such complex analytical devices; I do not usually *need to know* the kinds of information many of those formulas reveal; and, furthermore, I don't really *enjoy* that aspect of the profession.

Why, then, am I talking to you this afternoon? BECAUSE . . .

I believe that I can be a better teacher if I know something about research—about how to do it, and about what the results of other research mean.

I believe that I can be a better teacher if I can understand more of what happens in my classroom, of what my students do, of how they do it, what they think, how they feel about it. And I can understand that better if I can ascertain it in some *organized* and *valid* manner.

I believe that I can be a better teacher and I can help others be better teachers if I can share what I find with other educators and hope that they will share their findings with me.

And you can be a better teacher for the same reasons.

Most classroom teachers are not knowledgeable about research or statistics beyond those required in some basic education course where you learn what *means* and *standard deviation* are and then never again have to figure out. In fact, because we have few occasions to utilize that early learning, we forget even those rudimentary things and many of us grow to *fear* statistical things. Not only do the majority of classroom teachers shy away from statistical research, many even develop an anti-intellectual stance that says "That stuff doesn't really mean anything; you can make statistics say anything you want them to say."

While it is true that a clever researcher may be able to arrange some data so that the results are quite different from what they would have been with a different arrangement, and that someone can interpret the findings of a study differently from someone else because of their lack of background data, facts are facts, and results are results. If the research was done properly (and that's an important factor always to consider), the results must be considered seriously.

This past April in Seattle I presented some results of a recent study I did on the reading experiences of Connecticut students. We had surveyed hundreds of students in all kinds of schools, in grades 4 through 12. One of the open-ended questions was: "What's the difference between books you read on your own and books you are *assigned* to read by your English or language arts teachers?" Very few students said there were no differences between assigned and self-selected readings. Large numbers of students responded to this question in similar ways. Here are some typical responses:

Grade 5: "Mine have more action."
"They pick the dumb ones."
Grade 6: "I know what I like, they don't."
"Theirs are too stuffy and goody-goody."
Grade 7: "Mine swear and sometimes have sex. Teachers' books are dull and boring."

The most frequent response from students was "The books *I* read are more exciting." I'll conclude with three comments from 10th graders: "English departments are too stuck in their ways. [They] don't change authors or titles." "They are what the teacher likes, not us." "The books have nothing to do with me."

We also looked at the same thing in a different way, a way that yielded a more concrete and classifiable response. We asked: "Do you like the novels and other books you are *assigned* to read for school? ALWAYS/USUALLY/SOMETIMES/SELDOM/NEVER.

To that, most 4th graders said USUALLY or SOMETIMES. But overall in grades 4 through 6, 31% of the boys and 25% of the girls said SELDOM or NEVER! In grades 7–9 only 1% of the students said they ALWAYS like the assigned books, and 17% said USUALLY. (More girls than boys said USUALLY.) The plurality—44%—said SOMETIMES. But 40% of the males and 35% of the females said SELDOM or NEVER! (More boys than girls checked NEVER).

By grades 10–12, less than 1% of the students said ALWAYS and

24% said USUALLY. But again here, 41% of the males and 23% of the females said they SELDOM or NEVER liked the assigned readings! What we are seeing, then, is that *40% of the kids in our junior and senior high schools are not enjoying most of the books we require* them to read in school, while only 20% of the students in those grades USUALLY enjoy them.

After hearing those findings, one teacher in the Seattle audience said: "THOSE ARE STUPID STATISTICS!"

That's what I mean by anti-intellectual. She did not question our methodology. She did not try to see how the question might have been worded so that it elicited negative responses. She did not question our addition or multiplication. She simply could not accept the plain *fact* that a very large proportion of students had declared their dissatisfaction for what she thought were wonderful, educational, rewarding reading experiences.

If that teacher had had more respect for research—indeed, if that teacher had done some of the same kinds of research that I was sharing with her—she would have realized the truth and the significance of the responses of those students. And she should have made the necessary adjustments in her teaching to somehow counteract the kinds of objections students usually have to assigned reading. And even if students in *her* classes did not answer in that same way, she should have learned that she was reaching her students in more positive ways than the majority of her colleagues around the country were with their students.

Why?

By way of example, that provides a partial reason for why every one of us should be research-oriented in our own classrooms: *first*, it might make more of us more accepting of the research findings of others, and *second*, it might encourage more of us to determine where, actually, our students stand in relation to others, or where *we* stand, how satisfied or well-read or informed or unskilled our students are by doing original reseach in our own classrooms.

All of us have the potential for being researchers—by using what we normally do every day. Or at least what we do to some extent on most days:

- We observe students.
- We evaluate students (both formally and informally).
- We evaluate our teaching (at least at the gut-level).
- We draw inferences about those things; we arrive at conclusions about our successes and failures and about those of our students. And we make decisions on the basis of those things.

But we don't usually do those things *systematically*. And that's really what research is: it's a systematic way of assessing what we normally do—of *observing* the activities; of *collecting* and *recording* the information carefully; of *categorizing* and *analyzing* the data; and finally of *sharing the results* with others.

Where?

I'm suggesting that you need not go outside of your own classroom to be a researcher. (You may want to, of course). I'm suggesting that you begin simply, perhaps by giving a questionnaire to students in your class. Perhaps asking them to list the best book they read during the past year, or to give the name of their favorite author, or to tell you where they get most of the books they read. For the sake of comparison, or for a larger sample, you might ask the same questions of all fifth graders in your school, or all tenth graders, or whatever group you might wish to examine. You could do that whenever you wanted to know that information, or you could make it an annual investigation to be done every September 15 to see what kids had read during the summer, or every June 1, enabling you to track changes in reading interests over the years. I'm suggesting you do this using the results for guidance in planning the year's reading activities based on the interests of the specific students in your classroom.

You might decide that you would like to expand your study, to see how your school compares with a different school on the other side of town, or in a neighboring town. Perhaps you have a friend who teaches in another state where you could each survey similar groups of students to see how their responses match or differ.

Start small. Simple. Personal. Those are enough for you to begin with. And those should be significant enough to tell you some important things: what titles have been most special to your students; what types of books they seem to like; who their favorite authors are. I won't go into the many ways you can utilize that information, because I'm sure you can see the value of finding out who reads what and how much, and what types of books you might order next time you have a few extra dollars in the book account, or what kinds of writing or discussion assignments you could give.

Let me show you, quickly, some of the information we discovered on a large scale in Connecticut through those kinds of questions. Perhaps then you will want to compare, on a much smaller scale, how students compare in *your* classes next fall.

Favorite type of book. From a list of 25 topics, we asked students to circle the three that interested them the most. The following tables show how extensive the interest is in romances, mysteries, and sports.

The importance of romances for females is not very strong in grades 4–6. There, Romance is only fourth in importance, with Problems of Growing Up first. Romances take on their fullest importance in grades 7–12 where 57% of the girls noted that. For boys, Sports remains on top at all three grade level groupings. These data are presented below in Tables 1, 2 and 3.

Favorite Books. If those are the favorite topics, what are the favorite books? We asked students to list the best books (up to three titles) they had read during the previous two years and then we compiled the most frequently listed titles. The most obvious finding is that there are very few titles that stand out. That is, while most students listed a favorite title, very few students listed the same titles. Variety is therefore the most dominant quality of students' reading—in all grades. By grade, in Table 12-4, are the most frequently mentioned titles and the percentage of students noting that title.

In the elementary grades, the top three titles in grades 4, the top five titles in grade 5, and five of the top six titles in grade 6 were written by

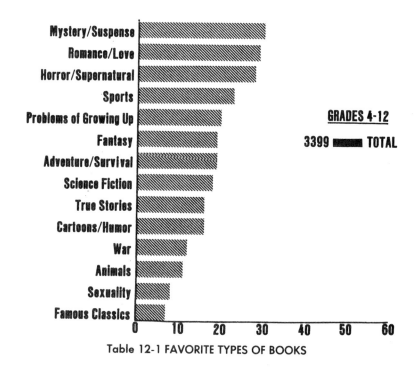

Table 12-1 FAVORITE TYPES OF BOOKS

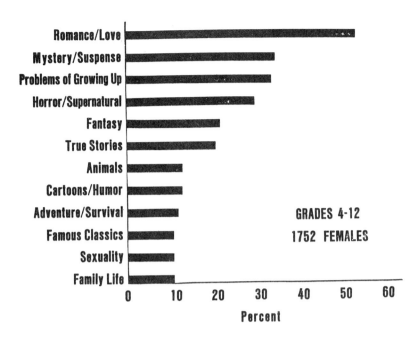

Table 12-2

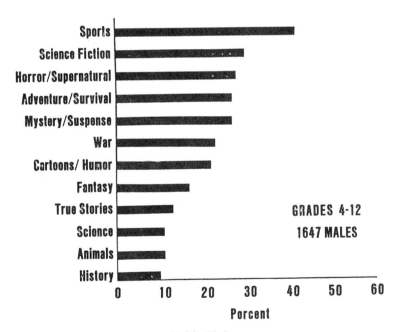

Table 12-3

Table 12-4. BOOKS FREQUENTLY IDENTIFIED AS FAVORITES

GRADE	TITLE	PERCENT
4	SUPERFUDGE	30
5	ARE YOU THERE, GOD? IT'S ME, MARGARET	18
6	SUPERFUDGE	7
7	WHERE THE RED FERN GROWS	7
8	FLOWERS IN THE ATTIC	7
9	FLOWERS IN THE ATTIC	8
10	THE OUTSIDERS	7
11	TO KILL A MOCKINGBIRD	8
12	OF MICE AND MEN	5

Judy Blume. *Flowers in the Attic* was not only the most popular title overall in grades 8 and 9, it was there almost exclusively because of its popularity among females. In fact, in grades 7–12, 11% of the females noted that as their favorite book. (Another 8% noted *Petals on the Wind*, while 4% noted *If There Be Thorns*.) Among males in grades 8–10, *The Outsiders* held top position; *Of Mice and Men* took over first place for males in grades 11 and 12.

Most Recent Title Read. Variety dominated also in the list of the most recent books students had read for their own information or enjoyment, everything from trash to classics. A few titles were repeated in each grade, though not many. These are presented in Table 12-5.

Table 12-5. MOST RECENT TITLES READ

GRADE	TITLE	PERCENT
4	SUPERFUDGE	9
5	(none)	—
6	BIG RED	1
	THE OUTSIDERS	1
7	WHERE THE RED FERN GROWS	3
8	FOREVER	2
	THE OUTSIDERS	2
9	THE AMITYVILLE HORROR	2
	FLOWERS IN THE ATTIC	2
	THE PIGMAN	2
10	NO ONE HERE GETS OUT ALIVE	1
11	THE CRUCIBLE	3
12	NO ONE HERE GETS OUT ALIVE	2

Table 12-6. ASSIGNED BOOKS

Grade	Best	%	Worst	%
4	Secret Garden	13	—	—
5	Sounder	18	—	—
6	My Brother Sam is Dead	10	A Wrinkle in Time	5
7	Where the Red Fern Grows	4	The Light in the Forest	4
			Johnny Tremain	
8	Cheaper by the Dozen	5	The Light in the Forest	5
	The Hound of the Baskervilles			
9	The Outsiders	11	Johnny Tremain	3
10	Romeo and Juliet	11	Romeo and Juliet	6
11	Macbeth	7	The Scarlet Letter	6
12	The Scarlet Letter	7	The Scarlet Letter	3

Assigned Books: Best and Worst. Variety still dominated on lists of best liked and most hated assigned books, but certain books gained a lot of responses because students in one school seemed to really enjoy a particular book, or a whole group really hated their assignment. The figures in Table 12-6 show percentages of students noting the most frequently mentioned title at each grade.

Authors. It is surprising that many students did not note a favorite author. It is also surprising that there was not as great a variety in the list of favorite authors as there was in the listing of favorite titles. Only a few authors' names came up again and again. And there wasn't much change throughout the grades, though the changes that did occur are very interesting, as Table 12-7 shows.

We also discovered some interesting information regarding where students find out about good books to read, where students get the books they read, and where students buy books most often. This information is presented in Tables 12-8, 12-9, and 12-10.

How?

Finding information like this—or finding data about students' reading skills or their ability to use study materials or the length of their attention span—can be done in a very short period of time. The questionnaire we used had over 30 items on it and took an average of half an hour to complete, longer for some kids. (In several classes it took more than one full class period, because many students wanted to discuss their responses right then and there. You see, nobody had ever asked them for that

Table 12-7. FAVORITE AUTHORS

GRADE	MALES		FEMALES		BOTH	
4	Blume	60	Blume	90	Blume	75
	Cleary	20	Cleary	44	Cleary	32
	Christopher	14	Silverstein	11	Christopher	7
					Silverstein	5
5	Christopher	30	Blume	81	Blume	50
	Blume	23	Cleary	35	Cleary	15
	Dixon	17	Keene	27	Christopher	15
6	Blume	13	Blume	63	Blume	38
	Christopher	7	Cleary	16	Cleary	10
	Hitchcock	6	Danziger	7	Hitchcock	4
7	Blume	12	Blume	52	Blume	30
	Tolkien	9	Cleary	7	Tolkien	5
	Hitchcock	4	Christie	6	Cleary	3
					Hitchcock	3
8	Hinton	10	Blume	42	Blume	23
	King	6	Andrews	12	Hinton	10
	Bradbury	5	Hinton	9	King	6
	Steinbeck	5				
9	Tolkien	11	Blume	29	Blume	17
	Hinton	8	King	9	King	7
	Steinbeck	6	Andrews	8	Tolkien	6
10	Poe	6	Blume	16	Blume	10
	Hinton	6	King	8	King	6
	Tolkien	5	Steinbeck	6	Hinton	6
			Andrews	6		
11	Twain	8	Blume	15	Blume	8
	Steinbeck	8	Poe	9	Poe	8
	Poe	7	Christie	8	Steinbeck	6
12	Steinbeck	9	Steinbeck	8	Steinbeck	8
	Tolkien	7	King	7	King	5
	Poe	5	Steel	6	Tolkien	5
	Shakespeare	4	Blume	5	Dickens	4
	Dickens	3	Christie	5	Shakespeare	4
			Dickens	5		

Table 12-8. SOURCES OF INFORMATION ABOUT NEW BOOKS TO READ

| | Grades 4-6 | | | Grades 7-9 | | | Grades 10-12 | | |
	All students	Males	Females	All students	Males	Females	All students	Males	Females
Friend's suggestion	36	25	47	42	28	55	38	25	50
Browsing in store	17	20	14	28	32	25	31	29	33
Browsing in library	28	25	31	27	27	27	18	18	18
Teacher's suggestion	12	15	9	8	11	6	11	13	9
Parent's suggestion	9	10	7	8	10	5	10	8	11
Store display	6	8	5	7	10	5	8	9	7
Advertising	5	6	4	6	6	7	9	9	10
Brother's/sister's suggestion	6	4	7	8	7	9	8	7	9
Bookclub catalog	17	18	16	7	6	8	3	4	3
Library display	7	8	7	5	6	5	-5	5	4
Librarian's suggestion	19	14	24	4	5	3	2	2	2
School list	3	4	2	6	6	6	3	4	2

Table 12-9. SOURCES OF BOOKS ALL GRADES

	Males	Females	Both
BUY THEM	27	27	27
TOWN LIBRARY	21	21	21
SCHOOL LIBRARY	20	14	17
FRIEND	6	18	12
PARENTS	6	6	6
BROTHER/SISTER	5	5	5
GIFT	6	4	5
CLASSROOM LIBRARY	6	3	4

Table 12-10. SOURCES FOR BOOK PURCHASES

	GRADE 4–6			GRADE 7–9			GRADE 10–12			ALL GRADES		
	MALE	FEMALE	BOTH	MALE	FEMALE	BOTH	MALE	FEMALE	BOTH	MALE	FEMALE	BOTH
BOOK STORE	40	34	37	49	52	51	60	66	63	53	56	55
LARGE DEPT. STORE	13	13	13	11	11	11	13	13	13	12	12	12
SCHOOL BOOK CLUB	21	27	24	7	14	11	<2	2	<2	7	10	8
SCHOOL BOOK FAIR	8	13	10	12	9	10	4	2	3	7	6	7
PHARMACY	2	<2	2	4	4	4	6	5	6	5	4	5

kind of information before, and they had never had a chance to express their opinions on some of those things before. And many of the teachers found out things they had never known before! Thus, there was a beneficial side effect to the research).

I repeat: if you have never done anything like this before and if you do not have unlimited free time, start with something simple. Just a couple of questions. Just simple totals or percentages. Just a few basic comparisons: for example, males vs. females; good readers vs. nonreaders; kids in advanced classes vs. kids in remedial classes; and so on. (Any of those, not all of them.) This kind of information is very easy to gather. But it is time-consuming to compile and to analyze.

For example, I have in my hand here several sheets of paper on which we recorded the responses to just one item on our Connecticut survey. On this item, we asked students to circle, from a list, any or all of the topics that would offend them and cause them to stop reading. So we had to record the number of students from each school and each grade, both males and females, who noted each of the 15 possibilities (including NONE). We could have broken this down further by each classroom, by type of school, by type of community, by academic success of the students. This set of sheets contains only the *basic totals*. So you get some idea of the complexity of the materials if you are not careful or if you establish goals that are too ambitious for the time you have or the information you want. (Certainly it is ideal if you can put all this data into a computer that will print out exactly what you need to know at the push of a button. But don't forget that nothing comes out of a computer that does not, first, get put in and, second, have a program of instructions/directions of what to do with the data. Those things cost time and money, and you need someone to write such a program for you unless you are an expert at that as well. I am not an expert at that, and I work at a state institution that has very few computers on its campus, nor would anyone in our computer center volunteer to write a program for our study. So we've been doing all of the compilations longhand. (Thank God for pocket calculators!)

In any case, start small. No matter how small you start, it will grow on you anyway. It's almost always more complex than you envision it when you begin.

If you are a good conceptualizer, you will also have an easier time doing any kind of research. Try to envision the responses to the questions you ask. Try to envision the way your directions are going to be received by students. Try to envision what the results will look like, so you have some idea of what you will need to do to handle them: Do you want to have predetermined lists from which students choose, or do you want to wade through open-ended answers and then try to categorize those? Do you want to provide only a limited number of alternatives that force students to choose only one of those, or do you want to provide a wider variety of possibilities? (For example, you could ask students if they prefer to read paperbacks or hardcover books; or you could ask if they prefer paperbacks, hardcovers, or either . . . or, indeed, neither; or you can ask students if they prefer paperbacks ALL OF THE TIME, MOST OF THE TIME, SOME OF THE TIME, SELDOM, or NEVER.)

The more you think those things through, the easier it will be for you to get the kinds of data you are looking for. (I don't mean that you should try to bias your questions to get predisposed answers.)

Of course you can always run a pilot study first—and perhaps you *should* run a pilot study first, to get the kinks out of your questionnaires or whatever devices you are using, but I never do that. I'm always too anxious to get to the real thing. So I try to think through all the details as thoroughly as I can. I think at the office, and while I'm driving to and from school, and when I awake in the early morning, or whenever I can find the time to get involved with the project. (Maybe that's why I don't produce very rapidly: I always think about it for a long time before I put it into action.) And then, when I feel as comfortable as I can feel about what I've planned, I do it. (Even if you do a pilot study, there's a good chance that you will find something in the final—real—study that you should have done differently, so why worry about it? Just do the best you know how to do in either case.)

I expect that you noticed, when I presented some of our findings from the Connecticut study before, that I did not present them in terms of means and standard deviations, or Chi squares, or F-ratios, or any of

those statistical terms. I didn't do so because I didn't need to do that
with these data. Certainly we can analyze some of our findings in that
manner. But I think the *kinds* of things we have been looking at—at least
at this point—are clear enough so that we don't need to see if the differences between one grade and the next are statistically significant at
the .001 level or whatever. The differences or the similarities, the pro-
gressions from grade to grade, the patterns are so obvious that we don't
have to resort to more sophisticated measures to prove anything. (Nevertheless, we will resort to those statistical devices if and when we want to
look at some of the finer points of the data.) My point is not that such
statistical measures are not useful. My point is that there is a lot of
information about your students, your teaching, your classroom activities
that can be gathered and analyzed and interpreted without your having
to know or to use sophisticated measurement techniques or statistical
manipulations. Most of you are classroom teachers; your time is limited;
the information you can use on Monday morning should be obtained
in the easiest ways possible. Let the professional researchers and the
doctoral candidates handle the more advanced statistics; or find a col-
league who is good at statistical measurement and work on the project
together.

What to Do with the Results?

Nothing bothers me more than teachers who discover interesting things
(or who do interesting things) in their classrooms but who never share
them with a wider audience. When you do a study, no matter how simple,
write it up. At least write a brief summary of something you discover.
Even if you discover nothing new, tell somebody about it.

Tell the students you surveyed or tested, first. They gave you the
information in the first place; they deserve to know the results. (That's
why small studies are better in a way than large studies. With small
studies you can usually analyze the data and present your findings to
the students the following week or so. With something as massive as my
Connecticut survey, it takes too long to analyze—it's been a year and a
half since we asked the questions. Hundreds of the students we surveyed
and a couple of their teachers have graduated or moved away, so we
can't share the findings with them. All of the teachers who participated
in the survey and who are still teaching, however, will receive a copy of
the findings.)

Beyond your own classroom, share the findings with members of your
department, with the school faculty, especially with your superiors. (I
realize that in some schools you will be singling yourself out as somebody

different from others, and that might gain you some disdain from your colleagues. But I hope it won't. And you should tell them about your findings anyway.) Send a report to the parents. Just letting the public know you are doing more than just teaching from 8:30 to 3:30 is important.

Take your most interesting findings and write a brief article for a professional journal: for *The Reading Teacher, The Journal of Reading, Reading Research, The English Journal, Research in the Teaching of English,* your state professional journals, or a journal in another state if yours doesn't have one. Say: Hey, here's what we did, here's what we found, and here's what we think it means. Ask to be on a program at a national, state, or local conference. Tell others about your discoveries, just as I've told you a little bit about mine today.

And, by all means, use that information to modify your teaching or to adjust your thinking about your students. No matter what you do, you are bound to discover things about your students that you never knew before. And even if you discover nothing new, you will have at least confirmed what you suspected all along. Only this time you will have concrete evidence in your pocket to use when you prepare your daily lessons or your worksheets, or when you ask the administration for new or different or more books and teaching materials. You will be, in either case, a better informed and thus a more aware, more effective teacher.

Author Index

Subject Index

A
Analysis of data, 6
Attention deficits, 141–142, 146–147

C
Chunking information, 107
Classification techniques, 138
Coding, 10–12, 158
Communicative competence, 4
Comprehension, 80, 85, 105, 119
Cooperative environments, 29–32
    accepting, 29–31
    advocating, 29–30
    facilitating, 29–31
    obstructing, 29, 31
Cognitive basis for limited representations
    of reality, 111–113
Cognitive separation of language skills,
    108–111
Computers in language arts, 130–133
    drill and practice, 130
    heuristic approach, 131–132
        Seeing Eye Elephant Network, 132
    simulations, 130
    tutorials, 130–131
        Story Machine, 131
Critical thinking, 86
Cross cultural miscommunication, 173–175
Cultural contexts of reading, 175–178

D
Data collection, 189
    categorizing and analyzing data, 189
    recording information, 189
    result sharing, 189
Data collection methods, 5–6, 8
    audio recording, 5
    communicative processes sampling, 6
    transription of tapes, 10
    video recording, 5
Decision making, 39–57
    action, 39, 54–56
        final or ongoing operations, 56
        initial phase, 55

medial phase, 56
        timing, 55
        worker performance, 55
    allocations, 39, 53–54
        of human resources, 53–54
        of material and economic resources, 54
    alternatives, 39, 48–51
        congruency with axiologicals, 48–49
        decision science elements, 49–51
        examination of axiomatic factors, 49
    appraisal, 56
    architecture, 39, 51–53
        designing the plan, 53
        selecting and defining the plan, 52
    axiologicals, 39–44
        complexities of values positing, 42
        values as behavior determinants, 42–43
        values changes analysis, 43
        values constancy, 41–42
        values definition, 40–41
        values development, 41
        values imperatives analysis, 44
    axiomatics, 39, 44–47
        organizational givens, 46–47
        significant coalitions as givens, 46
        significant people givens, 45–46
        socioeconomic givens, 45
        territorial givens, 44

E
Effective speaker, 4–6, 20
English for Special Purposes, 162
ESL, 151–153, 155, 159 *(see also* TESOL,
        Second language classroom)
    literacy, 151
    reading class, 153, 155
Ethnographic approaches, 25
Ethnographic approach to reading instruc-
        tion, 167–168 *(see also* Sociolinguistic
        approach)
Evaluation, 161

G
General immaturity, 143, 149